Because I Have a Voice
Queer Politics in India

Because I Have a Voice
Queer Politics in India

EDITORS

ARVIND NARRAIN
GAUTAM BHAN

YODA PRESS
NEW DELHI

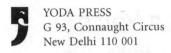YODA PRESS
G 93, Connaught Circus
New Delhi 110 001

Published in India
by YODA PRESS

© Arvind Narrain and Gautam Bhan 2005

The moral rights of the author have been asserted
Database right YODA PRESS (maker)

First published 2005

ISBN 81-902272-2-x

Typeset in Minion, 10/12
By Excellent Laser Typesetters, Delhi 110 034
Printed at Chaman Offset Printers, Delhi 110 092
Published by Parul Nayyar and Arpita Das, YODA PRESS
    G 93, Connaught Circus, New Delhi 110 001
Distributed by Foundation Books Pvt. Ltd. FOUNDATION
    Cambridge House, 4381/4, Ansari Road   B ⦿ ⦿ K S
    Daryaganj, New Delhi 110 002

To Famila

If you had told us,
  just one word,
On what was killing you inside,
When we danced that night,
When we smoked that evening,
When we hugged that afternoon,
When we met that morning,
  just one word...

and we would have screamed,
some more like we always do.
Your flesh is gone,
but your strength remains.
Your breath is gone,
but your voice remains.
We'll use it well to scream some more.
Scream...till our voices...
yours, mine, and all ours,
  will be heard.

Contents

Introduction

Arvind Narrain and *Gautam Bhan*

MY GENDER MY RIGHT The rumble of the cars zipping across the flyover directly above the ceiling shook the small room almost continuously, sending tremors through the bodies of the dozen or so people who had gathered there. It was a dusty Friday night, not unlike any other, in the middle of a long Delhi summer, and the sense of excitement in the room almost seemed out of place. At first glance, the reason for the excitement wasn't apparent—a mixed group of men and women, both young and old, were seated on *chatais* on the floor reading to each other, raising their voices to be heard over the cars rumbling overhead. They spoke, they would say later, queer words. Words of desire, of confession, of celebration, of empathy, and of resistance. Words that retold and reclaimed stories, poems, and narratives that had, till that night, excluded their identities, desires, and feelings. Queer words, read by queer people, with and for each other, finally being heard even as the city literally rumbled on its way above their heads.

There is a sense of freedom in the lives of many queer people in India today. It is a hesitant freedom for none of us can afford to forget how fragile the few accepting spaces we inhabit are, or how few of us have access to them. Nevertheless, this new freedom is a heady feeling, and it cradles within it a sense of hope that, even five years ago, seemed distant. New words surround queer lives today and they are words chosen by queer people themselves to be part of a new language that speaks of change just as it steps towards it. This book is written in this new language. It seeks to bear witness to its existence, add to its vocabulary, and teach others how to read it and understand queer politics and queer lives.

In what words does a queer language describe the India that we live in today? The idea of an inclusive and tolerant nation continues to be challenged by brutalities inflicted in the name of maintaining the purity of caste, class, religion and gender. Many of the signposts of post-independence India—the Mathura rape case in 1979, the destruction of the Babri Masjid in 1992, or the carnage and continuing injustice in Gujarat—are moments of rupture in our history. Yet each of these ruptures has had, as its counterpoint, an emerging moment of assertion. Such a moment may have been the beginning of the contemporary women's movement, the emergence of vocal anti-communal movements, or simply the initial stirrings of ordinary people getting together to work against ideologies of power and oppression. The story of queer people in India has, so far, been written and lived along the fault lines and margins of Indian history, but now the search for our own moment of assertion is gaining momentum. It is within this search that the present anthology is located.

Our effort is to give voice to a concept, an identity and a politics that is only now, and slowly at that, beginning to enter the consciousness of the nation. To speak of sexuality, and of same-sex love in particular, in India today is simultaneously an act of political assertion, of celebration, of defiance and of fear. For far too long, gay, lesbian, bisexual, and transgender people have simply been the distant and hypothetical subjects of theories and ideas, looked upon either with pity, curiosity or disdain. At each turn, we are constantly described and defined by other people's words as they stand codified in religion, medicine, law, and in the silent assumptions that form the reality of our everyday lives. We are told via our faith, our families, our laws, our bodies and our very imagination of ourselves, that we've got the script wrong, and are, in effect, playing the wrong parts.

The words of this anthology are our own scripts, written for us by ourselves as we question and challenge the right of others to script our lives. Finding our voice is the beginning of our politics, for it is in the naming of ourselves that we begin to question the cultural, social and political basis of those that seek to invisibilise us. The essays in this volume are a celebration, a defiant political resistance, an introspective reflection as well as a conceptual space. They write of the past, the present and the future of queer lives. They speak of desires, of identities, of languages and of spaces. They share stories of pain, joy, struggle and victory in equal measure. They are the voice of a community that refuses to be silenced, and that refuses to recognise the rules that deem its desires to be, at best, unnatural, and, at worst, beyond imagination. The words in these pages are, perhaps, the beginning of our own moment of assertion.

WHO ARE THE QUEER?

We live in a society where we are repeatedly told that there is only one kind ⊃∠ of acceptable desire—heterosexual, within marriage, and male. Social structures further define and defend what we call the hetero-normative ideal: rigid notions of what it means to be a man or a woman, how the two should relate and the family unit that should result from such a relationship. All those who dare to think outside this perfect ideal are considered threats to 'morality' and to society at large. There is a fundamental principle at work here—those in power create norms, rules and structures that enforce their vision of what is acceptable, and penalise all those that fall outside these rules. On the other side of 'normal' lie a host of those that are 'different'—an inter-religious or inter-caste couple, a daughter who has just realised that she has half the claim to her parent's land as her brother, a hijra whose body is the subject of public ridicule in a culture that claims to treat sexuality as a private issue, or a lesbian woman who must not only fight to be a lesbian, but simply to be a woman ⌐∫ in India who has (gasp!) sexual desires.

What we have chosen to call the queer movement encompasses a multiplicity of desires and identities, each and all of which question the naturalness, the rightness and the inevitability of heterosexuality. Historically used as a derogatory term to describe homosexual people in the West, and home to the rather unflattering meanings of 'odd' or 'strange' in the English language, 'queer' might seem a perplexing choice of name for a community or movement. Yet it is its very infamy that makes the term attractive to so many. By proudly calling themselves queer, homosexual people not only re-appropriate a word historically used as part of a language of oppression, they also reject the power of the oppressor to judge them in the first place. As Nivedita Menon has eloquently argued in the present volume:

> even at its best, society's response to the question of sexuality has been in the form of 'respecting choice'. Such a response as we have seen, leaves unquestioned heterosexuality as the norm—that is, 'most of us are heterosexual, but there are others out there who are *either* lesbian *or* gay *or* B, T, or K'. The alphabets proliferate endlessly *outside* the unchallenged heterosexual space. But if we recognise that this 'normal' heterosexuality is painfully constructed and kept in place by a range of cultural, bio-medical and economic controls, precisely in order to sustain existing hierarchies of class and caste and gender, then we would have to accept that all of us are—or have the potential to be—'queer' (Menon, present volume).

The term 'queer' is, in some ways, both a deeply personal identity and a defiant political perspective. It embodies within itself a rejection of the primacy of the heterosexual, patriarchal family as the cornerstone of our society. In doing so, it rejects the assumption of compulsory heterosexuality—society's firm yet unsaid belief that the world around us (and everyone in it) is heterosexual until proven otherwise. It captures and validates the identities and desires of gay, lesbian, bisexual and transgender people, but also represents, for many, an understanding of sexuality that goes beyond the categories of 'homosexual' and 'heterosexual'. It speaks, therefore, of communities that name themselves (as gay or lesbian, for example) as well as of those that do not, recognising the spaces for same-sex desire and sexuality that cannot be captured in identities alone. To speak of queer politics is, in some sense, different from just speaking of gay, lesbian, bisexual, transgendered, kothi, and hijra communities. Queer politics does not speak only of the issues of these communities as 'minority issues', but instead it speaks of larger understandings of gender and sexuality in our society that affect all of us, regardless of our sexual orientation. It speaks of sexuality as a politics intrinsically and inevitably connected with the politics of class, gender, caste, religion and so on, thereby both acknowledging other movements and also demanding inclusion within them.

Queer resistance is, therefore, about questioning the fundamental assumptions of our society. As Michael Warner puts it,

> because the logic of the sexual order is so deeply embedded by now in the most standard accounts of the world, queer struggles aim not just at toleration or equal status but at challenging these institutions and accounts. The dawning realisation that themes of homophobia and heterosexism may be read in almost any document of our culture means that we are only beginning to have an idea of how widespread these institutions and accounts are (Warner 1993).

Queer resistance takes different forms: an alternative reading of a mainstream Bollywood film, publicly holding the hand of someone you love, coming out to friends and family, living one's chosen sex/gender, embracing one's body and one's pleasure often in defiance of the ideas of how 'manly' men and 'feminine' women should live, protesting against instances of exclusion or violence, or simply existing in a daily-lived resistance that protests the hypocrisy of silence around the desires and needs of a community. The queer struggle is not just a public movement for rights and legal change. It is also a map of how people navigate their most intimate geographies: their bodies, their desires, their families and their selves.

In India, the word 'queer' is not as yet commonly used. However, the realities of the non-normative experiences—i.e., gender identities, sexual practices, sexual identities, culturally sanctioned forms of erotic behaviour—

which contest the embedded nature of heterosexism in our society have traditionally existed and continue to exist in the contemporary context. If one were to compile an open-ended register which would reflect some of the diverse practices that come under the political project of 'queer,' this list would minimally include:

- The Hijras: As a community, they represent an existing Indian tradition which clearly contests any hetero-normative understandings of gender, sexuality and the body. Hijras include men who go in for hormonal treatment, those who undergo sex-change operations and those who are born as hermaphrodites. The community has its own culture and ways of living, including its own festivals and gods and goddesses. Hijras divide themselves into *gharanas* or houses and the strength of the hijra community lies in its close-knit relationships, their sole source of support against the social ostracism they face in mainstream society (PUCL, K 2003).[1]
- The Kothis: The kothi is a feminised male identity, which is adopted by some people in the Indian subcontinent and is marked by gender non-conformity. A kothi, though biologically male, adopts feminine modes of dressing, speech and behaviour and would look for a male partner who performs masculine modes of behaviour, speech and dress. Most kothis also identify as non-English-speaking and coming from middle, lower-income, and working-class backgrounds (ibid.: 19–21).
- Lesbian, Gay, Bisexual and Transgender Communities (LGBT): Nearly all urban centres in India have large and diverse communities of men and women who identify as being gay, lesbian, bisexual or transgender. The use of the abbreviation LGBT is largely restricted to urban, English-speaking, middle- and upper-middle-class men and women.
- In addition, each region of India has traditional identities that are based on practices of gender and sexual non-conformity, such as the *jogappas* and *jogtas* in North Karnataka and Maharashtra, or the *shivshaktsis* and *ganacharis* in parts of South India (see www.sambhavana.org). There are many more gender- and sexuality-based identities in India today, and the categories above are part of merely an illustrative, and in no way exhaustive, list. Much more ethnographic work needs to be done to fully understand the forms of ritually sanctioned gender non-conformity in Indian culture.

Beyond the framework of such communities are stories of people and spaces where same-sex desires exist in permutations and expressions that we as yet do not have the language to describe or fully understand. How do we speak of the women couples who committed suicide rather than be parted from each other, but who never used the word 'lesbian'? Where do we draw the line between intimate friendships and queer relationships? How do we understand a concept such as *masti*—a term that refers to the sanctioned space for sexual activity between men—in our framework of sexual desire? How do we understand the marriage of Urmila Shrivastava and Leela Namdeo in 1988, two women from a rural background who were serving in the Madhya Pradesh constabulary? Whether they name themselves or not, what the lives and identities outlined above bring to the fore is the fact that our society and our culture have alternative visions and realities embedded within them. As the story of the queer movement itself unfolds, it is necessary to remember that our understanding of sexuality in itself is ever changing, and that the realm of same-sex desire and love in our country extends far beyond those that embrace a certain identity.

THE CONTEMPORARY QUEER MO(VE)MENT IN INDIA

The contemporary moment has seen the emergence of a more public queer articulation, as well as a change in the language and spaces of that articulation. Queer groups have consistently tried to map and understand the basis of the violence that is part of the reality of queer lives in India today. Much of the initial organising in queer spaces occurred as a response to such violence or in the context of the HIV/AIDS epidemic. Increasingly, however, the contemporary movement has begun to shift away from a discourse solely centred on violence and disease prevention to one rooted in rights, identities and the celebration of one's desires.

 To name, visibilise and counter the violence faced by queer people on a daily basis remains a critical part of the movement, but our understandings, both of the nature of violence itself (expanding it to emotional as well as physical violence), and its institutional roots (locating it within hetero-patriarchy and larger understandings of gender and sexuality), have changed. This implies that rather than simply speaking for the right to make different choices, or remain a 'minority' within a larger heterosexual 'majority', the queer movement tries to challenge the idea of a 'normal' and 'different' sexuality in itself. It argues that while hierarchies of desire are certainly not acceptable, neither are 'us-and-them' or 'separate/different but equal' assertions valid. The point is to object to all hierarchies and power structures, not just the ones that we happen to be on the wrong end of. It is within this framework that intersections are beginning to emerge between queer and feminist movements, and other movements at the margins. Similarly, rather than just responding to isolated cases of violence against queer people, the movement now speaks of the pervading institutionalisation and legitimisation of this violence in a locus of spaces, such as the law, family, medical establishment, popular culture, public spaces and work spaces (PUCL-K 2001).

How does a movement respond to such a multi-sited understanding of queer oppression and violence? What have been the methods of protest within queer spaces, and how do these reflect the tenets and paradigms of queer politics? What are the alternative ideologies that a queer perspective offers in each of these spaces? The following sections begin to answer each of these questions by documenting the work of queer activists and people in each of the different spaces identified above.

Challenging the Law

Legal challenges surrounding queer sexuality centre on Section 377 of the Indian Penal Code. This section, drafted in 1860 by Lord Macaulay reads:

> whoever voluntarily has carnal intercourse against the order of nature with any man, woman or animal, shall be punished with imprisonment...which may extend to ten years, and shall also be liable to fine. Explanation Penetration is sufficient to constitute the carnal intercourse necessary to the offence described in this section.

A look at the history of the use of Section 377 reveals that it has hardly been used to prosecute cases of consensual adult male sexual relationships. Mostly, it is used in cases of child sexual abuse (Gupta 2002: 9). Two important caveats have to be made here: the study cites only decisions that cite Section 377 in the higher courts, it does not account for lower and trial court decisions where the law may have been used. More importantly, we must realise that the true impact of Section 377 on queer lives is felt outside the courtroom, and must be measured in terms of legal cases. Numerous studies, including both documented and anecdotal evidence, tell us that Section 377 is the basis for routine and continuous violence against sexual minorities by the police, the medical establishment, and the state. There are innumerable stories that can be cited—from the everyday violence faced by hijras and kothis on the streets of Indian cities to the refusal of the National Human Rights Commission to hear the case of a young man who had been given electro-shock therapy for nearly two years. A recent report by the People's Union for Civil Liberties (Karnataka), showed that Section 377 was used by the police to justify practices such as illegal detention, sexual abuse and harassment, extortion and outing of queer people to their families, which are all forms of violence practised against queer communities (PUCL-K, 2001). The power of Section 377 lies both in its direct/indirect use within the law and the symbolic impact that it has on conceptions and understandings of queer communities in larger society.[2] The law is not simply a space of enforcement, but is an active arbiter of social norms and morality.[3] Foucault described this socially constitutive role of law in terms of the panoptic—the idea that the law is internally manifested within its subjects, and not just externally imposed upon them (2000). What Foucault is arguing is that the very existence of Section 377 shapes people's beliefs about queer sexuality as they internalise the prohibition that the law puts forth. The court, therefore, need not enforce or use Section 377 in its decisions to exercise its homophobia—such discrimination is inherent in the law's existence in itself. The real danger of Section 377 lies in the fact that it permeates all parts of society—the medical establishment, media, family, and the state. It becomes a part of ordinary conversations and ultimately a part of the very social fabric in workplaces, families, hospitals and the popular press. This helps to create an environment where violence against queer people gains a semblance of legal acceptability. Section 377 expresses a deep societal repugnance towards queer people and provides a fig leaf of legitimacy for the harassment of queer people by families, friends, the medical establishment and other official institutions. It is this nexus between social norms and legal statutes that the queer movement must challenge. Legal reform is just one part of a larger process of social change, and change in the law will have a real impact on the everyday lives of queer people only if it is used to challenge homophobia in larger society, and in the intimate spaces of our families, homes, relationships and workplaces (Bhan, present volume).

Much of queer activism in the last few years has come to be associated with a movement for legal reform, with Section 377 emerging as a significant rallying point with increasing calls being made for its reform. The movement against the law has taken multiple forms ranging from public protests and academic/legal critiques to the filing of a public interest petition in the Delhi High Court. The petition was recently dismissed by the Delhi High Court on technical grounds but, at the time of writing, the Supreme Court of India had overturned the technical dismissal and was beginning to hear the merits of the case.

It is not just Section 377 that affects queer people—laws against obscenity, pornography, public nuisance and trafficking are also often invoked in the policing of sexuality by the state and police. One also has to pay heed to the civil law regime where queer people are deprived of basic rights such as the right to marry, or to nominate one's partner and the whole series of rights which are based on the assumption of one being a member of a heterosexual family (Desai 2003).

Protests and Demonstrations

Protests and demonstrations always play a strong role in building an alternative culture as they are, most times, the first spaces in which many issues interact with and reach a wider public consciousness. The first recorded queer protest in India was organised by the AIDS Bhedbhav Virodhi Andolan (ABVA) which took place in 1992, when a rally was organised in Delhi against police harassment of gay men. Its slogan was indicative of its Marxist roots: 'Gays of the World Unite, You Have Nothing to Lose but Your Chains'.

The late 1990s witnessed a profusion of protests over a number of incidents—the Shiv Sena vandalism and the general controversy that followed the release of the movie *Fire* and, more recently, *Girlfriend*; the arrests of HIV/AIDS workers under Section 377 in Lucknow (see Bandopadhyay 2002:104); as well as repeated police violence and brutality against the hijra community.[4] Recalling the emergence of the Campaign for Lesbian Rights in India (CALERI) in the context of the protests around *Fire*, Ashwini Sukthankar notes:

> Hundreds of people showed up outside the Regal Cinema—the theatre that had been ransacked by the mobs—holding candles, chanting, raising placards. But for the first time ever in India, lesbians were visible among the other groups marking the specific nature of their anger. In the sea of placards about human rights, secularism, women's autonomy, freedom of speech, was a sign painted in the colours of the national flag: 'Indian and Lesbian'. Who would have thought that staking that saucy claim to our share of national pride would result in such a furore? (Sukthankar 2002: xxvii).

Since those early stirrings, the nature of the protests as well as the issues raised within them, have changed to reflect the changing social composition of the movement. The emergence of vocal and organised kothi and hijra communities has widened the class base of the queer movement beyond the middle class to include other subaltern groups. The slogans emblazoned across the signs at marches increasingly speak not just of freedom from violence but of rights and affirmation. Queer voices have begun to hold the state and society responsible for the discrimination against them, questioning the authority of law, medicine and even religion to pass judgement on their lives. The protests also no longer come only from queer-identified people. A recently formed coalition of groups in Delhi, called Voices against Section 377, functions as a coalition of women's rights, child rights, human rights and queer groups. Voices is the first time that non-LGBT-identified people have taken on a sustained campaign for queer rights as their own issue.

Voices members come from different fields of work, and they take issues of same-sex desire back into movements on health, women's rights, child rights and human rights. Since its inception, Voices has conducted consultative workshops with the Jan Swasthya Abhiyan—the largest network of health NGOs in India—on the intersections of sexuality and access to health; with the Network of Autonomous Women's Groups on sexuality and women's movements; with the Psychological Foundation of India on understandings of sexuality within mental health practice, along with public rallies, and outreach efforts in different parts of the city, including Delhi University. In progressive spaces, queer issues are raised from organisations seen not just as LGBT organisations, but as existing members of these networks. In outreaches to mainstream society, Voices presents a forum that cannot be dismissed easily.

Perhaps the most visible example of a newfound assertiveness in queer organising was on display at the World Social Forum, organised in Mumbai in January 2004. Amidst the cacophony of literally thousands of people propounding diverse social causes right from the environment to children, the Rainbow Planet as a coalition of sex workers, PLWHAs (Persons Living with HIV/AIDS) and sexual minorities were a dramatic presence. As the flyer succinctly noted, *'All are Different—All are Equal'*.

Apart from bringing the violence suffered by queer people into dramatic focus, public actions have had a celebratory side as well. For the last two years, Kolkata has celebrated a Pride Week with queer people marching openly through the streets of the city. It is interesting to note that this spirit of celebration has had spin-offs in the highest places. As Vivek Diwan, a lawyer working with Lawyers Collective noted, 'Judges hearing the Section 377 petition referred to the Kolkata Pride and asked the advocate for the Government of India how we could hold on to such archaic laws when, the culture even within India was changing.'[5] Similarly, Bangalore is home to Hijra *Habba*, the annual celebration of the hijra community, organised by Vividha—a non-funded autonomous collective of hijras, kothis, and other queer people. In its second year, the festival was symbolically held in Town Hall, the cultural heart of the city, and drew over 2,000 enthusiastic participants.

Queering Culture and Creating Queer Culture

For most queer people much of our early lives were spent wondering if there was anyone else in the world who shared our feelings. It would not be far-fetched to say that there is no queer person who doesn't understand that moment of utter loneliness on realising that the world isn't exactly designed for people like us. At this point, we scavenged. We took the novels we read and changed the pronouns of the protagonists. We saw films and changed the gender of the hero or the heroine. We read between lines, we found spaces between cracks, we desperately looked at any gesture of affection between friends that seemed to last a fraction of a second too long. Anything to know that somewhere, in someone, somehow, there was a mirror of our reality, a name to our desire, or simply a companion to our confusion. We have all come out to a friend and realised that they know next to nothing about same-sex desire. We have all ached to tell our parents—'read this, look at that, see this…it's not just me!' Until recently, however, there were barely any films, no magazines, no TV characters, no space in history or in culture. Queer people were invisible.

However we define 'culture'—a common ethos, a shared history or set of experiences, common identities, self-expressions, or as the creation of social spaces and norms—queer expression as culture is at a highly productive moment. What is different is that this is an era of extraordinary cultural production. Today, there is a self-consciously queer representation that seeks to speak to an emerging queer community. An increasing number of queer people across a diverse array of spaces are feeling able to write their own histories, construct their own communities and tell their own stories. For more and more young queer people today, there are reflections of themselves and their lives in art, media, films, on the Internet and in other cultural spaces; many of which are created and produced by queer people themselves. Alternative histories are accessible, as are the spaces within which to meet other queer people and share each other's lived realities.

Perhaps one of the most important works to emerge in the realm of queer culture has been Ruth Vanita and Saleem Kidwai's *Same-Sex Love in India*, an effort that applies a queer lens to Indian literature. By citing stories ranging from the *Panchatantra* in ancient India and the love story of Madho and Hussayn in medieval India to texts in modern India in Kannada, Urdu, Bengali and other Indian languages, the authors demonstrate that queerness has always existed in Indian culture, and dismiss any claim that queer sexuality is a 'newfangled Western import'. The publication of such a book takes the hidden and alternative narratives of queer lives away from the margins, and places them firmly within the annals of Indian culture and history.

Let us take cinema as another case in point. A growing subculture of queer films or queer representations in 'mainstream' films has found an eager audience in urban India. In addition to consciously queer representations, queer viewers have also interpreted mainstream culture on their own terms, and they are—if the Kantaben episodes of *Kal Ho Na Ho*, or the gay couple of *Rules: Pyaar Ka Superhit Formula* are anything to go by—being recognised as audiences in their own right. Contemporary critical work indicates that it might not be correct to suppose that, 'Indian cinema is fundamentally addressing "straight" (sic) viewers'. One queer interpretation of Malayalam cinema understands films as a 'series of views and sensations to their audience rather than following a linear narrative logic'. This allows for a different reading of a close friendship between two male heroes regardless of a final closure that subscribes to heterosexual norms.[6] Other such engagements with the history of Hindi, Punjabi, Tamil and other regional cinema might throw extraordinary light on the history of queerness in Indian cinematic culture. Other films speak more directly to the queer experience: Mahesh Dattani's *Mango Souffle*, Sridhar Rangarajan's *Gulabi Aaina*, Riyadh Wadia's *Bomgay*, and Nishit Saran's *Summer in my Veins* are all examples of queer films made by queer filmmakers to project the emerging queer culture on screen. Other documentary films, such as the recent *Many People, Many Desires,* offer another perspective—the actual voices of lives which are gay, lesbian, kothi, transgender, bisexual and hijra, which speaks to the diverse experiences of the queer community.

In contemporary fiction, we have authors like Raj Rao, who has no problems representing himself as a gay author and who does not fear being 'confined' as a gay writer. When mainstream publishing houses like Penguin commission anthologies of gay and lesbian writing, there is the understanding that there must be queer people who will form a significant part of the market for this form of literature, and that there is a need to reach out and acknowledge their presence. Bhupen Khakkar self-consciously used gay imagery in his paintings since the late 1980s to queer the art world, just as Mahesh Dattani's *On a Muggy Night in Mumbai* took homosexuality to the theatre stage. Posters, pamphlets and t-shirts from various events and public actions have created their own queer subculture, be it the 'Don't think straight, think people' t-shirts from the Gay Rights Seminar in the National Law School Bangalore in 1997, or the 'My Gender, My Rights' poster carried by a hijra protestor at the World Social Forum in 2004.

Another form of contemporary cultural intervention that uses media as a tool of activism has been pioneered by media activist collectives such as Nigah in Delhi, Larzish in Mumbai, Pedestrian Pictures/Swabhava in Bangalore and Sarani in Kolkata. Using the queer film festival—a space where films are used to initiate discussions on gender and sexuality—these spaces not only challenge the 'straightness' of mainstream culture, but also create alternative cultures, especially amidst younger Indians at colleges and universities across the country. As Nigah puts it , 'these are spaces where we break the silence around our bodies and our sexualities, both as an act of conscious resistance and as a means of exploration and expression.'[7]

Contemporary queer culture is also evident in the emergence of community magazines. These are often the efforts of groups that get together to produce magazines ranging from *Bombay Dost* in Mumbai, *Sangha Mitra* in Bangalore, *Darpan* in Delhi and *Naya Pravartak* in Kolkata. Though many of these are short-lived, they still provide a means for building a sense of community by providing a forum for the expression of same-sex desire. These magazines are in effect attempts at articulating a worldview, an ethos and a sense of shared community forged under often difficult times. Besides these examples there are also, traditional cultural expressions rooted in gender and sexual non-conformity which are widespread. For example, the annual beauty contest and festival at Koovagam held by the hijra and kothi community is only one of the many cultural practices of the hijra community that are part of a living culture that contest heterosexism by their very existence.

Queer Lives as Political Project(s)

In many ways, it is the lives of queer people that lie at the heart of the queer movement. In the structure of this book, and indeed in the ethos of the movement, we see the ways in which queer people live their everyday lives as creative acts of resistance, and a kind of living theory. This living theory today has much to teach us about new ways of relating, of expressing desire and relating to notions of our identities and our selves, and ultimately, new notions of personhood.

Key to this act of political resistance is the formation of identities that arise out of an understanding of one's sexuality. The contemporary movement has produced a profusion of identities, be they lesbian, kothi, gay, hijra or queer. These identities have given a space to many same-sex desiring people to name their desires, as well as putting a face to the queer movement. The shared sense of common identity, and the emergence of increasingly visible communities that openly name themselves as gay, lesbian, bisexual, kothi, hijra and transgendered, has in effect become the foundation of a young queer movement.

One recalls with great fondness the courage of Famila, one of the foremost queer activists in the country who recently died at the young age of 24. When called upon to speak, she would always begin by stating that she was 'a bisexual hijra sex worker' in the most matter-of-fact tone. This stunning reversal of everything our society holds sacred was usually met with a shocked silence. Famila's statement simultaneously disrupted the multiple assumptions that biological sex determines gender, that prostitution is not work, that the categories of lesbian, gay, bisexual and transgender are neatly divided and separated from each other without overlap, and also that sexual orientation/ gender identity is something that Western-educated élites called 'gays and lesbians' have imported from the West.

What Famila's deployment of her identity as a conscious political strategy brings to the fore is the ability of queer lives to disrupt the 'normalcy' of everyday life. It is not so much the sexual act which is transgressive as the forms of everyday living which make up the way a queer person lives his or her life. There are forms of intimacy and friendship that have a subversive potential to disrupt the received certainties of our culture and to open up the possibility of constructing a new culture.

Michel Foucault recognised the potential which queer life has to disrupt when he noted:

One of the concessions one makes to others is not to present homosexuality as anything but a kind of immediate pleasure, of two young men meeting in the street, seducing each other with a look, grabbing each other's asses and getting each other off in a quarter of an hour. There you have a kind of neat image of homosexuality without any possibility of generating unease, and for two reasons: it responds to a reassuring canon of beauty, and it cancels everything that can be troubling in affection, tenderness, friendship, fidelity, camaraderie, and companionship, things that our rather sanitized society can't allow a place for without fearing the formation of new alliances and the tying together of unforeseen lines of force. I think that's what makes homosexuality 'disturbing': the homosexual mode of life, much more than the sexual act itself. To imagine a sexual act that doesn't conform to law or nature is not what disturbs people. But that individuals are beginning to love one another—there is the problem (Foucault 2000: 136).

Identity, apart from being an important performative statement with the potential to disrupt straight culture, also seems to answer a deep personal need. A hijra narrative captures this powerfully. Roopa, a 30-year-old hijra states: 'Ever since I can remember I have always identified as a woman. I lived in Namakkal, a village in Tamil Nadu. When I was studying in my tenth standard I realised that the only way for me to be comfortable with my self was to join the hijra community' (PUCL-K 2003). What emerges clearly is dissatisfaction with seeing identity that is based solely on sex, and not sexuality and gender. For Roopa, comfort with her self is linked to becoming a part of the hijra community. For the hijra community, the sex one desires to be as well as the sex one desires to be with are both linked to a form of self-identity called hijra.

A friend and fellow activist once remarked:

> When I was 13 or 14, what probably saved me through the horror of an adolescence where none of my desires made any sense to anyone but me, was the ability to say 'I am not straight, I am gay'. I remember the first time I said it. I had language. I had a kind of identity. I had space. I could talk to my parents and I had something to say, some way to explain. I had my other identities and now I had the final piece of the puzzle. As I grew older, I found others who felt the same way, who shared the same community.[8]

The proliferation of identity and identity politics is closely tied to both a new political language that uses rights-based and community-centric ideas (for instance, gay rights as human rights), as well as the emergence of support spaces where the lives of same-sex desiring people can be validated and shared, rather than be judged and condemned. Cities across India now have support spaces and meetings—GayBombay, LABIA, or Aanchal Trust meetings in Bombay, Good As You (GAY) in Bangalore, SAATHI or Sappho meetings in Kolkata, Sangini or meetings at the Naz Foundation (Humraahi, Humnawaaz, and Humjoli) in Delhi, or at Olava or the Queer Studies Circle in Pune.

Challenges Facing the Movement

Regardless of the pressure of our activism, many questions continue to be asked of the queer movement in India. Perhaps the most relentless construct which assaults queer people is the conceptualisation of their lives as the preoccupations of a small, Western-educated, and élite minority, whose understanding of sexuality is thus aped from the West. This perception has old histories and continues to compel writers on sexuality in India to respond to the charge that they are talking about an issue that is either not relevant to the 'Indian' context, or one that deals with a lesser politics in the face of greater oppressions. Janaki Nair and Mary John respond to these critiques strongly. They argue:

> We cannot but draw upon western theories, since they determine at an unconscious level, the reading practices we bring to bear on our work. But this still leaves us with the task of theorization, which can never take the form of the application of a theory that one possesses in advance, but must resemble a process, a historical and political mode of conceptualizing sexual economies that

would be true to our experiences of an uneven modernity, calling for multiple levels of analysis and the forging of articulations between the global and local (John and Nair 2000: 7).

What Nair and John are arguing is that while the West might inform certain discourses of sexuality (and, indeed, on any and all other issues), it is neither our sole language to speak of sexuality, nor the only conceptualisation with which we understand our desires. Understandings of what it means to be queer in India are constituted within local discourses that reflect the realities of our own socio-political contexts, and extend far beyond the Western framework of sexual identity—hijra and kothi identities are perhaps the most easily identifiable examples of this argument. For a country that lives under a constitution and a penal code modelled on the nations of the West, and which firmly and desperately seeks to be a larger part of a Western, globalised, consumer culture, the larger question here is why the 'tag' of Western (however wrongly applied) is construed as an invalidation of passionately felt sexual desires and strongly defended identities, *only* when it comes to sexuality.

Beyond the 'Western' tag, there lie other challenges. Ideally, queer spaces would be free from the hierarchies and exclusionary politics of mainstream society. Yet the reality of queer spaces is that they must also struggle against their own biases and hierarchies, particularly along the lines of class and gender. The movement is rightly criticised for still being largely urban-based, and queer spaces often reflect the patriarchal biases of our society, being more easily accessed and safer for men. There are far fewer lesbian women who are able to live their lives as freely as most gay men, and hijra and kothi communities remain marginalised from the leadership of the movement in many ways. While there is still often far more freedom in queer spaces than in mainstream society, there is still a need to ensure that the hierarchies of our hetero-patriarchal context do not seep into these newly emergent spaces.

There are also more fundamental questions in the minds of many. While identity politics and the emergence of identity-based communities have made several positive and important contributions, there are also perspectives within the community that lament the strict categorisation of same-sex desire into neat and often exclusionary boxes. What happens to those who do not identify as one or the other? What happens to our understanding of sexuality itself if any inkling of desire has to be instantly codified or named?[9] Is the categorisation of same-sex desire a first step towards a community where our named identities divide us within ourselves? At what point is a space 'autonomous', and at what point does it become 'exclusionary'?[10] As a movement slowly gains momentum, these questions remind us of the challenges that exist even within the queer community, alongside the discrimination that exists in larger society.

THE STRUCTURE OF THE ANTHOLOGY

Efforts at writing on queer-related themes that have come before us have focused either on mapping the relentless violence inflicted by state and civil society on queer people, or on the stories of queer people as they live their lives. The former has been pioneered by groups such as ABVA , Stree Sangam, CALERI, and the PUCL-K. The latter has emerged through the anthologies on gay and lesbian writing edited by Hoshang Merchant and Ashwini Sukthankar respectively. The two forms of writing have shared little common ground. While one sketches the larger conceptual frameworks of the politics of sexuality, the other documents the reality of queer lives that must live and negotiate these very frameworks. Neither has, as yet, fed into the other, understanding how the everyday lives of queer people are politics in themselves, or how the politics of sexuality must emerge from the realities of queer lives. This anthology will attempt to break this dualism by bring together writings that show how political and conceptual spaces impact queer lives, and also how queer lives shape these frameworks in turn.

Towards this end, the anthology begins with a section on the theoretical paradigms that describes our understandings of gender and sexuality and lays out the central tenets and perspectives of queer politics. Following this is a section that documents the experiences of activists working for queer rights in myriad spaces. Writings in this section not only document the victories, the setbacks, and the challenges ahead for the movement, but also serve as spaces of self-reflection as the writers/activists reflect on how the complex field of sexuality constantly forces them to rethink their own foundational assumptions. Finally, there are the personal stories of queer people as they document their own negotiations through the maze of identities, desires, loves, faiths, and politics. These personal narratives don't just need to be documented but require to be seriously reflected upon as an aid to further conceptualise the nuances of queer life.

The authors who have contributed to this anthology include some well-known names, but the significant majority of contributors are being published for the first time. We consciously tried to get narratives that cut across class, religion, gender and language. A special effort was made to include hijra and kothi perspectives. Apart from this strategy, we also sent out a general call for contributions through the email list lgbt-india@yahoogroups.com. The sheer depth of talent within the queer community, and the eagerness of so many to write openly about their lives and beliefs both excited and humbled us. These are perhaps some of the most telling indicators of how far the queer movement in the Indian context has come.

It is important to acknowledge the many limitations we could not overcome. Though we made efforts to get as diverse a range of voices as possible, hijra and kothi voices still continue to be underrepresented. While Maya Sharma's work has been translated from Hindi, and Revathi's from Tamil, we were unable to get more non-English texts. We hope that readers and activists alike will see this anthology as a stepping stone to take on projects of their own that fill such gaps.

Theoretical Paradigms

The first part of the book attempts to place the diverse sexuality-related struggles we have outlined above within a conceptual framework. The fundamental questions that preoccupy the authors in this section strike at the very heart of our understandings of gender and sexuality. The purpose behind having a section on conceptual frameworks surrounding sexuality is two-fold. One, we believe that unthinking activism, that is, a politics that doesn't grapple with larger paradigms of thinking, will lead to a dead end as will any theory which loses its grip over the reality of people's lives. Two, there is a constant need for introspection and a questioning and rethinking of the frameworks within which our politics is conducted. This section outlines the contours of the political debate, mapping the strands of thinking that exist in queer spaces, and posing new questions that queer activists and all those thinking on sexuality continue to grapple with.

The first piece by Nivedita Menon explores the idea of 'natural' and 'normal' sex and sexuality. Menon's argument is stunning in its sheer simplicity, as it exposes how scratching just a little below the surface shakes the foundations of what are some of the deepest assumptions of heteronormative society. Speaking of the construction of heterosexuality as being the only 'natural' sexuality, Menon wonders: 'if normal behaviour is so natural, then why does it require such a set of controls—from religion to law to the state—to keep it in place?' Arguing that 'patriarchy needs the institutions of compulsory heterosexuality to survive', Menon's piece speaks to both feminists and the public at large to understand the institutional roots of gender and sexuality that make one form of union—the heterosexual, patriarchal family—paramount above all others.

The subsequent pieces extend Menon's questioning to other spaces. Arvind Narrain and Vinay Chandran trace the emergence of homosexuality within medicine, and, in particular, mental health. They present a history of the way in which medicine has treated and understood homosexuality, and in doing so, challenge the power and presumed objectivity of the medical discourse. The authors argue that a possible way of resisting the all-pervasive heterosexism of the medical establishment might be through forms of queer activism which question the power of the medical discourse to define and pathologise the very category of the 'homosexual'.

T. Muraleedharan, in his queer reading of Malayalam cinema, takes us to a space beyond the law and the state. Cinema in India is a realm in which literally millions of people participate, and Muraleedharan draws a fascinating picture of how cinema also caters to a queer sensibility. By re-reading the assumed 'straightness' of Malayalam cinema, he opens out an entire field of inquiry into how queer desire is constituted and how it is nourished through queer subtexts that insistently pop out of the otherwise seemingly 'straight' narrative.

The two other essays in the section turn their gaze onto queer political spaces themselves. Akshay Khanna raises fundamental questions about how we understand sexuality itself—a space, a process, an identity, a way to describe who we are or simply a way to name ourselves? Khanna challenges the proliferation of identities in queer spaces, and reminds us that we are creating and defining the language in which sexuality will be spoken about in the future. He asks a critical question—'how does the way we name ourselves impact the way in which we participate in political processes?'—and answers it by locating sexuality in a historical framework, and by challenging the language of sexuality activism which, he argues, is limited by the postcolonial framework through which we understand personhood.

Gautam Bhan tackles the place of legal reform and its intersections—both as points of convergence and divergence—with a larger process of social change. His argument warns of the danger of the movement being confined within the space and the language of the law, and reminds us that legal challenges must be seen as 'being located as part of a larger political struggle,' one that does not limit itself to the courtroom, but challenges 'not just pieces of legislation, but the larger understandings of gender and sexuality that allow such legislations to exist in the first place'.

Stories of Struggle

In conceptualising this section, we wanted both to tell untold stories of activism, and critically reflect on the directions of the Indian queer movement. We asked our writers—all of whom are activists in the queer movement—to write about their own experiences, looking at their lives as activists and as queer people. The lines, as expected, are often blurred—personal desires blend into and often become political objectives, and public protests often speak of private lives. These narratives are perhaps the most telling reminder that there is no one queer reality and that there is not just one, but indeed many, queer struggles. This section is also an attempt to raise various difficult questions, as we ask ourselves, as queer people, how inclusive our movement truly is.

One gets a sense of the various trajectories of activism and the changing nature of queer spaces right from the feeling of complete isolation with which Elavarthi Manohar started his activist career in the early 1980s to the almost celebratory mode in which Tarun and Mario D' Penha write about their experiences in the National Law School and Jawaharlal Nehru University in the late 1990s and early 2000s. Manohar's struggle to raise sexuality as a human rights issue, speaks to the dilemmas faced by many activists when he argues that, 'sexuality issues are considered irrelevant and élitist and hence routinely excluded from the human rights agenda in the Indian context.' Just as Manohar grapples with his attempts to seek spaces where the politics of sexuality are taken seriously, other authors echo his concerns and document their efforts at broadening the reach of queer politics. Tarun and Mario D'Penha take us to a newly emerging frontier for the queer movement—college campuses. Documenting two contrasting campus climates, they not only tell the tale of their efforts to build queer-friendly spaces within colleges, but also identify the factors that made such a movement possible, including supportive faculty, visiting speakers, and already existing campus political spaces.

Sexuality movements share a complex relationship with other movements at the margins. Even as some women's groups have begun the process to fully accept same-sex desire as a part of the women's movement, there are telling silences, within, for example, the Dalit or labour movements. Several queer groups stress the interconnectedness between queer politics and other politics that oppose hetero-patriarchal norms, arguing that casteism, classism, communalism and homophobia ultimately emerge from the same place. Yet how does one begin to realise these interconnections in a meaningful and practical way? What brings movements together, and what keeps them together? Chayanika Shah, writes in this volume about activism at the intersections of feminist politics and queer politics. She shares the pain of feeling trapped between trying to validate queer struggles in feminist spaces, as well as feminist struggles in queer spaces.

Ashwini Sukthankar takes up on Chanyanika's critique and notes that coming from an ideological framework of being a feminist and a lesbian activist, she was troubled by the implications of transsexual rights. She argues that she felt as if:

> a transsexual rights movement in India would only aggravate the phenomenon where two women seeking to make a life together are encouraged to believe that one must metamorphose into a man in order for the relationship to exist as a phenomenon acceptable or recognisable to society (Sukthankar, present volume).

What makes Sukthankar's essay fascinating is that she moves from this belief to examine her own stance—a rare and insightful self-critique as she struggles to balance the theory in her mind with the reality of the lives and heartfelt viewpoints of the two transsexual people she interviews. A similar self-reflexivity characterises Deepa V.N.'s piece on Sahayatrika—a queer women's support space in Kerala. The very first line of her essay alerts readers to her awareness of Sahayatrika's politics:

> The Sahayatrika Project was problematic by almost all indices of political correctness. It was a political initiative that was made possible through foreign funding—in our most active period, we operated through a ten-month grant from an international agency concerned specifically with sexuality minority issues. It was coordinated by a non-resident Indian (myself) whose major life experiences and political experiences were with gay/lesbian communities in the west (Deepa V.N., present volume).

Deepa's essay addresses the experience of working with an often tenuous and fragile group of women struggling with their same-sex desires, who are fleetingly present and often quickly disappear. She powerfully documents the way the idea of the 'lesbian' is constructed in Kerala. As she notes, in the popular imagination in Kerala, a lesbian is 'someone who will have sex with anybody'. Her work speaks to working with women who love other women and creating an identity for same-sex desire in an overwhelmingly patriarchal context. There are moments of victory and of loss—for every woman who calls and then is never heard from again, there is a letter with a green Kathakali face and the words 'Express Yourself' emblazoned across the front.

Alok Gupta in his essay brings out the sheer diversity of the queer community and traverses the complex divisions which class engenders in queer spaces. He recounts how being called 'Englishpur *ki* kothi' startled him into realising that, even amidst people with whom he shared a sexual orientation, his class status made him seem like he was literally from another country—the mythical land of Englishpur. His essay goes on to map the varied ways in which class enters queer spaces, and also recounts the different approaches to class amongst various groups. While gay men seemed indifferent to class, he argues, kothis identify it as a central issue in the community. It is this gap that Gupta defines as a particular fault line, the transcending of which he posits as a critical challenge for queer activism.

Pawan Dhall, a long-time queer activist from Kolkata, recounts the earliest days of the queer struggle in his city. His essay is as much the story of his own journey to a sexual and personal identity, as it is an in-depth account of organisations, clubs, spaces and magazines that came and went in the many years that he has been an activist. He speaks of these fleeting efforts at queer organising with a sense of tenderness, recognising how much they nurtured him and the spaces he inhabited, and how they were, in so many ways, building blocks of the contemporary queer movement.

Bina Fernandez and N.B. Gomathy in their piece on the film *Fire* discuss the enormous possibilities that the film and the various protests around it opened out. The piece speaks not so much about the film as text but rather the act of going to the film as a pivotal experience it ultimately became for lesbian and bisexual women. As the authors note:

> For those of us who identify as women who love women, that such a film should have been made at all and shown in India in mainstream theatres seems almost unbelievable. The experience of sitting in a theatre full of women and watching the film with its scenes of love and caring between two women, and not a man and a woman was moving in a way that prevented immediate analysis or critique. Foremost was a sense of exultation that in the barrage of constant heterosexist imagery was (one possible) representation visibilising and validating the ways in which women can love women (Fernandez and Gomathy, present volume).

The second piece by Fernandez and Gomathy reports a study undertaken under the aegis of the Tata Institute of Social Sciences, where the authors document the nature of violence suffered by lesbian and bisexual women in India, drawing upon the narratives of numerous women. This piece locates the institutional roots of violence against lesbian and bisexual women, and, critically, expands its definition, speaking of emotional and intangible violence as well as that which is physically manifested. This piece raises fundamental questions as to whether we as activists do yet have any understanding of the institutional roots of violence against lesbians. If the family remains a key part of the framework of violence against lesbians, then maybe one needs to move towards a reconceptualisation of the family itself The piece also implicitly raises the larger question as to why violence faced by lesbian women in these spaces has not yet become a human rights issue in the same way that, for example, Section 377 of the IPC has become.

One of the concerns that queer activists have to face is the urban location of much of our activism. Fact-finding reports such as the PUCL-K report on violence against the transgender community make clear that rural spaces are often the site of violence against hijra and other transgender communities. This fact is also evidenced by the number of hijras deciding to escape the intolerance of the rural to make a life in the urban context. However, in spite of these narratives it is fair to say that the history of 'queer' desire in the rural context is yet to be written, and the queer person in the rural context still awaits the telling of her story. Maya Sharma's work (see Personal Lives below) is perhaps one of the first attempts at documenting the oral histories of queerness among women in rural areas.

However, semi-urban spaces that are neither fully urban nor rural are slowly emerging as new sites of queer activism as evidenced by the story of Amitié, a friendship group set up in a small subdivisional town called Chandanagar in West Bengal. What emerges from this narrative is the striking similarity in the nature of violence which is inflicted in both big cities and small towns. Queer activism in small towns often defines itself in a relationship to the big cities which is often understood in terms of 'lack,' with the town seen as lacking facilities, resources, and so on, which are more easily accessible in the city. We are still in need of narratives from rural areas and small towns which are examples of organisation and contestation which in some ways predate the influence of the big cities and are accurate reflections of how resistance happens within the rubric of more traditional ways of living.

Personal Lives

Politics in the queer context is not only a political performance engendered by group activism, but also remains a personal, and sometimes lonely and frustrating, struggle against the insistent everyday pressure to conform to the dominant notions of what it is to be an ideal (read: heterosexual) man or woman in society. This pressure plays itself out in our most intimate spaces—our families, our friendships, our workplaces and in the way we see ourselves. Coming to terms with ourselves and our desires, finding a voice to tell others around us, learning to celebrate our sexuality, refusing again and again to let it be silenced, and searching for and creating spaces in which to be ourselves—the personal journeys of queer lives are stories of daily resistance that these authors have fought long and hard to be able to tell.

This section has a critical place in this anthology. If it is to succeed, a larger politics must build itself on an understanding of people's lives. The nuances of what it means to live a life on the margins of societal institutions like marriage, monogamy and family, needs to be told, reflected upon, and conceptualised. Any genuine queer history must go beyond the outward and public expressions of politics and try and decipher the contestations of social and cultural codes which emerge through the daily act of living a queer life.

Perhaps emblematic of the struggles of queer people around the world is the act of 'coming out'—the first voicing of our desires to ourselves and then to others—which has a central place in defining queer identity. Vaibhav Saria, in his narrative on coming out, captures the drama and the pathos which a Marwari boy who remembers himself being called *chakka* in school faces when he comes out to his mother. The insistent failure to acknowledge Vaibhav's homosexuality as anything but abnormal, the reference to Indian society and its inability to accept such a thing, and even the failure of his mother to state her love for her son are all evoked in a story that will strike a chord with many queer people.

While Vaibhav's story documents open confrontations, Sheba Tejani's story speaks of a more hidden and layered hesitancy. She writes of her life in Mumbai at a point when she and her girlfriend are contemplating moving to an area in which a lot of her family members live. Sheba is forced to ponder what the move would mean in terms of her daily intimacies. What if her cousins decided to 'drop in'? What would she do about the multicoloured postcard with the word 'homo' blazing across the front? Or what would happen if she bumped into her aunt when she and her partner were feeling especially amorous? Would she be able to hold her girlfriend's hand on the street and not worry about bumping into a relative?

Coming out as an act of political assertion also emerges strongly in Satya Rai Nagpaul's piece. The essay, almost deceptive in its simplicity, documents that first moment of the end of a journey, one across genders as a sex reassignment surgery brings a body in line with a deeply felt gender. Nagpaul's need to tell Noor Sahib that the reason he does not know how to tie a dhoti is because he is a transman is perhaps the heart of the queer political impulse— a desire to be recognised for who we are.

Maya Sharma's piece articulates the culturally bounded nature of the entire discourse of coming out. What happens to people who are not part of a discourse which enables you to come out? What is the nature of their political expression? Sharma illustrates this by calling close attention to the nuances of the way same-sex desire expresses itself in the case of Hasina and Fatima. Hasina's entire description of Fatima is a male who 'comes from the world of the spirits'. As Sharma notes,

> Hasina has gone beyond the limits of the socially permissible. Paradoxically, in a male-dominated location where male-inspired and male-authored laws were

interpreted and applied by men in favour of men, her vision was rooted in the realm of the illegal. Somehow, either miraculously or through sheer strength of will, she had generated possibility from the matrix of the impossible. Her private world materialised its substance from the very same public ground that completely excluded both her and her desired other.

Thus in Hasina's case, there is no coming out, but rather a mixture of affirming certain traditional values as well as articulating a mystical fantasy which encapsulates the extent to which her desire would be tolerated by her and by society around her. The 'coming out' dilemma naturally leads to larger questions: what is one coming out into? What changes when one 'comes out'? What is so different or so special about queer life? What is its everyday nature composed of? Other essays in the section offer different answers.

The letter exchange between the father of a gay son, A. K., and a Kolkata-based queer activist exemplifies the varied nature of perceptions of the everydayness of queer life. In Mr A. K.'s worldview there is place for love between two men, but what he cannot understand is whether coming out is about the right to get affection, or simply about the right to have multiple partners? The letter was written on one of the gay e-mail lists, and its response tries to illustrate the varied nature of life in the queer community, arguing that it is difficult to draw any line as to what queer life is about. The activist notes that there are committed relationships as well as multiple-partner relationships within queer spaces and being judgemental about either is problematic.

Prathiba Sixer Rani in her piece evokes a culture which is a striking synthesis of Western queer culture and existing Indian traditions to evoke a kothi identity, one which shows a familiarity with both the Yellamma of North Karnataka and the protests on Stonewall day. In her narrative, Revathi evokes what coming out into the hijra community means for her. In a compelling account she writes about how her desire to be a woman led to her joining the hijra community. The narrative documents an extremely difficult journey as Revathi negotiates the intolerance of her family, the police and goondas. What is remarkable about Revathi's story is her insistence on struggling for a better world for others like her. As she puts it, 'Even if my dreams had to be bundled up into a gunny bag and forgotten I felt that others like me should not end up the way I did.'

Sandip Roy questions the very idea of the freedom others are searching for. In his essay, he captures the dissatisfaction and loneliness of coming out into the 'freedom' of Western gay culture with its clubs and muscle boys. He articulates a need for community, belonging and acceptance which for queer people of Indian origin in the West, neither Indian families or Western gay culture is quite able to provide. As he says, 'I am trying to make myself a family. But I never know if I get the recipe right.'

Sonali, in her poem, captures the oppositionality which marks queer existence. The 'Sum Total' of lesbian existence is understood as a constant struggle to defy the norm—be it the norm of marriage as a dutiful obedient wife, the norm of getting a job as a doctor or engineer or the norm of wearing 'long beautiful hair'. Sonali asserts queer life as

> Divided by abusive demons
> Multiplied by
> A will to survive
> Sums me up.

How do our queer selves interact with our other identities along the lines of class, religion, and gender? All of us are a complex intersection of many identities and writers in this section remind us of the ways in which other aspects of personhood intersect with sexual orientation to either limit the expression of sexual orientation or enable it. In Maya Sharma's essay, for example, she notes: 'Hasina was well aware of exactly to what extent a woman of her class, whether Muslim, Hindu, Christian or Dalit, is permitted to live in the way that she wants to. She was also aware that to violate the social norms was, in literal and psychological terms, a dangerous action that could have serious psychological consequences.' Mario D'Penha's narrative on the other hand is a brave attempt at reconciling different seemingly conflicting aspects of selfhood. What does one do if one is born a Christian and identifies as gay? Do you disown the gay part of your self or the Christian part? In his essay, Mario attempts to get past this problematic by reinterpreting Christianity on his own terms, and finds that the spirit of his faith allows him the space for multiple identities.

For Ali Potia, the effort at reconciling the different parts of his identity brings him up against a blank wall. He is critical of those who 'wander around searching for meaning in a religious tradition which says that they don't have a right to exist'. Based on this understanding he concludes that:

I see no problems in defining my identity exclusively in terms of my sexuality. After all, being gay is about so much more than just sex. My queer, urban family and I have much more in common with each other than just the fact that we sleep with members of the same sex. We face the same discriminations, we fight the same battles, and we share the same spaces. In fact, everybody else also seems to think we are identical—look at our portrayal in the mass media—so maybe we do have just that one identity after all. We are all just queers.

The narratives of Roy, Potia, D'Penha and Revathi all address the contemporary experience with identity and its limitations, and how any identity is by itself a form of exclusion. This has particular salience within the queer community where there are always those who define an identity in terms of how they look and how they dress. Gym-toned bodies, military cuts and tight t-shirts are a common sight in gay male clubs in the West, and one is increasingly witness to the same kind of 'look' in Indian gay parties and clubs. For Revathi, while her identity as a hijra is important, she also feels trapped by the constraints to which she is exposed because she is a hijra. What needs to be recognised is that as we form a certain queer culture and a collective identification, people who do not fully subscribe to the norms of the culture—be it gay, lesbian or hijra—are, once again, excluded.

However, one also needs to keep in mind that regardless of the complexities and limitations of identity, the world where identities don't exist and only sexual acts are allowed to exist is not exactly the proverbial Garden of Eden. Devdutt Pattanaik's narrative alerts us to the fact that these narratives of 'coming out' are few, with possibly most people leading lives in which the 'queerness' is completely invisible. In his piece, Pattanaik captures the pain and poignancy which is an inevitable part of the end of someone who is forced by circumstances to lead a 'double life', that is, straight in the day and gay at night. When death ends such a gay life, then the gay part of the person's life is rendered completely invisible and the dead person is venerated as a good nephew and a good son, but his identity as a lover of men, stands erased. The pain of 'invisibility', and erasure seems to be the natural end point when identity is not an option.

Parting Words

In an ideal world, this book would end with a tightly-written summary of the limits, beliefs, and tenets of a queer politics, with which one could agree or disagree. It would lay out a philosophy, argue a case, and even present an identifying label that 'queers' could then use to name themselves to others. It would offer solutions, find mediations, neatly label and define communities, give shape to paradigms, while also giving solace and the assurance of a better tomorrow. Ours being far from an ideal world, however, this cannot be the case. Hopefully, the words in this anthology will be some part of each of the above. Even if they do nothing else, perhaps that will be enough. The true test of queer politics will only come with time, for like with other living histories, the future is as yet an unwritten part of the story.

Acknowledgements

Like all efforts that seek to capture the voice of an entire community this volume was, perhaps from the very beginning, fated to be a necessary, but never sufficient, effort. Yet even the little we have done would not have been possible without the help of many. Our editors, Arpita Das and Parul Nayyar, of Yoda Press, who in themselves are a queer space of comfort and inclusion, and who are the reason this book exists at all; our families—both biological and chosen, and especially our parents whose pride in us is our sustenance; our colleagues in the queer movement who inspire us every day; and, more than anything else, each and every one of our contributors, who have taken the time to share their thoughts, beliefs, and stories with us, and also trusted us enough to do their amazing lives some measure of justice. To you, our eternal debt. We would also like to thank Arul Mani for enthusiastically translating Revathi's story from Tamil to English.

We owe much to a few in particular. Gautam would like to thank Jaya and Lesley for a queer home away from home; his own urban queer family spread which has sustained him in so many ways across so many geographical divides: Siddharth, Maya, Aarti, Richa, Nais, Dubey, Arvind, Famila, Kajol, Bombay Grrls, Anokhi, Akshay, Alicia, Ponni, Sophia, Sheena, Abhi, Sharmi, Mario, Parth, Ali, Rohit, Ekta, Vinay, Arvind, Tarun, Monica, Pramada, Vivek, Prateek, and Priya. He would also like to pay homage to his few shelters in the big bad streets of queer Delhi: PRISM meetings at India Coffee House, Friday's at Nigah, Bhagwan Nagar, Jagah, the ALF office, JNU (who would have thought?), Anjuman, Saheli @ Defence Colony, Hash, P'n'P, and the IIFT Dhaba. A special thank you to Arvind—for everything.

Arvind would like to thank his comrades at the Alternative Law Forum (ALF) for creating a space of comfort which made this anthology possible: Lawrence, Namita, Jaga, Clifton, Anu, Tahir, Neeraj, Alok, Anuja, Geetu, Aarti and Vishwas have been central to making ALF what it is. Special thanks to Curt, Sanjeev, Anna, Vinay, Tarunabh, Siddharth, Gautam and Nanu for being there in so many different ways. He would also like to thank his mother, father and sister for being consistently supportive of his many endeavours.

NOTES

1. Also see Revathi's piece in this volume.
2. See also Voices Against Section 377. 2004. *Rights for All: Ending Discrimination Under Sec 377. Copy on file. Available on request: voicesagainst377@hotmail.com.*

3. For a powerful analysis of the constitutive role that law plays in producing a regime in which gays and lesbians are ultimately encouraged to police themselves and the way in which sodomy laws function as symbolic statements and as threats of criminal punishment and disempower lesbians and gays in a range of contexts, see Goodman 2003.
4. The most recent protest was in Bangalore in 2004 around the case of Kokila, a hijra who, when she went to the police to report a crime of rape against her, was further sexually abused and tortured by the police itself.
5. In the recently released documentary film, *Many People, Many Desires* (2004).
6. See Muraleedharan, present volume.
7. See www.geocities.com/nigahmedia.
8. Personal Communication. Name withheld upon request.
9. See Khanna, present volume.
10. Our gratitude to both Gupta (present volume), and Shalini Mahajan, of LABIA in Mumbai for this conceptualisation.

REFERENCES

Bandopadhyay, Aditya. 2002, 'Where Saving Lives is a Crime: The Lucknow Story'. Personal Communication, Copy on File.

Desai, Mihir. 2003, 'Law and Discrimination against Homosexuals', *Combat Law*, Vol. 2, No. 4, October–November.

Goodman, Ryan. 2003, Beyond the Enforcement Principle, *California Law Review*, Vol. 89, No. 643.

Gupta, Alok, 2002, 'The History and Trends in the Application of the Anti–Sodomy Law in the Indian Courts', *The Lawyers Collective*, Vol. 16, No. 7, p. 9.

Fernandez, Bina (ed.). 2000, *Humjinsi*, Bangalore:Combat Law Publications.

Foucault, Michel. 2000, *Ethics, Vol. 1*, London: Penguin.

John, Mary and Janaki Nair (eds). 2000, *A Question of Silence*, New Delhi: Kali for Women.

People's Union for Civil Liberties, Karnataka (PUCL, K). 2001, *Human Rights Violations against Sexual Minorities in India: A Case Study of Bangalore*, www.pucl.org.

———. 2003, *Human Rights Violations against the Transgender Community: A Study of Kothi and Hijra Sex Workers in Bangalore*.

Sukthankar, Ashwini. 2000, 'For People Like Us', in Brinda Bose (ed.), *Translating Desire*, New Delhi: Katha.

Warner, Michael (ed.). 1993, *Fear of a Queer Planet*, London:University of Minnesota Press.

I

Conceptual Approaches to Sexuality as a Form of Politics

1

How Natural is Normal?
Feminism and Compulsory Heterosexuality*

Nivedita Menon

 Anyone who has ever tried to raise sexual preference as a political issue in India would be familiar with the stern admonition—there are many more serious issues we have to deal with first: poverty and class conflict, caste and communalism. This bit of wisdom though, is useful far beyond the context of sexuality—it is a neat all-purpose argument that serves to set aside and trivialise any issue that challenges the dominant common sense, whether of Left politics or of the conservative middle class. For instance, on the question of reservations, you will often hear the sonorous pronouncement that Dalits are not well served by reservations in jobs—only when structural changes like land reforms have taken place will their position improve. Why go in for piecemeal measures? Until the huge radical transformations have taken place, let us not disturb the status quo. This kind of argument sets up a hierarchy of oppressions along a scale decided by one set of opinions. What if your opinions don't tally, you don't agree with this hierarchy, and you insist, cussedly, that the oppression your particular stigmatised group faces is as important and as immediate as any other? Then you are engaging in 'identity politics', and breaking up the possibilities of a broader unity.

The term 'identity politics' is used as a term of abuse by those who see themselves as occupying some unmarked identity such as 'Indian citizen',

* This article is based on two presentations, one made at the Larzish Film Festival, Mumbai, October 2003, and subsequently published in *Scripts* Number 4, April 2004 and the panel organised by PRISM at WSF 2004, Mumbai, and subsequently published as 'Unnatural Sexuality versus Natural Justice' in the *Indian Express*, 21 January 2004.

rather than an 'identity' such as 'woman' or 'muslim' or 'dalit' or 'homosexual'—but believe me, you have to be pretty damn privileged if you can afford the luxury of that unmarked designer label of 'citizen'. Only if you are privileged by your class position can you forget that you are any of those identities, and even then, most women and non-heterosexuals and Dalits and Muslims know to their cost that they can shout for all they are worth that they are simply 'citizens'—they are stigmatised, *branded* (now in a different sense—not branded as in designer label, but branded as in cattle), by their 'identity', whether they like it or not. This is not to say that all forms of identity politics are by definition democratic, because there can be anti-democratic assertions of identity. But by the same token, not all forms of identity politics can be simply denounced without taking into account how they define themselves with reference to the larger society.

Now, as far as patriarchy is concerned, this 'hierarchy of oppressions' argument is something feminists have heard since the time feminists first walked the Earth—you'll get the vote after the white working-class men, then after the black men, we'll get to your stuff after the revolution, after the nation is free. At best, gender gets treated as an add-on to what is called a 'broader understanding'—add gender to class, to caste, to communalism, to development, just a little soupçon to improve the flavour. Then you get questions like—how are women and children (why isn't it ever 'men and children', just to be even more irritating and cussed) affected by communal violence/caste oppression/development strategies that marginalise the powerless? The more questions are posed in this way, the more the fundamental point lies unrecognised, that if you take 'gender' seriously as an axis of oppression, then Class and Caste and Nation themselves look very different. You can't simply 'add gender and stir'.

But it seems feminists have learnt the lesson too well from patriarchy when it comes to sexuality. If not being actively homophobic, our movement's best response tends to be along the lines of 'not now, this is not the time'. But is 'sexual preference' (a term that tames and domesticates the really scary issue at stake here, but we'll come to that later)—a mere add-on to feminism? Or, to translate the question in a way that any feminist would understand: is gender merely an add-on to nationalism/development? Did we feminists spend over half-a-century of scholarship and politics challenging the 'add gender and stir' formula, only to apply it to sexuality ourselves?

What we need to recognise, particularly as feminists, is that the normalisation of heterosexuality is at the heart of patriarchy. Patriarchy needs the institutions of compulsory heterosexuality to survive. (Note 'compulsory' as opposed to 'natural', we'll be coming back to this.) But compulsory heterosexuality undergirds most other forms of identity too. Caste, race and community identity are produced through birth. So too is the quintessentially modern identity of citizenship. The purity of these identities and social formations and of the existing regime of property relations is protected by the strict policing and controlling of women's sexuality. Thus, the family as it exists, the only form in which it is allowed to exist—the heterosexual patriarchal family—is key to maintaining both nation and community.

A recent-striking illustration of my point is the debate over Sonia Gandhi's 'foreign origins'. Is there any doubt that had Indira Gandhi had a daughter who married an Italian man, that man would have zero chances of being considered for political office even by those who now support Sonia Gandhi's case? Once a woman marries, she assumes her husband's identity, and far from the Italian husband becoming Indian, the wife would become Italian. After all, much of the mass support for Sonia comes from the understanding that *bahu ki koi jaat nahin hoti* (the daughter-in-law has no caste). The *bahu* becomes ours—whatever she was to begin with. (Well, not *whatever*—as a reader asked rhetorically in a weekly, what would have been the acceptability of a blonde, Japanese or black *bahu?*) As for daughters, in the context of inheriting political mantles, some do and some don't, the latter more so if there is a brother to take over. But with other kinds of inheritances, of family name, lineage and property, daughters have no status, they barely even exist except as tokens to be passed on.

Another instance of the assumed naturalness of the patriarchal family— the vivid scene from the Hindi film *Mrityudand* in which the visibly pregnant Shabana, whose husband is known to be impotent, is asked *'yeh kiska bachha hai?'* ('Whose child is this?') She answers simply, *'mera'* ('mine'). It is very evident that the baby is inside her body, that it is hers, but the absurd question makes absolute sense in a patriarchal society—who is the father of this child, is what the question means. Whose caste does this child bear, to whose property can he lay claim? Clearly, if this form of the family falls apart, then neither national, race, caste nor community identity can be sustained. Not in the form they now exist. Nor can property arrangements exist. In other words, challenging patriarchy, capitalism and anti-democratic forms of identity politics is inescapably linked to challenging the naturalisation of the heterosexual family.

Incidentally, this may be the main reason behind the Hindu Right's opposition to Valentine's Day. Many of us have our own objections to the commercialisation of 'love'—apparently it's not enough to love someone, you have to buy something to prove it. However, there is a subversive potential to individuals 'falling in love', the possibility that young people could find someone of a different caste or community or of the same gender. What sort of community would it be in which every family has Hindus and Dalits and Muslims, and homosexuals with adopted children from god knows where?

Policing of social boundaries is not the only work done by the institution of marriage. A Delhi High Court judgement in 1984 ruled that the Fundamental Rights to Equality and Freedom have no place in the family. To bring constitutional law into the home, the learned judge ruled, is like 'taking a bull into a china shop'. And of course, he was absolutely right. The family in India is indeed premised on extreme inequality—beginning with the wife changing her surname on marriage, to the property to which no sister has equal rights with her brother. Freedom and equality among individuals would certainly destroy the family as we know it. Consider the other feature central to marriage, assumed to be as natural as breathing—the sexual division of labour which legitimises the unpaid domestic labour of women. It's done 'for love'—is it only in tennis that 'love' means 'nothing'? The ideology of marriage ensures that the physical and mental work (bearing and rearing of children, cooking, cleaning) that goes into reproducing human beings and ensuring their capacity to labour is classified as 'not work'. And this 'not work' is performed exclusively by women. The oppressiveness of this is unrecognised, indeed, women themselves fail to understand why they are unhappy with this thankless, endless drudgery, for after all, they do it for those they love.

But we, feminists in India, have hesitated to attack the primacy of the heterosexual family as such. We have of course, continually pointed to the oppression of women and children within the family, but we nevertheless reinforce existing family structures in many of our interventions, for example, on the issue of the Uniform Civil Code, or over the practice of dowry. In both these instances the target of our critique is not the heterosexual, monogamous, patriarchal institution of marriage—we attack only the practices that surround that institution: polygamy, dowry, domestic violence. With each such intervention we assert in effect, that a *good* marriage would not have these features. Of course, we cannot stop such interventions. But do we have anything beyond such fire-fighting tactics?

Let us go back to the notion of 'sexual preference'. One way of mounting a limited critique of homophobia is to assert the liberal credo that everyone has the right to her privacy, and feminists must recognise that many people (many many people!) are not heterosexual. This is better than nothing, but it is not a radical challenge to heterosexuality, in that it does not recognise the *compulsory* nature of heterosexual institutions. Underlying the argument that as long as consenting adults are involved, sexual preferences are private matters from which the law should keep out, is the assumption that 'sexuality' is a private matter, that 'normal' sexual behaviour springs from nature, and that it has nothing to do with culture or history. But if we recognise that sexuality is located in culture, we have to deal with the uncomfortable idea that sexuality is a human construct, and not something that happens 'naturally.'

Consider the possibility that rules of sexual conduct are as arbitrary as traffic rules, created by human societies to maintain a certain sort of order, and which could differ from place to place—for example, you drive on the left in India and on the right in the United States of America. Further, let us say you question the sort of social order that traffic rules keep in place. Say you believe that traffic rules in Delhi are the product of a model of urban planning that privileges the rich and penalises the poor, that this order encourages petrol-consuming private vehicles and discourages forms of transport that are energy-saving—cycles, public transport, pedestrians. You would then question this model of the city that forces large numbers of inhabitants to travel long distances every day simply to get to school and work. You could debate the merits of traffic rules and urban planning on the grounds of convenience, equity and sustainability of natural resources—at least, nobody could seriously argue that any set of traffic rules is natural.

Let us apply this argument to sexuality. First of all, if 'normal' behaviour were so natural, it would not require such a vast network of controls to keep it in place. Take some random examples. Item one: gendered dress codes. Imagine a bearded man in a skirt in a public place: why would this shake the very foundations of 'normal' society? Unless 'he' is recognisably a *hijra*, and that puts him on the margins of normal society in a different way. Just the wrong kind of cloth on the wrong body, and the very foundations of natural, normal sexual identity start to quake! Two: the disciplining of thought through schools, families, the media, education, religion. All telling you that desire for someone of the same sex is a sin, or insane, or criminal. Three, if all else fails: violent coercive measures to keep people heterosexual, from electric shock therapy to physical abuse to using the coercive apparatus of the state. For instance, recently a lesbian couple in Kerala had to seek court intervention to stop police persecution initiated by their parents. Four: laws; in our case, the notorious Section 377, which penalises 'sexual acts against the order of nature'. Why would we need laws to maintain something that is natural? Are there laws forcing people to eat or sleep? But apparently you need a law to ensure people have sex the 'natural' way.

The point of real interest though, is that human beings do not, in fact, live particularly 'natural' lives. The whole purpose of civilisation seems to be to move as far away from nature as possible. We clothe our naked bodies (indeed, the same people who condemn homosexuality as unnatural would insist that natural nudity be covered up). We cook raw food derived from nature, we build elaborate shelters from the natural elements. We use contraception (again, most of those who condemn homosexuality on the grounds that sex is only for procreation would not question the need for contraception). Clearly, equating 'unnatural' with 'immoral/wrong' is simply a way of suffocating debate.

But the more important question is—what is the social order that the rules of 'normal' sexual behaviour keep in place? Why is it so crucial to ensure that men have legitimate sex only with women? Note the word *legitimate*, because of course sex between people of the same sex is as old as human civilisation. Why the need to ensure that women only have sex with the men they are married to (because again, everyone knows that the rules of chastity and monogamy are enforced strictly only for women)?

If families were only about material and emotional support structures, then any such group of people would be recognised as a family. Isn't it also more likely that humans experience sexual desire in a variety of ways, of which the heterosexual is only one? But the point precisely is that only the heterosexual, patriarchal family is permitted to exist. And this family is about the passing on of property and lineage through men. The 'normality' that this requires is produced, maintained and rigorously policed by the state, laws and social institutions. It is far from being natural or private.

In other words, Section 377 does not refer to some queer people out there, whose unnatural sexual practices normal people can gaze upon like anthropologists at a bizarre tribe. Section 377 is, on the contrary, about the painful creation of Mr and Mrs Normal—it is one of the nails holding in place the elaborate fiction that 'normality' springs from nature.

Maybe we have not seriously recognised the subversive potential of the 'queer' identity. This term is, of course, untranslatable into Indian languages, because it comes out of a specific political appropriation of homophobic discourses by the non-heterosexual movement in the West. The term has its history and cultural moorings in that struggle. But the point is not simply to translate the word, which would raise legitimate questions about why we should not instead look to 'our' histories. The point is to use the experience of that struggle and of that term 'there', to remind ourselves that there are discontinuities and fluidities to the ways in which sexual desire has been experienced, constructed and appropriated 'here'. The beginnings of scholarship in this area (for instance, that of Geeti Thadani or Ruth Vanita and Saleem Kidwai) point to the instability of sexual identities in pre-modern social formations in South Asia, and to the normalisation of heterosexual identity as a part of the processes of colonial modernity. I don't mean to valorise the 'pre-modern' as the space of unambiguous freedom by any means, but merely to suggest that a recognition of sexualities outside heterosexuality, should radically destabilise what is understood to be heterosexual in the first place.

At its worst, the Indian women's movement has been, and is, homophobic. But even its best response to the question of sexuality has been in the form of 'respecting choice'. Such a response as we have seen, leaves unquestioned heterosexuality as the norm—that is, 'most of us are heterosexual, but there are others out there who are *either* lesbian *or* gay *or* B, T, or K'. The alphabets proliferate endlessly *outside* the unchallenged heterosexual space. But if we recognise that this 'normal' heterosexuality is painfully constructed and kept in place by a range of cultural, bio-medical and economic controls, precisely in order to sustain existing hierarchies of class and caste and gender, then we would have to accept that all of us are—or have the potential to be—'queer'.

2

Challenging the Limits of Law
Queer Politics and Legal Reform in India

Gautam Bhan

 For many queer activists, there is a heady sense of freedom in our lives today. No matter what obstacles lie ahead, there is a feeling of having broken new ground in our struggles, and of having found a new language that speaks of real change just as it leads us towards it. This new freedom is a heady feeling, and our first taste of it has seen us rushing to question, to interrogate, to assert, to defy, to testify, to confess, and to celebrate all at once. As we lose ourselves in this freedom, however, we must be careful to realise that a deep responsibility also lies before us. We live in a country that has innumerable histories of struggles against dominance and oppression along the lines of caste, race, religion, empire, and class. Today, sexuality is increasingly joining that list, and the words of this volume are, in a sense, some of the first public stakes of our struggle. We are demanding a right to be heard, and therefore, we must step back and reflect on what our demands are. If we speak of sexuality and of change, what is that we are asking for? What are the ends of our struggle, and what means will we employ to get there? How will our methods reflect our beliefs? Who are we addressing, and what do we want them to believe?

This essay is an effort to begin to answer these questions. In it, I look at the law—one of the prime spaces of protest and change that queer activists have repeatedly turned to—in contrast with movements that seek to challenge hetero-patriarchy outside it. Since 2002, a petition has been traversing the corridors of the Delhi High Court (and, at the time of writing, the Supreme Court of India), in order to read down Section 377. The petitioners are part of the queer rights movement in India, and locate the petition as part of the new language of queer activism I have described above. While most queer activists, including this author, support the petition for what seem to be obvious reasons, I believe that few of us have reflected deeply on what the implications of this legal challenge are for the movement and for queer communities in India. In this essay, it is precisely this reflection that I hope to begin.

How do we understand legal challenges versus efforts at social change in larger society, that is, a protest march, a film festival, the politics of everyday queer lives, or a mass movement? I do not believe that these are two mutually exclusive methods of protest, and I will be the first to admit that the line between the 'law' and 'larger society' is often hard to define. Yet even within these broad generalisations, I believe that there is a distinction to be made between efforts at social change within and outside the law. This difference arises because the languages and logics of protest one employs within the law and outside it are radically different. Not only do these logics often lead to divergent and, at times, contradictory ends, they also require us to use different methodologies of protest, each demanding its own pound of flesh. My attempt in this essay then is not to find the 'right' method of protest, or to pit movements of legal and social change against each other, but instead to remind us that we are making —consciously or not—critical and defining choices within each of these spaces of protest. These choices will shape the queer community of tomorrow in myriad ways, and as such, must be taken with, if nothing else, a deep knowledge of the consequences of our actions as activists.

MAPPING CHALLENGES: WHAT DOES LEGAL REFORM ASK FOR?

Section 377 of the Indian Penal Code effectively criminalises same-sex sexual activity between men, even if it is consensual, between adults, and in private. Studies have shown that its use has been largely limited to cases of child sexual abuse involving young boys, though this does not account for incidents where the law is cited or used in trial court decisions (Gupta 2002). The paucity of court decisions under Section 377, however, does not reflect the tremendous and debilitating impact it has on the lives of queer people for the story of Section 377 plays out mostly outside the courts. Example after example, ranging from documented violations to anecdotal evidence, shows how violence, intimidation and fear in the lives of queer people are legitimised in the name of this law. There are more stories that can be told: the arrest of NGO workers in Lucknow who were charged with Section 377 because they worked on HIV/AIDS prevention efforts with Men-who-have-Sex-with-Men (MSM); the refusal of the National Human Rights Commission to entertain the complaint of a young man who had been given electric shock therapy for two years to 'cure' him of his homosexuality; the routine and continuous violence that queer groups, especially hijra and kothi communities living outside the privileged classes, face at the hands of the police on almost a daily basis (Narrain 2004); or the parents who fear for their queer son or daughter because the law legitimises the homophobia that they see in society around them.

There is currently a petition pending in the Delhi High Court that is asking for a reading down of Section 377. At the time of writing, this petition was being heard by the Supreme Court of India after being dismissed on a technicality by the High Court. Reading down is different from asking for a repeal—the petition is not asking for the law to be removed, but only asking for its interpretation to be changed. If the petition succeeds, then same-sex sexual activity when it occurs between adults, with consent, and in private, would no longer be a criminal offence. The petition names the Government of India and the National Aids Control Organisation (NACO) amongst its respondents. Though NACO had yet to file a reply at the time of writing, the Government's thinking on the issue is now infamous. The government response was as much a doctrine on prevailing social values as it was a legal response to a court petition. They argued that the 'purpose of Sec 377 is to provide a healthy environment in society by criminalizing unnatural sexual activities'. Completing their rhetoric of moral panic, the government went on to describe how 'changes in the law could well open the flood gates of delinquent behaviour and be construed as providing unbridled license for the same'. What does it mean for a government to be able to respond to a legal petition in this manner? When the government uses the argument that 'by and large, Indian society disapproves of homosexuality', to then say that this 'disapproval is strong enough to justify it being treated as a criminal offence'; how do we understand a conception of law where social opinion carries the weight of justice? Perhaps more importantly, how do we, as activists, respond to such a conception of law and justice, and what are the implications of our response?

Let me answer this question by using an example from the Indian women's movement. In the infamous Mathura Rape case (1979), thought by many to be the galvanising force that started the contemporary Indian women's movement, a 16-year old tribal girl accused two policemen of raping her while in custody only to see them released by the court on the grounds that she was 'a loose woman who must have consented to the sexual intercourse' (as cited in Sukthankar, 2002). Sukthankar further argues that the fundamental objection to the judgement by those in the women's movement was the court's measurement of sexual offence against 'societal values of modesty'—the idea that a woman's modesty was a necessary part of the definition of sexuality and, therefore, a marker of her ability to consent to sex.

The court's response in the Mathura case and the government's response to the 377 petition both consider prevailing social norms to be grounds for legal judgement. In doing so, they bring to the surface an often overlooked fact about institutions of justice: the law is not an objective and autonomous space but an institution firmly located in prevailing social hierarchies. In India, the women's movement has long struggled to internalise the realisation that the values of heterosexist patriarchy are just as rampant in the courts as in other parts of society, and that the court will not hesitate to use these values in its conceptions of justice.

The argument that the law legislates on, and on the basis of, morality, is far from revolutionary. Its implications for our challenge to Section 377, however, are tremendous. Speaking of the place of law in feminist movements, Nivedita Menon (2002)has argued that:

> Dominant modes of constituting the self—as woman, as criminal, as victim—are maintained and reinforced through the conventions of legal language... judgment is passed not only on the 'crimes' defined by the code, but on 'the shadows lurking behind the case'—in short, on the deviations from the dominant norms.

Menon is reminding us that the law does not just legislate on crime, but through the process of justice, legislates on social norms—it is not just a sexual act that is being judged under Section 377, it is the desires and lives of gay people that are being branded as unnatural. The cycle is complete: a law that uses societal disapproval to justify a 'crime' then uses the same law to reinforce that very disapproval. It is here that we arrive at a crossroads. What do we respond to—the law itself, the social norms that are being used to justify it, or both? How do we respond to one or the other? Can we use the law to challenge social norms, or vice versa?

In its response to Mathura, the women's movement rejected the right of the court to use 'modesty' as part of a definition of sexuality and sexual violation. By focusing on the use of modesty by the court, they both challenged the normative joining of sexuality-modesty-privacy so rampant in Indian society as well as the court's use of social norms within a process of legal judgement. When we respond to Section 377, therefore, our own legal challenge must also simultaneously challenge—both outside and through the petition—the notions of hetero-normativity, modesty, privacy, and patriarchy that are encoded in the law and that allow queer desire to be considered unnatural. At the heart of this argument is my understanding that Section 377 is not the cause of homophobia in our society today, but merely its tool. Its legitimacy arises from assumed and imposed definitions of Indian culture, and a larger hetero-patriarchal system that legitimises discrimination and prejudice against queer people. It is this hierarchy of normal/abnormal (read: natural/unnatural, public/private) desire that the government's response draws upon, and it is this hierarchy that we must contest—both in larger society and within our own communities.

Let me be clear—my argument here is not to say that legal reform does not have an impact on social understandings, or to undermine the need for Section 377 to be challenged. I am arguing that the process of legal reform must not be seen simply as a challenge within a courtroom, for the law itself does not recognise those boundaries. Instead, we must see legal challenges as being located within a larger political struggle, and indeed, see them as being impossible and harmful without such a location. If we do not do so, then reading down Section 377 will have little impact on the lives of queer people. The first step towards this goal requires us to be aware of the traps of legal language that Menon warns us against and position ourselves to counter them, both inside and outside the law. As the women's movement did with Mathura, we must fight not only a piece of legislation, but a system of hetero-patriarchy.

Let me contextualise this argument within the current petition. In the next part of this essay, I look at two parts of the petition—the idea of 'unnatural' sexual desire and the caveat of privacy—and show how both of these parts represent strategic and necessary legal tactics to ensure the success of the petition, but simultaneously play into dominant hetero-normative understandings of power and privilege. In the section that follows, I look at ways in which we can respond to this bind while still supporting the de-criminalisation of same-sex sexual relations within the court.

THE LIMITS OF THE LAW: WHAT OF 'UNNATURAL' AND 'PRIVATE' DESIRES?

The distinction between not asking for a repeal of Section 377, and instead asking for a reading down, is a telling example of how the constraints and language of the law define the spaces of protest that we are allowed to inhabit. Given the absence of a separate law on child sexual abuse (CSA) against underage boys[1] in India, it is difficult for lawyers to ask for Section 377 to be repealed. The most commonly made argument is that one cannot leave the victims of child sexual abuse without recourse to justice, and hence until a new child sexual abuse law is created, one cannot tactically or ethically ask for Section 377 to be fully repealed.[2] There is little that any queer activist will find objectionable in this strategic stance—indeed, queer activists have long stood by child rights activists in this regard.

Yet where does this leave us? If we read down the law, we decriminalise same-sex sexual activity between consenting adults in private. What we do not do is challenge the idea of 'unnatural' sexual activity in the first place. At present, there is a clear and hierarchical division between natural/unnatural, public/private, heterosexual/homosexual sex in our legal code, and an understanding (given the government's response) that this hierarchy is reflective of the way Indian society thinks. Reading down the law would simply ensure that we do not fall under the 'criminal' category anymore, but it would not, in any way, challenge the very idea that the state, law and society has the right to decide that certain sexual acts are 'unnatural'. Was this not the very point of the queer movement in the first place—to challenge the arbitrary and narrow definitions of Indian values, culture and of 'natural/normal' desires? Are we now to leave the idea of unnatural sexual desires within the law unchallenged? In responding to the Mathura Rape case, activists in the women's movement challenged the conflation of modesty with sexuality. By not filing for a repeal (which we, understandably, cannot at this stage), we have lost the ability to challenge the normative stance taken by the government. My intention here is not to demonise the decision to file the petition, which I work to support as an activist, but to bring to our attention the boundaries that the space of the law has imposed on us so that we may be aware of these boundaries and work in other spaces to push against them. The main question I raised earlier in this essay echoes again here: are we looking to challenge systems of domination and exclusion, or simply making sure that we don't end up on the wrong end of one of them? Tomorrow, in a wild but perhaps instructive hypothetical, what will we do if the state decides to expand the definition of 'unnatural' once again, and says that while same-sex sexual activity is no longer criminal, inter-caste gay couples *are* 'unnatural'? Or, in the all too close to home case of Sri Lanka, where the government changes the law to add lesbians under its ambit as well as gay men?

A second trap of legal language is the notion of privacy. When the AIDS Bhedbhav Virodhi Andolan (ABVA) filed the first petition against Section 377 in 1991, they appealed to the Court to consider the right to privacy. Sukthankar describes how, when criticised by women's groups, they admitted that the 'appeal to privacy has been a tactical move suggested by the senior members of the Supreme Court, rather than a principled stand' (ibid.: 50).

The current petition again highlights that de-criminalisation will only apply to private consensual acts. What does this understanding of privacy imply? Let alone that for most queer men and women outside the middle and upper middle classes, the notion of privacy is far from the reality of their everyday lives, or the fact that even the homes of hijra sex workers are not considered private since the police have the right to walk into any suspected 'brothel' without even a warrant. The real question here is simple—is an appeal to privacy any different from an appeal to modesty? Is it any different in its judgement on understandings of sexual desire and sexuality in Indian society than the court using the sexual history of a woman to determine her 'modesty' as part of a rape trial, or the Indian Penal Code not recognising marital rape or violence that occurs within the 'private' sphere of the family? Have we not learnt anything from two decades of the women's movement that has sought to pierce the barrier of family privacy to expose the violence and silencing of sexuality that lies within? Are we now submitting to the same dictates? Tomorrow, will we be unable to speak of domestic violence within gay couples because we consider sexuality a 'private' affair? The feminist movement said that the personal is political, the queer movement fought to speak openly of its desires—are we, as a tactical legal strategy, now going to go back on those words?

The Law and Social Norms

I have argued that the law cannot be seen to be 'objective' and distant in any way from its prevailing socio-political contexts—social norms and thinking both shape the law and are, in turn, shaped by it. In this context, how do we understand the law's ability to change social norms? There is no doubt that the success of the pending petition against Section 377 would be a positive and welcome outcome for queer people in India. The question is: will it be enough? I began this essay by arguing that Section 377 is a law whose power is mostly symbolic. It hangs like the sword of Damocles over the lives of queer people and their ability to live lives free of fear. Yet the removal of Section 377 will impact the fear that governs queer lives today only if the challenge to it—legal and otherwise—targets not pieces of legislation, but the larger understandings of gender and sexuality that allow such legislations to exist, and that allow the government to use social norms as an argument to protect them.

Reading down Section 377 tomorrow will not make most Indian queer people feel any less fearful of coming out to their peers, their families or their friends, unless the change in the law becomes part of a larger movement that challenges the way we think of sexuality in India today—not just of queer sexuality, but of all those who fall outside the hetero-patriarchal norm: single mothers, widows, sex workers, inter-religious couples, and so on. We must challenge the idea of hierarchies in themselves, not just the one hierarchy that victimises us. We must not only protest the right of queer people to live lives free of violence, we must challenge the thinking that allows many people to see such violence as legitimate. Legal reform cannot become the end point of our struggle, neither can it overtake the process.

I will go out on a limb here: I don't believe that we can, given the expressed views and history of the Indian state, expect any kind of positive inclusion under the law. By approaching the courts at a time when a majority of Indian people are less than willing to openly accept homosexuality (though many will tolerate it in private), we have given the government and the courts the right to judge our existence. There is a real danger here. The filing of the legal petition has inevitably become tied to the entire queer movement—the judgement that comes will impact the legitimacy of all our struggles in the eyes of the larger public. The defeat of the petition, therefore, will inevitably be read by many as a decision on the legitimacy of our struggle—recall Menon's argument here about how legal decisions are given the status of 'truth', a power that we have acknowledged by filing the PIL.

To prevent the decision of the court, whatever it may be, from having such an impact, we must try to ensure that our struggle never becomes one synonymous with the ongoing legal challenge—that the battle for legal reform constantly positions itself as part of a larger movement that is fought every day by queer activists in the media, in film festivals, in workshops, in public events, and simply by queer people living openly gay lives against all odds, and changing people's opinions even if it is one person at a time. In many ways, the creation of forums like Voices Against Section 377 and the articulations of a queer politics are recognising this need.[3]

We must build new spaces instead of simply protesting within existing structures that constantly tell us how unworthy we are. If we get change in law, we must use it to challenge the real spaces of homophobia—the family, the workplaces, the streets we walk, and even in our private and personal relationships. The law cannot acknowledge our identities, it can simply decriminalise one aspect of our lives. It cannot acknowledge queer lives and desires, it can only remove one part of its definition of what is 'unnatural'. We must build the spaces which we want to inhabit, not by relying on the law alone, but by changing thoughts and lives, not just by echoing words in a courtroom that exists in a society whose homophobia it not just condones, but encourages.

NOTES

1. There is also no law for CSA w.r.t to girls, whose cases are heard under Sections 375 or 376. Though also inadequate for the purposes of a CSA trial, I refer to CSA cases against boys only here because those are the cases that are heard under Section 377.
2. It is worth noting here that many child rights groups have repeatedly supported the petition to read down Section 377, and argued against the often posited public misconception that gay rights are against child rights. See Voices Against Section 377 (2005). *Rights for All: Ending Discrimination under Section 377.* Voices: New Delhi.
3. See Introduction, present volume. Also see Bhan, 'Re-Appropriating Desire: The Rise of Queer Politics in India', Paper presented at Graduate Student Conference of the University of Chicago, 2005. Copy on file and available upon request.

REFERENCES

Gupta, Alok. 2002, 'The History and Trends in the Application of the Anti-sodomy Law in the Indian Courts', *The Lawyer's Collective*, Vol. 16, No. 7.

Menon, Nivedita. 2002, 'Emobodying the Self: Feminism, Sexual Violence and the Law', in Brinda Bose (ed.), *Translating Desire*. New Delhi: Katha.

Narrain, Arvind. 2004, 'There are no Short Cuts to Queer Utopia: Sodomy, Law and Social Change' (copy on file), www.lines-magazine.org.

Sukthankar, Ashwini. 'The Dangers of Dignity and the Hazards of Health: Sexuality, Law and the Language of Reform in India'. Unpublished Manuscript (copy on file).

3

It's not my job to tell you that it's okay to be gay
Medicalisation of Homosexuality: A Queer Critique

Arvind Narrain and *Vinay Chandran*

> Being gay and growing up in Bangalore in the late seventies was a curse....
> I approached a psychiatrist, assuming he would help me. 'It's all in the mind', he
> said. My bouts of depression (which I now realise arose from bottling up my gay
> orientation), he glibly informed me, was a disease called schizophrenia. 'Your
> gayness is the cause of delusions and hallucinations.' He prescribed Orap and
> Serenace which are powerful neuroleptic medications. The nightmare began in
> earnest, lasting fifteen years, ravaging body and soul, rendering every living
> moment an excruciating torment, a journey through hell. I failed my courses and
> I took an overdose of Orap, hoping to die. I was rescued and given shock therapy,
> which played havoc with my memory for over two years. I had to discontinue
> college. Efforts to reason with my shrink were shot down perfunctorily. Instead
> he prescribed a weekly dose of Semap. None of these medicines 'cured' me. When
> all else failed, the shrink suggested I get married. To prepare me for marriage,
> my shrink had more (mis)prescriptions. Out went Orap and Semap and in came
> an anti-epileptic medication, to 'enhance sexual performance!'
>
> Excerpt from *My Story* cf. *Gay in the Garden City*, Radha Thomas,
> *The Bangalore Monthly Update*, September 1998.

INTRODUCTION

 Who is the homosexual in India today? In law, a criminal committing unnatural sexual offences; in religion, a sinner who vio-
lates God's laws; and in medicine, a mentally ill person who needs
treatment. These three systems of knowledge—law, religion and
medicine—deeply impact our understanding of homosexuality in India. The
story of one gay man, quoted above, is actually representative of a large

number of others—whether gay, lesbian, bisexual or transgender—who have been put through the moral grinders of an oppressive society due to their sexuality or gender identity.

These powerful ways of understanding the 'truth' about homosexuality are, however, increasingly being questioned in India through the emergence of a queer movement. The gaps in knowledge, the underlying contradictions and assumptions within these discourses, as well as the pervasive and near invisible heterosexism, are all increasingly being exposed. Just as the queer discourse questions the incoherence of a century-old anti-sodomy law within the framework of constitutional freedoms; just as voices that affirm both their faith and their sexuality challenge a religious discourse that refuses them space, questions are today being asked about the 'objectivity' and 'neutrality' of the medical discourse that declares the desires of homosexual people as abnormal and pathological.

In this essay, we will concentrate on trying to understand the ways in which homosexuality has been understood within the medical discourse and how this attempt to define, understand and ultimately control the homosexual has been questioned by the rise of the queer rights movement. After briefly tracing the emergence and understanding of homosexuality in early Western medicine, we will focus on the ways in which issues of sexuality are understood by Indian mental health practitioners, located particularly in Bangalore. Finally, we explore the ways in which the queer movement has challenged and continues to challenge the construction of sexuality within medicine showing how prevailing social norms and prejudices against homosexual people are often the driving force behind 'medical' diagnosis that deem their desires 'abnormal'.

How Western Medicine Got to 'Know' the Homosexual

There are many traditions of thinking about sexuality in Western medicine. These traditions have played a constitutive role in the emergence of the realm of 'abnormal sexuality' as a recognised discipline of study. Disciplines as diverse as sexology, psychology and psychiatry have produced thinking about the 'abnormal' in sexual terms, contrasting it with the only acceptable or 'normal' form of desire—within heterosexual marriages.

Historically, to understand the 'normal', one has needed to stigmatise 'perverse' sexualities. As Weeks put it:

> The negative side of this classificatory enthusiasm was a sharp reinforcement of the normal...the debates over the causes of the perversions and the eager

descriptions of even the most outrageous examples inevitably worked to emphasize their pathology, their relationship to degeneracy, madness and sickness, and helped to reinforce the normality of heterosexual relationships (Weeks 1981: 71).

The founding father of the tradition of classifying sexual diversity as sexual abnormality was Viennese psychiatrist Richard Krafft-Ebbing who, in *Psychopathia Sexualis* (1894), viewed human sexual behaviour as a collection of loathsome diseases. These 'deviations' from this 'normal' pattern Krafft-Ebbing viewed as perversions, including sadism, masochism, necrophilia, urolagnia, fetishism, nymphomania, satyriasis, homosexuality, voyeurism and exhibitionism (Brecher 1976).

Joseph Bristow notes, 'Given the overwhelming quantities of evidence that Krafft-Ebbing subsequently produces on the topic of sexual perversion, *Psychopathia Sexualis* makes the distinct impression that the highest form of heterosexual love is menaced on all sides by an epidemic of perverse sexual behaviours' (Bristow 1997: 30). Though Kraft-Ebbing wrote his work towards the end of the nineteenth century, his conceptual framework of abnormal sexuality as opposed to looking at the above as an example of benign sexual diversity, remains remarkably resilient and continues to influence abnormal psychology textbooks even in twentieth-century Bangalore.[1]

When Kraft-Ebbing's thinking is specifically applied to homosexuals it results in conclusions such as the one arrived at by Beiber. Beiber, after a study of 100 homosexuals and 100 heterosexuals, concluded that homosexual orientation was a result of a pathogenic family with a domineering mother and a detached or absent father. Beiber in his study went on to pathologise various aspects of homosexual existence. He noted that, '...Because of its pathological status, the possibility of establishing a stable and intimate homosexual relationship is precluded... hence there is ceaseless, compulsive, anonymous cruising' (Bayer 1981: 46).

This conclusion by psychoanalysts resulted in efforts to treat this pathological condition. Early efforts at treatment included the use of surgical techniques. For example, Stienach in 1917 was the first to use a surgical technique to 'cure' homosexuality. He performed a unilateral castration on a homosexual man, and then transplanted testicular tissue from a heterosexual man into the castrated patient, in the hope that he would be cured. 'At least 11 men were operated on from 1916 to 1921. The experiments were not successful' (Silverstein 1991: 107).

In 1962, Roeder introduced a new surgical technique. Since then 75 men considered sexually abnormal have been subjected to hypothalamotomies (surgical removal of the hypothalamus). Most of these men had either been imprisoned or were involuntarily committed to medical institutions (ibid.).

Apart from these surgical experiments there was also the attempt to treat homosexuality using hormones based on the theory that 'homosexuality means that the men are inadequately masculine and the women are overly masculine'.

However, the therapeutic method, which achieved a culturally hegemonic status in the Western world, was what is today called behavioural therapy. Behavioural therapy was based on the work of physiologist Pavlov who showed that repeated exposure to a certain stimuli in a certain environment could succeed in eliciting a behavioural response from a patient. His work showed that:

> previously neutral environmental stimulus (for instance, a bell) when tempo-
> rarily preceding a naturally occurring automatic response (for instance, salivation
> in the presence of food) could acquire the power to elicit the automatic reaction
> after many such pairings—in simple terms, if you heard a bell immediately before
> seeing food often enough, the sound of the bell would then make you salivate
> in expectation of the food. This phenomenon was later described as 'classical
> conditioning' and a number of the current treatment strategies used by behaviour
> modifiers are derived from the principles of classical conditioning (see Introduc-
> tory comments in Herzen et al. 1975: 2).

When behavioural therapy was applied to the treatment of homosexuality it took the form of exposing, say, a male patient to male nude pictures and subjecting the patient to a mild electric shock so that the patient would begin to link the imagery to feelings of pain. This was followed by techniques wherein one tried to increase the pleasure in heterosexuality. One of the methods used was orgasmic reconditioning which:

> involves masturbation to 'deviant' imagery, with a heterosexual image substituted
> just before ejaculation. The appropriate image is then gradually substituted at an
> earlier stage of the masturbatory sequence until it becomes its sole content. Case
> studies have demonstrated the usefulness of this technique for increasing hetero-
> sexual arousal in subjects seeking treatment for homosexuality (Brownell et al.
> 1975: 613).

What is interesting to note is that there is a gap between the diagnosis and the proposed treatment. Studies in the aetiology of homosexuality have pointed to everything from the pathogenic family to lack of heterosexual contact as the cause. Homosexual orientation is seen as a product of a deep psychic process, but the proposed treatment (in the form of behavioural therapy) addresses homosexual orientation as a mere question of behaviour. It seems inexplicable how, if something is so deeply rooted and pathological as homosexuality was believed to be, it was still considered possible to bring about change by treating it as a behavioural pattern.

QUESTIONING HOMOSEXUALITY AS A SEXUAL PERVERSION

It was not till the emergence of the gay and lesbian movement that the hegemonic status of the pathology paradigm was seriously ruptured. It was the beginning of gay militancy after the Stonewall riots in 1969,[2] which resulted in a dramatic transformation of the existing social milieu surrounding homosexuality. While previously homophile organisations requested inclusion and stressed a gradualist approach, Stonewall changed the nature of gay activism. As one of the activists noted, 'We consider the Stonewall riots to mark the birth of the gay liberation movement, as that was the first time that homosexuals stood up and fought back' (Bayer 1981: 93). This new culture of militancy found a worthwhile target in the psychiatric treatment of homosexuals. Gay activists used various strategies to question the framework of pathology.

First, activists arrived at a more political understanding of the cultural power of psychiatry. Psychiatry was no more seen as a science but rather an elaborate body of knowledge which had replaced religion as the arbiter of social values. The critique of psychiatry's inclusion of homosexuality as an illness in fact drew upon a wider critique of the very process of the medicalisation of social life. It drew upon anti-psychiatrist work such as that of Thomas Szasz and others who in their work went on to:

> expose the ways in which psychiatry had assumed the social function previously performed by religious institutions. As a guarantor of the prevailing social ethos, he argued, it sought to redefine deviations from ethical, political and legal norms by first the invention and then the expansion of the concept of mental illness (ibid.: 54).

Second, the authority of psychiatry to speak on behalf of a silent population was questioned. Gay activists such as Frank Kameny questioned the right of psychiatrists to speak on their behalf. Kameny quite simply asserted that, 'We are the true authorities on homosexuality whether we are accepted as such or not' (ibid.: 82). This viewpoint was taken forward by repeatedly asserting the right of homosexuals to speak in forums of psychiatrists where homosexuality was the object of discussion, and deny narratives that portrayed them as deviants.

Third, the critique of pathologisation tapped into a cultural current, which was delinking procreation from pleasure. The hegemonic status of the ideology of sexuality as procreation was questioned by the rise of the feminist movement.

Finally, the critique was successful only because the strategy built upon the new culture of fighting back as opposed to reasoned speech. Activists disrupted the functioning of psychiatric conferences, through sit-ins and what were called 'zaps'. Conferences were disrupted with gay activists taking the microphone and denouncing psychiatry as the enemy incarnate. Bayer concludes:

> To those who had so boldly challenged the professional authority of psychiatry it was clear that only the threat of disorder or even of violence had been able to create the conditions out of which such a dialogue could occur. That lesson would not be forgotten (ibid.: 104).

SHIFT IN THE CLASSIFICATION OF HOMOSEXUALITY

Due to the factors outlined above, the classification of homosexuality as a mental illness under the Diagnostic and Statistical Manual (DSM II) came under increasing pressure. Finally in 1973, after years of bitter dispute, the Board of Trustees of the American Psychiatric Association (APA) approved the deletion of homosexuality as a mental disorder. The APA also passed a far-reaching civil liberties resolution, which clearly opposed discrimination against homosexuals and called for repeal of anti-sodomy laws.

The APA noted, '...whereas homosexuality in and of itself implies no impairment in judgement, stability, reliability, or vocational capabilities, therefore, be it resolved, that the American Psychiatric Association deplores all public and private discrimination against homosexuals in such areas as employment, housing, public accommodation...' (ibid.: 137).

Following this historic development, the opponents of the decision asked for a referendum on the decision by the entire membership of the APA. Through this democratic process, the APA by a majority vote of 58 per cent who supported the decision of the APA versus 37 per cent who opposed it decided that homosexuality was not a mental disorder (ibid.: 148). Thus in the entire controversy over the inclusion of homosexuality as a mental disorder, the scientific basis of classification was itself exposed to ridicule as it showed that the inclusion of homosexuality was as political a position as its deletion.

The position adopted by DSM IV should be understood in the context of the various APA statements made since 1973, which have been supportive of gay and lesbian civil rights. Among the most recent is a 1998 statement regarding so-called reparative therapies. It states that:

the American Psychiatric Association opposes any psychiatric treatment, such as 'reparative' or 'conversion' therapy which is based upon the assumption that homosexuality per se is a mental disorder or based upon the *a priori* assumption that the patient should change his/her sexual homosexual orientation.

In specific regard to the issue of civil unions, in 2000, the APA's Board of Trustees voted to affirm that, 'The American Psychiatric Association supports the legal recognition of same sex unions and their associated legal rights, benefits, and responsibilities' (http://www.finnqueer.net/juttu.cgi? s=116_47_2).

MENTAL HEALTH AND HOMOSEXUALITY IN THE INDIAN CONTEXT: TOWARDS A HISTORY

Homosexuality in India was never a medical category, and neither the subject of furious debates as it was in the United States of America. Within India, medical categories were themselves more complex, with ayurveda, *unani* and homeopathy as more traditional systems of medicine positioning themselves in opposition to allopathic systems. Outside the framework of all these systems of medicine there exist various faith healers, godmen and peddlers of miracle cures for a whole series of ailments. Particularly in the area of sexuality, these informal systems of medicine undoubtedly serves the needs of a majority of the Indian population.

The 'treatment' of homosexuality is located within this complex field of competing systems of medicine. However, the most well-articulated position with respect to the treatment of homosexuality encompassing both theoretical viewpoints and treatment protocols remains the domain of Western medicine. Historians of Western medicine in India have seen the very introduction of Western medicine into India as a part of the colonial project of pacification and control of the Indian subject. The disease of plague for example was seen as providing the rationale for the segregation of the European from the Indian.

Comparatively there has been little discussion on the history of the mental health field in India. It is in this context of a limited critique that we need to locate the 'non-discussion' around the clinical category of ego-dystonic homosexuality. The Indian medical establishment, i.e., The Medical Council of India, the Indian Medical Association and the Indian Psychiatric Association, has adopted the World Health Organisation (WHO) system of classification of mental and behavioural disorders known as ICD-10 (International Classification of Diseases-10) (1992). This system distinguishes between ego-syntonic and ego-dystonic homosexuality and specifically mentions ego-dystonic homosexuality, bisexuality and heterosexuality as psychiatric disorders.

In ego-dystonic homosexuality, bisexuality or heterosexuality the gender identity or sexual preference is not in doubt, but the individual wishes it were different and seeks treatment. In such a case, according to the WHO, treatment is warranted. In ego-syntonic homosexuality, by contrast, the individual is comfortable with his or her sexual preference or gender identity and treatment is not warranted. Apart from the ego-syntonic/dystonic distinction, if a person faces problems in maintaining a sexual relationship due to the person's sexual preference or gender identity, then the ICD-10 classifies it as a sexual relationship disorder, which also warrants treatment.

There has been no pressure on the mental health profession to re-evaluate the notion of dystonicity. The following of the category of ego-dystonic homosexuality by the Indian mental health profession is itself a testament to the power of discourse. How once a 'truth' is produced by a certain form of knowing, that 'truth' has a life of its own. We become the servitors and defenders of that 'truth'. Mental health professionals have become the uncritical defenders of a category, which is the product of a certain history. The West might have moved on due to the social pressure exerted by the gay and lesbian movement, but Indian professionals remain hostage to the category which was implanted at a certain point in time, and today constitutes nothing but a historical residue impacting the very perception and treatment of homosexuality in India with long-term implications for the lives of those with homosexual desires in India.

Ego-dystonic Homosexuality: What do Doctors Mean?

To figure out the contemporary meaning of 'ego-dystonic' homosexuality, we interviewed a section of Bangalore's mental health community. The dominant opinion really flowed from an understanding of the diagnostic category itself. As one psychiatrist noted:

> Ego-dystonicity is a Freudian term and is to do with the lack of coherence of the self. The dystonic patient is often deeply distressed over his/her condition. As a psychiatrist, I cannot ignore the patient's distress. It is not my job to tell him that it's okay to be gay, but rather my duty to deal with the patient's distress by treating him. I have to help the individual.
>
> Dr PE (Psychiatrist)

The decision to 'treat' flows from the understanding that there is a category of ego-dystonic homosexuality. Once the category exists, then doctors diagnose the patient and if they find that he or she is ego-dystonic then there is no choice but to treat him/her. Through this positivist construction of helplessness in the face of an already given category, which needs to be followed, mental health professionals effectively absolve themselves of any ethical responsibility. Since they are following what already exists they are outside politics and decidedly neutral. It is, therefore, not their responsibility to tell a person that it is okay to be gay as their role is merely confined to addressing the person's distress.

The question of whether the distress can be dealt with by making the person more comfortable with himself or herself is not contemplated. The underlying assumption leaves the primacy and inherent superiority of heterosexuality in the minds of the practitioners unquestioned—the best result for a patient is to make him/her heterosexual, even if briefly and as a conditioned response. This opinion shows no understanding of the histories of the category of ego-dystonicity, instead a preference to take the ICD classification as the 'truth'.

However, an even more basic problem exists: the very understanding of dystonicity itself. The scientific character of dystonicity itself comes into doubt, as Dr CPB (Clinical Psychologist) notes, 'the problem is much more when the person is not distressed about homosexuality but about its consequences. Since you cannot separate the individual from the society, the attraction leads to a problem.'

What Dr CPB is articulating is the sheer difficulty in actually specifying what the distress associated with the clinical category of ego-dystonic homosexuality is. The distress is often because of the consequences of being homosexual, i.e., lack of family support, no peer group approval, and so on. It has nothing to do with the abstract supposedly scientific category of ego-dystnonic homosexuality, or an inherent discomfort with one's sexuality, rather it is fear rooted in the lack of social acceptance—a fear of violence, of alienation and of phobia. In this context ego-dystonicity remains more a social category than a clinical category, and in diagnosing it as a disorder, it merely makes homophobia seem acceptable and inevitable.

THE CAUSE OF HOMOSEXUALITY:
A CEASELESS ETIOLOGICAL PREOCCUPATION

The question as to why are people homosexual exercised considerable fascination among the interviewees. Everyone has an opinion on the question:

> I feel that young people are being trapped in Bangalore, on the roads, in pubs, they are enticed by offer of food and drinks and once they get addicted then they

feel there is no way out. There are so many young people who come to me, that it is really quite shocking. In a meeting with gay activists, I told them that you are trapping people into homosexuality; they kept quiet because they knew it was the truth.

CB (Counsellor)

At a particular age the person of the opposite sex appears very mysterious and there is no outlet in our society, so what people do is that to release sexual tension they adopt whatever is available and get fixated on it. People do have friends of the same sex and they can care a lot about each other. But development of interest in the opposite sex is natural. However, if they get fixated, then they continue with their homosexual behaviour. We try finding out at what age these feelings start? What is the aetiology? When did this orientation become a fixation?

Dr CPB (Clinical Psychologist)

Homosexuality doesn't do any good...the homosexual himself was not the problem but his condition was due to poor parenting. People who feel they are homosexuals and want to change should come in early to cure the problem... if a homosexual is happy then there's no problem, but if they aren't then I will help them.

Dr CA (Counsellor)

The answers themselves illustrate the way the issue of aetiology has been elaborated by existing discourses. Among the most powerful influences has been the discourse of psychiatry with the theories of homosexuality resulting from a pathogenic family. Thus the 'homosexual fixation' is explained by the lack of normality in the family environment which could include the 'victim' suffering from child sexual abuse. A further theorisation contends that the fixation, which interferes with the normal route of sexual development, might be the result of a particularly Indian context where the two sexes are rigorously separated. There is also the link between early childhood experience and pleasure, which could lead to the formation of a homosexual orientation. Finally, the homosexual orientation is linked to the trapping of young boys by people who are already homosexual. Within this discourse there is a vigorous resistance to the idea that homosexuality could be natural and continued insistence that there is an active 'recruitment policy' by homosexuals themselves.

Whatever might be the diverse discourses from which these ideas of origin come, what is clear is that the very focus on producing these forms of knowledge about the aetiology of homosexuality is itself a process of stabilising a form of heterosexism. The very production of homosexuality as an object of knowledge leaves heterosexuality as a neutral position beyond the pale of study. As David Halperin notes, 'By constituting homosexuality as an object of knowledge, heterosexuality also constitutes itself as privileged stance of subjectivity—as the very condition of knowing—and thereby avoids becoming an object of knowledge itself, the target of possible critique' (Halperin 1995: 47).

THE HOMOSEXUAL AS PERVERT: DOCTORS SPEAK OUT

What are the ideas which form part of the very way the physician thinks? Where do these ideas come from? These ideas come from not only what the medical field has to say, but also as importantly, they are constructed by the ideas prevalent in the discourse of the law and of religion. The value systems, and ways of thinking of the doctor acquire crucial importance particularly when a heterosexual doctor is treating a homosexual patient. Very often, there is a wide gap between what the heterosexual person sees as 'right behaviour' and what the homosexual person's behaviour is. To give a few examples of what doctors in Bangalore think about homosexuals:

> Homosexual people, because of the societal pressure, do not have relationships which last long. They change their partners frequently. They have issues of how to deal with the pain of break-ups etc...there are those who go to seek sexual satisfaction by paying others for sex.
>
> Dr PA (Psychiatrist)

> The entire issue of multiple partners can create depression, feelings of rejection, jealousy when break-ups happen, as there is no support within the group for partners who experience this form of rejection.
>
> Dr PD (Psychiatrist)

> I feel that gays also have other problems such as depression, personality disorders etc. Some of these are due to a lifestyle with multiple sexual partners.
>
> Dr CPA (Clinical Psychologist)

> In today's world, young people have to fight both against peer pressure and the media, both of which are very strong. I believe that people should be free, but not free to commit suicide or to commit homosexuality. When we talk about freedom, we should ask the question, if God would want you to do that particular act.
>
> CB (Counsellor)

> Sodomy is illegal in India.
>
> Dr CPB (Clinical Psychologist)

In the narratives above, the beliefs about unstable and distressing homosexual relationships first constructed by Western psychiatrists in the early twentieth century, find voice through the experiences of mental health professionals in Bangalore. Multiple partners, cruising for sexual contact, short-term relationships, rejection and depression, are all mentioned in passing as problems that homosexual people have to face without exception. There is little or no questioning of the social pressure behind the cause for many of these so-called unstable components of homosexual relationships. Additionally conservative notions of relationships (both from religious roots or otherwise) as being monogamous, single-partner, marital and procreative only, permeate unconsciously through these assumptions.

The one fact assumed at the start by these mental health practitioners is that heterosexuality is the objective of all sexual development. That being a heterosexual is the 'natural' thing. And that people are homosexual because of unhealthy fixations, same-sex experimentation, same-sex sexual abuse and peer pressure. Yet again, the norm of heterosexuality is beyond question, and its primacy requires no explanation. Everything outside heterosexuality becomes 'different', and, therefore, suspect. What is different must be explained in ways that do not threaten the norm, and hence difference becomes pathologised, and acceptably classified as abnormal under the all-legitimising banner of medicine.

From this assumption to move into classifying heterosexuality as superior to any other form of sexual desire or attraction also seems inevitable. The following example speaks about how the counsellor, a sexologist, views the differences between homosexuality and heterosexuality, with an analogy about cycles and scooters. It is automatically assumed that pleasure through heterosexual sex is better, like riding a scooter, in fact.

In another case, a patient told me that he was standing in a bus and another man with his erect penis poked him. I told him that he should not feel guilty that he had enjoyed. I instead told him that he was going to have better and better enjoyment once he got more and more involved with girls. If you are riding a cycle you are happy just riding it. But once you know that a scooter is better than cycle you would prefer to ride it.

Dr SB (Sexologist)

Counselling processes that involve religious sanctioning breed a whole host of assumptions about the ideal man or woman and ideal relationships that disavow any effort to experience sexuality differently. Coupled with 'scientific' theories of poor parenting, fixations and habits forming homosexual experiences, and the connections with HIV and other sexually transmitted infections, the counsellors attempt to paint homosexuality as an undesirable as well as dangerous condition.

> I consider homosexuality akin to an addiction like alcoholism and drug abuse. And many boys and young men, because of homosexual sex, have sexual diseases like AIDS, and some boys wear colostomy bags because of anal tears.... Homosexuals who came to change obviously felt there was a deficit in their lives compared to heterosexuals...condoms and safer sex are also dangerous.
>
> CB (Counsellor)

Yet another form of belief about homosexuals expresses itself in the notion of homosexuals who articulate their identities as 'flaunting' it or 'wearing it on their sleeve'. One doctor we spoke to felt disturbed by this and said that heterosexuals don't wear their sexuality on their sleeves.

> The problem we have had in our hospital is that it being a teaching institute we have presentations on homosexuality. I have always felt we should look at it objectively and not get too carried away by activism. Even in our hospital we have some people who wear their sexuality on their sleeve. This I feel is unnecessary, as heterosexuals do not assert their sexuality all the time.
>
> Dr CPA (Clinical Psychologist)

This calls attention to the many subtle ways in which heterosexism expresses itself. In a culture where heterosexuality is the norm, even the slightest questioning of the 'norm' provokes resistance. The fact that heterosexuality always flaunts itself through every conceivable discourse, and that heterosexuals ceaselessly flaunt their identities, becomes invisibilised, when heterosexuality is the very standpoint of the speaking subject. In one rare self-reflective interview, a psychiatrist provided a glimpse into where all these opinions were coming from:

> Many heterosexual doctors are often very uncomfortable with the issue of homosexuality and when they deal with homosexuals, there is distaste and an anger, which gets expressed. The expression hides under the label of ego-dystonicity. Many doctors often mock homosexuals, they feel they are threatened by homosexuals because the sexual difference has some affinity with themselves. It is distasteful (for heterosexual doctors) to deal with homosexuals (speaking personally) and it takes some preparation before one is even willing to be compassionate.
>
> Dr PA (Psychiatrist)

What emerges is that there is no objective space from where these professionals can claim to speak. Their statements emerge from the medical discourse as well as being formed by their own notions as to what homosexuality is and who homosexuals are. The background belief which underlies every shade of opinion expressed above is that heterosexuality, marriage, family and procreation are the natural objectives of the development of each individual. These beliefs are the very formative ground out of which mental-health categories on homosexuality have emerged and continue to influence treatment options.

THE CONTEMPORARY 'TREATMENT' OF HOMOSEXUALITY: A STATE OF SHOCK

Homosexuality has a biological basis and if we find this basis one can treat homosexuality. I think they will definitely find a treatment. For example in some mental illnesses especially depression, if we treat the T2 receptors using drugs, the patient feels better. Similarly if you compare normal heterosexuals and homosexuals and do a neuro-imaging and see the difference in biological parameters then one can pinpoint possibly two or three factors and try and change them.

Dr PE (Psychiatrist)

Anyway, aversion therapy causes less tissue damage than anal sex.

Dr CPB (Clinical Psychologist)

We have examined the way the discourse of the physician operates when it comes to treating homosexuals. The deep-rooted beliefs of physicians are in some ways a product of the medical discourse and in other equally powerful ways emerge from discourses such as law (homosexual acts as an offence) and religion (homosexuality as a sin). Such being the powerful social influences which construct 'homosexuality', what can the physician do? What happens when the discourses of law, religion and medicine come together to treat the homosexual? There are three modes by which homosexuals are treated in Bangalore.

First, there is the mode of prescribing behavioural therapy including 'shock' therapy. For example:

In (the leading mental health institution in this city) they have behavioural therapy in which they try to suppress the homosexual response by shock therapy. They show pictures of homosexual activity and then give the person a mild shock. They show pictures of oral sex, on seeing which the patient feels happy, and then give him a shock. The idea being that the person associates shock and not pleasure with the activity. I believe in behaviour modification, the positive way. What I do instead is to show a series of pictures of heterosexual activity. Combined with this I teach him how to enhance pleasure by the use of lubricant. I try and introduce him to the idea that a woman feels nice and the pleasures of living together and how sex is the root cause of that. I give him an idea of what is the vagina and how one can masturbate with lubricant so that the organ slides into the vagina. I create a sense of anticipation about the vagina so that when he finally encounters a vagina he feels pleasure. My objective is to replace the feeling of pleasure in homosexuality by pleasure in heterosexuality. This is what I call replacement therapy.

Dr SB (Sexologist)

The idea is to decrease interest in homosexuality and increase interest in hetero-sexuality. That apart, we use treatments like orgasmic reconditioning—which is basically a treatment to redirect a person's stimulus for pleasure. For example, if a person can be made to think of a woman instead of a man at the moment of orgasm then we succeed in reconditioning their pleasure in the female direc-tion. We make the person get an erection with physical stimulus, the person is then made to imagine a person of the opposite sex and made to masturbate. We start by showing pictures of the same sex but move towards replacing it with pictures of the opposite sex. As an adjunct to orgasmic reconditioning we also use aversive therapy (10 to 20 sessions). We may follow up with booster sessions, which may be for four to five days consecutively.

Dr CPB (Clinical Pscyhologist)

There seems to be a widespread understanding that homosexuality is a behaviour and one can get patients to stop exhibiting that form of behaviour through aversive therapy, positive reconditioning, orgasmic therapy and various other ways in which sexual pleasure is sought to be changed. The violence of the process of behavioural therapy has its roots in its very beginnings. The comprehensive textbook of psychiatry notes that, in an experiment conducted in Pavlov's very laboratory it was discovered that:

As usual, the unconditioned stimulus was food powder and the unconditioned response was salivation. In this case the conditioned stimulus was a mild electric shock on the dog's skin, which might be expected to elicit defensive reactions competing with salivation. Still, the conditioning was going well up until the point when the shock was administered to one new location after another on the animal's skin. When this was done, conditioning broke down, and the animal developed a lasting disturbance of its overall behaviour (Routh 1976: 22).

The 'violence' of the process lies not only in the physical pain of a mild aversive shock which increases in intensity going up to 10 amps, but in the exposure of ones deepest fantasies to the clinical gaze of judgement. The fantasy is the subject of the doctor's gaze as pleasure is then monitored, calibrated and judged. The patient gets the approval of the doctor when he is successfully able to exhibit the 'right' kind of pleasure. When we speak of the clinician's gaze, the gaze not only functions to capture the homosexual body in an embrace of power but aims in fact to change desire under its relentless judgmentality. In bringing about this change the clinician becomes God in damning the very flow of human desire and changing its course to a more acceptable direction.

By being told that your desire needs to be changed, the patient's sense of self and internal coherence instead of being validated, is deeply challenged. As one doctor noted, behaviour therapy gives the patient a low sense of self-esteem as he is told through verbal and physical means that what he feels and indeed what he is has to be changed. The tragedy lies in the fact that there remains a historical continuity that links the dog in Pavlov's laboratory and the homosexual in contemporary Bangalore. Such is the power of the belief that is formed at the intersection of law, medicine and religion.

Second, we also have the recent development of religion-based therapy in Bangalore. This therapy, which offers homosexuals, through prayer and belief, the opportunity to become heterosexuals, gained prominence when Exodus International visited Bangalore. An organisation whose members have converted from homosexuality to assert heterosexual identities, Exodus International, with the help of local religious groups, organised a series of meetings to speak on how homosexuals can be converted through reparative religious therapy. Their practices are also endorsed internationally by another organisation called NARTH (North American Reparative Therapy for Homosexuals), an association that believes that homosexuality can be cured and offers aversion therapy. In the present context, we have faith-based support groups operating out of the office spaces of a religious group offering support for people to come out of homosexuality.

Recent developments show that even founders of Exodus International now state that their programmes were 'ineffective…not one person was healed'. They stated that the programme often exacerbated already prominent feelings of guilt and personal failure among the counselees; many were driven to suicidal thoughts as a result of the failed 'reparative therapy' (Davison: 159).

Third, one has to note that there are counsellors and doctors who do take a non-judgemental position towards homosexuality. When one tries to isolate the reasons for this position, how does one category of an admittedly small number of doctors function outside the powerful discourses outlined above? Is it the nature of a singular proactive empathy for patients or does the articulation of this position point to the beginnings of another discourse?

There is a hint that it is really the emergence of a gay and lesbian voice that has resulted in the abandonment of 'treatment' of homosexuality. There is also the understanding that readings in the contemporary history of Western psychiatry have resulted in a different stand. The question of clinical practice, which shows that treatment does not work, is also hinted at. Thus one can note that there is the incipient formation of a counter-discourse which questions the heterosexist assumptions of the discourses of medicine.

THE QUEER CRITIQUE: AN EPISTEMOLOGICAL CHALLENGE

In India, the three discourses of religion, science and law acting through prayer, therapy or punishment condemn homosexuals and homosexuality. The queer movement has challenged these forms of intervention and tried to liberate the homosexual voice from the power of these discourses. The queer discourse is not only an activist intervention but is also an epistemological intervention, which challenges the very foundational terms within which homosexuals have been defined and treated. The key analytical category through which this challenge has been mounted is the understanding of how the basis of law, science and religion is heterosexist. The critique can be viewed as:

1. Challenging the framework of heterosexism.
2. Offering a different epistemological framework.

Challenging the Framework of Heterosexism

When it comes to violence against homosexuals the first conceptualisation was the notion of homophobia. George Weinberg introduced the word 'homophobia' into literature in 1972 in a publication titled *Society and the Healthy Homosexual*. He defined homophobia as:

> the dread of being in close quarters with homosexuals which is consistent with the formal criteria for a phobia in psychological literature. Five key differences distinguish homophobia from a true phobia. First, the emotion classically associated with a phobia is fear, whereas homophobia is often characterised by hatred or anger. Second, a phobia generally involves recognition that the fear is excessive or unreasonable, but homophobic responses are often considered understandable, justified, and acceptable. Third, a phobia typically triggers avoidance, whereas homophobia often manifests itself as hostility and aggression. Fourth, a phobia does not usually relate to a political agenda, while homophobia has political dimensions including prejudice and discrimination. Finally, unlike homophobia,

people suffering from a phobia often recognise that it is disabling and are motivated to change (Plummer 1999).

Ironically, the starting point of critique by the queer movement was the use of the very medical discourse which had pathologised homosexuals to define those who hated homosexuals as suffering from a form of phobia. This in turn led to the use of other medicalised categories such as 'homosexual panic' as a defence acceptable in a court of law when a heterosexual person murdered a homosexual man. We would argue that medicalisation should not be the approach used when we are looking at structural modes of discrimination against homosexuals. The word homophobia individualises and locates the 'problem' in a phobia which some people suffer from. However, what happens in this analysis is that one forgets that the violence and discrimination suffered by homosexuals is not the result of a 'problem' that some people suffer from, but rather the result of the way society structures heterosexuality and homosexuality hierarchically. If one uses a parallel analogy and says that the reason why men beat their wives is because they suffer from gender phobia, the ridiculousness of the use of the word homophobia becomes clear.

Thus we need a structural conceptualisation of why homosexuals are subject to discrimination on the lines of the use of categories like racism and sexism. Similarly, we must adopt a framework for analysis that does not medicalise homosexuality but instead looks at how various epistemological frameworks function with the assumption of heterosexuality. In this connection we would like to use the concept of heterosexism to understand how knowledge is constructed and how this paradigm frames and conditions the violence to which queer people are subjected. Heterosexism operates by constructing the homosexual as the object of study and hence as the source of the 'problem'. Within the medical discourse the object of study is ego-dystonic homosexuality, not heterosexuality, with behavioural therapy being prescribed for homosexuality and not for heterosexuality. Of course, the question of whether heterosexuality is natural or normal is never posed with the assumption being that it is always heterosexuality which is the natural outcome of sexual development. Thus we see that the medical discourse as a system of knowledge ends up constructing homosexuality as the problem thereby leaving heterosexuality as the location from which the study is conducted. This form of construction of knowledge is what we would call heterosexism.

Heterosexism as a framework can be used to understand not only the medical discourse but also the discourses of religion, law and even popular culture. It is wider than 'homophobia' as it is not just a problem located in one individual, but is instead a way of looking at the world. So even violence has its roots in the structural foundations of heterosexism as we have shown, in the context of the medical discourse.

Towards a Different Epistemological Foundation

The medical discourse has traced the aetiology of homosexuality to medical causes. What the queer discourse in India has done is to show how the concept of ego-dystonic homosexuality is a product of heterosexism. If such is indeed the understanding of what is homosexuality, then even the treatment of homosexuality will be very different. The queer community believes that the best way of dealing with what the medical profession describes as ego-dystonic homosexuality is by exposing the heterosexist roots of the very category. While this critique functions as questioning the very need of medical intervention, the queer community also intervenes to provide its own form of 'therapy' for those characterised as ego-dystonic. The very simple answer which the queer community has come up with is the formation of support groups for homosexuals. Such spaces by their very nature portray homosexuality as a lived reality for a certain number of people. This might be the best way of ensuring that dystonicity is exposed for the social category that it is.

Support groups and other services like drop-in centres, documentation and research on homosexuality alongside counselling provided in NGOs in India have been sites where the traditional understanding of homosexuality is being challenged. More and more individuals can access these support services through the visible queer movement and through the vast resources thrown up by the Internet. While the Internet now also provides some of the anonymity and connectivity that was once the mainstay of public places, several e-groups and e-mail lists have provided space for the articulation of and resolution of homosexual desire. Support groups around India are strong sites of articulation of queer rights as well as spaces for becoming comfortable with one's own identity. In one sense support groups for homosexuals are spaces which affirm identities and experiences without judgement and moralism. By attempting to help its members gain some sense of individuality and self-esteem through contact with others who have gone through similar experiences, support groups also function as self-help groups.

A support group meeting provides many answers for homosexuals participating in them. The issues raised and discussed in a support group are the same ones that are raised with psychiatrists, clinical psychologists and counsellors. Issues of self-identity, marriage pressures, coming out to friends and family, are spoken of regularly in these meetings. Members of the group share their own experiences on these issues and thereby help others to realise that they are not alone in the feelings that they experience. Merely through the process of interaction with a diverse range of people, newcomers to the group realise that feelings of loneliness, guilt and depression are products of a dominant social morality. The moment the isolation is broken, and a sense of community forms, many of the problems disappear. While these feelings of low self esteem and crisis of identity may become problematised and 'treated' by supposedly 'neutral' counsellors and doctors, by the very nature of their existence, support groups through a process of sharing of experience, make queer people feel comfortable with who they are.

The very idea of a support space, therefore, is to do away with the need for medical intervention. It is argued that homosexuals themselves can best deal with the problems of homosexuals. To escape the gaze of the clinician might be the starting point of doing away with the category of ego-dystonicity. If counsellors have the humility to send homosexual clients to support groups of queer people, rather than professionalise and medicalise the lives of queer people it might be the starting point for a lasting solution.

NOTES

1. As recently as three years ago, a text book on abnormal psychology prescribed by Bangalore University for graduate and postgraduate studies noted in the chapter on sexual perversions:
   …it is a wrong notion with some persons that homosexuality is character-istic of only children and adolescents. In fact, this perversion may be found in any person at any age and in both the sexes. Innocent children and adolescents pick up this habit through association with perverted persons. Homosexuality in women may be found in those who are either unmarried, widows or deserted by or separated from their husbands on certain grounds. Such women seek partnerships with other such women who also desire their sexual gratification through the same process… (Chaube 1995: 438–39).
2. Outside a bar called the Stonewall, in New York, the riots marked the first time that patrons of a gay bar fought back against policemen who tried to raid the bar, a common practice with gay bars at the time.

REFERENCES

Bayer, Ronald. 1981, *Homosexuality and American Psychiatry*, New York: Basic Books.
Brecher, Edward M. 1976, 'History of Human Sexual Research and Study', in Alfred M. Freedman et al., *Comprehensive Textbook of Psychiatry*.

Bristow, Joseph. 1997, *Sexuality*. London: Routledge.

Brownell, Kelly D. et. al. 1975, 'The Behavioral Treatment of Sexual Deviation', in Michel et al. (eds), *Progress in Behavior Modification*.

Chaube, S.P. 1995, Abnormal Psychology. Agra: Lakshmi Narain Agarwal.

Davison, Gerald C. 1991, 'Constructionism and Morality in Therapy for Homosexuality', in Gonsiorek et al., *Homosexuality*.

Freedman, Alfred M., Harold I. Kaplan and Benjamin J. Sadock. 1976, *Comprehensive Textbook of Psychiatry*. Baltimore: Willams and Williams.

Gonsiorek, C. John and James D. Weinrich (eds). 1991, *Homosexuality: Research Implications for Public Policy*. London: Sage Publications.

Halperin, David. 1995, *Saint Foucault Towards a Gay Hagiography*. Oxford: Oxford University Press.

Michel, Richard M. Eisler and Peter M. Hersen Miller. 1975, Progress in Behavior Modification, Vol. 1. New York: Academic Press.

Plummer, David. 1999, '*One of the Boys: Masculinity, Homophobia and Modern Manhood*. New York: The Haworth Press.

Routh, Donald K. 1976, 'Hippocrates Meets Democritus: A History of Psychiatry and Clinical Psychology', in Freedman et al., *Comprehensive Textbook of Psychiatry*.

Silverstein, Charles. 1991, 'Psychological and Medical Treatments of Homosexuality', in Gonsiorek and Weinrich, *Homosexuality*.

Weeks, Jeffery. 1981, *Sexuality*. London: Routledge.

4

Crisis in Desire
A Queer Reading of Cinema and Desire in Kerala

*Muraleedharan T.**

Queer reading of Indian cinema is an academic project that has barely begun. In the conspicuous absence of any significant gay representations in Indian cinema, the early studies in this field tended to focus on the 'queer dynamics' that structure the seemingly straight narratives of mainstream films. Unfortunately this has persuaded some people to consolidate their assumption that Indian cinema is fundamentally addressing 'straight' (sic) viewers. Subsequently the queer reading is appreciated and immediately dismissed as just a 'reading,' perhaps an interesting intellectual exercise that is 'possible', nevertheless not 'real'. The political sites inspiring such readings are often read as further evidence that supports this assumption. For example, Gayatri Gopinath's analysis of the queer spaces in mainstream Hindi cinema was sited in a 'queer diasporic framework' arguing that 'cinematic images which in their *originary* locations simply reiterate conventional nationalist and gender ideologies may, in a South Asian diasporic context, be fashioned to become the very foundation of a queer transnational culture' (Gopinath 2000: 284). My own earlier reading of 'the queer dynamics' in some Malayalam films was articulated from a consciously occupied political location, claiming intellectual support of the poststructuralist debates, and legitimised on the basis of an international (Western?) perspective (Muraleedharan 2001).

Such validations frequently lead to certain vexing questions: are we merely inscribing and then reading 'marginal' desires (which appear not to signify

* I am grateful to Professor Carolyn Dinshaw, Professor Gayatri Gopinath and Mr Arvind Narrain for their valuable critical comments and suggestions.

for the rest of humanity) on and of a seemingly 'innocent' screen that is sincerely catering to heterosexual instincts? Is same-sex desire fundamentally foreign to Indian cinema's arbitrations with pleasure? Is the pleasure that self-identified queer viewers seem to derive from Indian cinema fundamentally superfluous and, by all means, 'unintentional'? Moreover, doesn't a queer reading have any significant contribution to make to our understanding of Indian cinema and its negotiations with evolving schemes of gender politics?

The main factor facilitating such confusions is a simplistic usage of the term 'queer'—one that obscures the complexities of signification it was destined to elucidate. The term queer, when used as a synonym for 'gay' or 'homosexual', fails to accomplish the political intervention it sets out to undertake and, instead, ends up refurbishing the very binarism of thought that it strives to dismantle. One should not forget that the emergence of queer theory in the early 1990s was not only as an extension but also a striking departure from the gay and lesbian studies of the preceding decades. For, queer designates an approach that neither acknowledges nor subscribes to dualisms in thinking. It is anti-essentialist and deconstructive in spirit. It embodies an inherent critique of the scheme of naming restricted by either/ or options and strives to reveal the constructed nature of categories such as homosexual and heterosexual. In the process, it seeks to unsettle the intellectual assumptions and methodological conventions that motivate any study of gender and sexuality using binary terms (Corber and Valocchi 2003: 1). According to Anna Trip, queer theory offers an understanding of sexuality not as something god-given, natural or innate, but as a series of culturally and historically specific classifications, definitions, moralisations and contestations (Trip 2000: 15). Moreover, queer empowers a mode of enquiry that refuses the grid of sexual/non-sexual divisions in conceiving pleasures. In other words, it repudiates conventions that classify pleasures as 'innocent' and 'sexual' or even 'corporeal'[1] and 'spiritual,' highlighting zones of fluidity that blur such distinctions, in order to generate fresh perceptions of human intimacies and corporeality. In short, a queer reading is NOT one that attempts to look at things from a 'different' angle, but one that seeks to demolish those very angles that perpetuate hetero-patriarchal visions.

Judith Butler's celebrated theorisation on the performative constructions of gender and desire was very much the foundation for much of the early developments in queer theory (Butler 1990). Butler's work, influenced by Michel Foucault's philosophical musings on the discursive nature of power and knowledge, effectively countered some of the fledgling enterprises in life sciences and clinical psychology—anchored in an assumed normalcy of heterosexual, patriarchal designs, however discreetly articulated—to identify genetic or social reasons (sic) for non-normative sexual preferences.[2] What Butler, as well as her contemporaries like Eve Sedgewick, accomplished was an understanding of normative heterosexuality also as socially engineered, just like all other sexual practices. In recent times theorists like David Halperin have built on these formulations to lead the study of sexualities beyond examinations of identities and subjectivities, towards investigations of social spaces, historical conventions and cultural institutions within which such formulations are fabricated. In other words, sexualities are no more studied with reference to individuals or bodies, but in terms of schemes that make them possible (Halperin 2002).

A crucial point stressed by Halperin is that the gay/lesbian identities, as they exist in some of the Western metropolises of today, are very much a con-temporary phenomenon (Halperin 1993). They are assemblages engendered within the evolving socio-economic structures of the post-industrial scenario and not in any way stable or eternal. Hence there is not much point in trying to locate or recover the same kind of identities from other historical and cultural locations. If comparable identities and lifestyles are emerging in some of the urban spaces in contemporary India, it is due to the similarities in the economic structure and patterns of social formations evolving in these locations. At the same time, the seeming absence of such identities elsewhere in India does not in any way indicate the irrelevance of queer politics to these regions. A queer perspective, if allowed to outstrip the hetero-patriarchal grid through which these societies and spaces have so far been perceived and understood, could unravel 'visions' that could undermine the 'reality' and subsequently the hegemony of the normative sexual order.

Cinema has become an important tool in the study of identities and sexualities today because of its ubiquitous presence as a popular medium and, consequently, a powerful ideological apparatus negotiating with subjectivities and pleasures. Having the most productive film industry in the world, cinema in India has a much stronger social presence than anywhere else. While film studies in the 1970s and early 1980s concentrated on the ideological function of the cinematic text, more recent projects in this field undertake to study the viewer also as a text, already constructed by a mul-tiplicity of discourses, actively engaging with and evolving through the process of signification. The viewer, however hypothetical, is forever in a process of getting written, 'a text in the making' within the shifting seams of the social and cinematic fabrics. Such a conceptualisation of the spectator could undermine rigid categorisations and highlight the significance of what Judith Butler has described as a 'critically queer' (Butler 2000) perspective—

i.e., a point of view that rejects predetermined categories (for instance, hetero/homo) of spectatorial desire.

Subsequently the purpose of a queer reading of Indian cinema is not to reveal any hidden agenda within a particular film text to address and please self-identified homosexuals among the target viewers, nor a (more danger- ous?) plot to convert some 'innocent' heterosexual viewers to homosexuals (sic). As a popular cultural artifact, cinema does not reflect the 'real'—it reflects on the 'real' and creates visions and imaginations that help us to construct the real, and construct ourselves within that real. A queer reading could examine the function of cinema in remoulding subjectivities, desires and pleasures. Like gender, desire also is an ongoing effect of meanings and definitions, culturally produced and circulated, and crucially, these defini- tions have very real material consequences in our lives. A queer reading could help us perceive the ways in which patriarchy and its allies negotiate with the potentially disruptive instincts, striving to maintain a normative order that complements their agenda. Simultaneously it could also reveal the conflicts and cracks that appear in the seemingly smooth evolution of social desires. How are our notions and experience of gendered identities and bodies redefined in the context of the readjustments in lifestyles and practices of domesticity, made inevitable by economic and social transformations? Cin- ema could tell us not only of the cultural construction of gender but, as Kate Millett has put it, also about the construction of gendered inequality—i.e., the ways in which gender and desire get remoulded within the power struc- tures. This essay is an aspiration to conjure a language that could help to perceive the complex transactions of desire and power that define masculinities in Kerala and I shall try to do this by examining the male intimacies in some recent films. I shall try to read these films from a queer perspective to tease out the implications of same-sex/gender desire deployed in their narrative construction of masculinities. I shall also try to highlight how these films both arouse an active exchange of desire between men and subsequently block it within an economy of 'acceptable' pleasure.

DESIRING THE MALE BODY

Male bonding has always been an important theme for Indian cinema from its earliest days and it has so far been read mainly through a heterosexist perspective that turns a blind eye towards the complex articulation of physi- cal intimacies and desire they regularly appropriate. For example, in an otherwise insightful analysis of mainstream Hindi cinema, Fareed Kazmi has recently described the relationships of 'obsessional, *almost unnatural* love' (emphasis mine) between men portrayed in Hindi films as an effort to recapture the residue of lost pre-capitalist values of mutual devotion and sacrifice, still entrenched in the superstructural consciousness of the people (Kazmi 1999: 7). Such assessments miss the strikingly gendered nature of these (*almost unnatural!*) relationships, explicit physicality through which they are increasingly getting defined and the significant investments they have in the consolidation of patriarchal power.

The male body started featuring as an object of visual pleasure and desire in Malayalam cinema with the emergence of Kamalahasan as a significant star in the early 1970s. This is obvious when we look at the publicity campaigns of some of his early Malayalam films.[3] The publicity material should be considered as an integral part of cinematic signification as it undertakes the task of doing the necessary 'ground work' to facilitate the pleasurable deployment of a film text in a particular context. Advertising campaigns invariably constitute a pre-text that configures the potential signification of a film text and have to be seen as a crucial part of the construction and circulation of cinematic pleasures. From his very first film, *Kanyakumari* (1974), Kamalahasan's bare-bodied appearance was one of the 'commodities' offered by the publicity materials as a promise of visual pleasure. The interpellation of desire in these films was routed through either a 'frustrated married woman' (Sheela in *Vishuvijayam* [1975] and *Eeeta* [1978]) or a young widow (Jayasudha in *Rasaleela* [1976]). Thus, it became a conjuncture when Malayalam cinema started engaging with 'female desire,' though always defined with reference to the institution of marriage.[4] Yet these women were either absent or had only a marginal presence in the publicity posters. Thus the posters preferred to offer the bare male torso as an object of visual fascination, frequently employing conventions of framing and lighting till then used mostly in the representation of female sex icons like Vijayashree. I consider this an important transition in the erotic imaginary of Kerala, as it marks the inscription (or re-inscription) of the male body, defined 'masculine', as the 'object', rather than subject, of desire. A 'feminised' male body had been functioning as an object of desiring gaze from much before this, and its history will have to be traced in the earlier centuries. The *stree veshams* (female characters, invariably performed by men) in Kathakali had been highly fetishised objects of desire in the early years of the twentieth century, evoking '*moham*' (allure/desire) among the male spectators.[5] Later, popular actor Prem Nazir appeared in drag in several films of the late 1960s and early 1970s, promptly to be wooed by another male within the diegetic space.[6] I consider such representations as an extension of the configuring of the 'feminine' (rather than the female) as a palpable object of desire and visual pleasure, which dates back to the earliest phases of patriarchal imagination, though it undertakes distinct trajectories within specific socio-historical locations. The 'male' desire, in such contexts, is deployed towards a 'feminine code'—i.e., the saree or any other 'female guise' worn by the 'male' performer. Thus the desire continues to be relayed from an active/masculine position of power to a seemingly passive/powerless location. What makes the Kamalahasan phase interesting is its substitution of the 'feminine' with the 'masculine' as an object of erotic gaze and desire.[7] In other words, desire is relayed *towards* a form that signified as 'powerful' and 'active'. Incidentally, *Vishuvijayam* was based on a James Hadley Chase novella, *An Ace up my Sleeve* (1971), in which the male character is gay and it is this 'consolidated sexual identity' (sic) that helps him to avoid having sex with the female protagonist in spite of having seduced her. In the Malayalam film, Vishnu (Kamalahasan) does the same, but without any similar explanations. Instead, he keeps referring to his intimate friend Unni who never appears in the film—thereby leaving the nature of the male extra-diegetic 'friendship' ambiguous.

The rise of Jayan as perhaps the first superstar in Malayalam cinema marked another important stage in the eroticisation of the male body. Kamalahasan, during the early phase of his career, projected a boyish, almost androgynous, identity. Jayan's 30-plus looks and hirsute, muscled torso marked a radical shift in the defining of 'male corporeality' as spectacle and it dominated the film publicity campaigns in Kerala during the late 1970s. He frequently portrayed a social outcast or criminal thereby, belatedly, intro-ducing existential isolation to popular Malayalam cinema.[8] Though the desire relayed to his body was also routed through the agency of a 'frustrated adult woman' (for instance, Sheela in *Sarapanjaram* [1979], Prameela in *Karimbana* [1980]), his popularity was mostly among male children and young men. A caricatured revival of this fanfare has recently swept through Kerala.[9]

If the transformations in representing the male figure in the publicity programmes are to be seen as shifts in the defining of desire, the late 1990s mark another important stage, as the 'heterosexual' figures in publicity posters have started getting replaced by same-sex pairs.[10] This, I would argue, is another significant shift in the configuration of male corporeality. Particu-larly striking is the publicity campaign of the recent Tamil film *Samasthanam* (2002) which featured an important star from Malayalam cinema. The film is supposed to be about a very 'normal' male friendship. The publicity programme of this film (i.e., which appeared in Kerala) was entirely focused on the two male stars, Suresh Gopi and Sarath Kumar. The other performers, especially the female leads, received scanty attention in the posters. Hoardings and billboards portraying the two men appeared everywhere much before the film's release, and one could hardly miss the physical intimacy of the two males they prominently featured. If the purpose of a publicity campaign is to offer the potential viewers with a taste of what they were to expect in large doses in the film, what this film seemed to promise was not merely the friendship of two men, but also the (fetishised?) spectacle of the physical intimacy of two handsome males. The most telling poster was one which showed the faces of the two in a close-up, with Suresh Gopi blowing into the eyes of Sarath Kumar, ostensibly to soothe a sore eye. Yet the picture could also give an initial impression that one man is going to kiss the other. I consider these posters important as they mark a transformation of the agency through which desire for the 'male body' is routed: the desiring self is no more a 'frustrated female' nor an 'absent and hence ungendered' (sic) spectator, but a male icon with a celebrated masculinity. Yet, the film presents these men as married to women, functioning as protective husbands and respectable members of a traditional social order. Thus the physical intimacy between two men is inscribed into a pleasurable spectacle, offering multiple locations of identification, without raising any significant disruptions to the patriarchal order. I shall return to this point a little later, when I discuss the reception of the male friendship films.

STAR, FAN AND THE POLITICS OF DESIRE

Many of my readers will now be raising their eyebrows—if not their voices and hands—in disagreement, ready to scream that these representations of 'sexy male bodies' were addressing female pleasure and nothing else. They might also contend that expressions of physical intimacy among men is common in India and does not ever indicate 'homoeroticism'. Gayle Rubin, in one of her celebrated essays, observes: 'Hunger is hunger but what counts as food is culturally determined and obtained...sex is sex but what counts as sex is equally culturally determined and obtained' (Rubin 1975: 165). Anyway, my purpose was not to indicate that every male in Kerala derived pleasure from watching the bare torso and biceps of Kamalahasan or Jayan and, I am sure, many females would also have been least impressed by the same. Neither do I wish to suggest that the directors of these films were 'consciously' portraying 'homosexual' love. My attempt here is to emphasise that the 'act of seeing and deriving pleasure' needs be seen as a dialectic with an ever-slipping trajectory of signification. The viewing subject, constituted as *he* is at the conjuncture of a variety of discursive formations, also functions as a text in his own right, sliding the signification and pleasure of cinema on to ambiguous realms of inter-texuality.[11] And the apparent (relative) absence of 'gay and lesbian life styles' of the Western or metropolitan mould in Kerala shall not tempt me to believe that this region is embedded in a pre-cultural innocence about non-heterosexualities.[12] I consider the eroticisation of male-bodies in cinema significant as it accomplishes the creation of a powerful discursive framework within which male-bodies are redefined in relation to desire and pleasure, in the process constituting a perceptual force field within which the spectator, irrespective of *his* gendered identity, finds *himself* located. The masculine pronoun I have used to refer to the hypothetical film viewer is not unintentional, but a conscious strategy to invite attention to the present sociology of film viewing in Kerala which, researchers point out, is increasingly becoming a male act.[13] Recent studies indicate that fan associations in India are primarily male domains, devoted to male stars and comprising male fans, and this explains the conspicuous absence of female membership in most of the fan associations. Both Malayalam and Tamil cinema do not seem to have had any significant fan associations devoted to female stars in the recent past.[14] According to Caroline Osella who has conducted extensive sociological research on the fan associations in Kerala, 'girls and women participate less strongly in the cinema-going culture (in Kerala); and … females are entirely absent from fan clubs and fan activities.' (Osella and Osella).

In the relationship of the male fan to the male movie star lies one of the keys to an understanding of the politics of screen masculinities in Indian commercial cinema, as it is a bond mediating between identification and desire. Osella has also pointed out the popularity of male pin-ups among the young male film fans in Kerala, citing the many instances when a heterosexually identified male informant instinctively slipped into an 'alternate' subject location and talked about how 'women' would find a particular male star very 'attractive,' or 'sexy.' A film that relies chiefly on the popularity of its male star for commercial success directly addresses this fascination and takes care to present the star as both an object of desire and a figure of identification. The male friend of the hero becomes a convenient location from which this fascination is addressed, thereby providing the fan/viewer a comfortable site of identification. The opening sequence of *Aaram Thampuran,* which I have discussed in detail in an earlier essay, is a telling example for this.[15]

The sequence in question appears immediately after the titles, but has a preceding prelude that introduces its superstar hero Mohanlal, who initially appears in the film as a hired muscleman and the saviour of his wealthy male friend (Sai Kumar) in distress. The episode has a structure similar to the 'damsel in distress' trope that conventionally initiates a heterosexual romance. But the distress confronting a damsel will invariably be a threat to her life or 'chastity' while the one which confronts the male friend in this film, risks his patriarchal authority as a successful business tycoon. The timely intervention of the star-hero and a subsequent performance of aggressive, violent machismo effectively avert the crisis. While, the need of a macho protector momentarily emasculates the male friend, his reinstatement into a position of economic power, retains his position of patriarchal authority. This leads to a sequence in which the two friends meet in the wealthy man's room (hotel suite). The encounter defines their intimate friendship as inter-woven by complementing hierarchies of power. The sequence also marks a striking shift in the pattern of framing. The preceding sequence, which introduces Jagan, conforms to what Ravi Vasudevan has termed the 'darsanic pattern' narration and portrays the hero as a deified figure of authority, with a series of low-angled shots. The following sequence slowly shifts to the style of 'domestic' realism, assuming medium close shots. It opens with the close-up of a glass of liquor into which Sai Kumar drops a cube of ice, directly shifted to a medium close-up of Jagan (Mohanlal) entering the room with a sedate smile. Thus an association is made between the inebriating liquid and the incoming male. Subsequently Sai Kumar addresses Jagan with a stream of endearing terms, hugs him repeatedly, fondles his face, offers him expensive gifts including a joint pleasure trip to Europe and finally settles on a night together in bed, in each other's arms.[16] The sequence is woven with shifting seams of power and complementing subordination in which the hero and his friend take turns to locate themselves, thereby offering the adoring fan with multiple locations of pleasure for identification and desire.[17] The sequence etches two masculinities that appear complementary, as they are unified in a mission to sustain and consolidate male power that is amicably distributed, thereby constituting a cultural space in which physical intima-cies between two men become a desirable, pleasurable spectacle that is not threatening. In the process a 'safe' framework, that does not disturb the imagined 'heterosexuality' of the character or the spectator, is created to define the male star as 'desirable' to the male viewers.

Similar portrayals of masculinities, defined through male intimacies, feature in many recent films. *Harikrishnans*(1999) and *Thenkasi Pattanam* (2001), elaborate this by presenting men who have set up an alternate domestic system—including an adopted child who is invariably a girl. *Chakram* (2003) has further extended the language of male–male domesticity by presenting two men in a far more 'unequally' constituted family formation. The younger male in this film assumes a subordinate role that borders on a replication of patriarchal heterosexual domesticity. The character played by Vijeesh cooks and washes for the older male, Chandrahasan (Prithviraj), and even declares 'I have been serving/taking care of him like a wife.' His relentless womanising seems to be specifically constructed as a precautionary measure to safeguard his 'masculinity'.

An explicit invocation of the sensual in a location of male intimacy appears in *One Man Show* (2002), in the sequence in which the hero Jayakrishnan (Jayaram) enters his decorated bedroom on his wedding night, wearing the groom's dress, only to encounter his eccentric male friend Hari (Lal), also in groom's attire. In his deranged fancy, Hari supposedly imagines himself as the groom who married Radhika (Samyukta), Jayakrishnan's wife. What follows is a surrealist game of hide-and-seek in which both the men recurrently end up in bed with each other. The situation is complicated by the presence of a lunatic (Salim Kumar), also in groom's attire, who strays into the same bedroom, adding to the confusion. The wedding night is a regular trope in Malayalam cinema, charged with obvious eroticism and corporeal desire. In the present situation, Hari and Jayakrishnan seem to erase the element of 'erotic' through exaggerated disavowals of any 'desire' for each other, while the mad man re-inscribes it with equal vehemence by openly soliciting it. On one occasion Jayakrishan mistakes the mad man, covered by a sheet, to be his wife and embraces him. His prompt reply is, 'Sorry, wrong number, but go ahead.' Thus, his 'madness' becomes the trope that pleads guilty, in this situation, of inadvertently seeking to undermine 'masculine' power. Incidentally, a striking picture of Lal and Jayaram, dressed as grooms and sitting on a decorated nuptial bed, was one of the prominent publicity posters of this film.

HOMO-SOCIAL OR HETERO-SOCIAL?

Even those who acknowledge such random expressions of queerness in films consider it relevant to point out that these moments are not only marginal to the main 'attractions', but also transient and hence irrelevant to the narrative significations. The sporadic sojourns to the domain of 'queer' intimacies are immediately reiterated in most films by the quick re-establishment of a normative order. This is generally accomplished through a re-inscription of the main characters into the heterosexual matrix that, in most films, constitutes the final marriage of the hero and heroine. A heterosexual domestic unit features in some of these films as an ideal, momentarily unavailable, yet coveted by some of the men in the male bond. Hence many prefer to describe these films as 'homo-social' yet heterosexual.

Even though I endorse some of these observations, I would like to disagree with the subsequent conclusion. I do not consider the heterosexist resolutions as necessarily impairing the pleasure of same-sex affinities that structure these texts. This becomes particularly relevant when we ponder on the characteristic narrative of mainstream Indian cinema, which rarely preserves the narrative unities that designate classic realism. Temporal and spatial continuities are frequently disrupted by the song and dance sequences that constitute a crucial component of Indian cinema's technology of pleasure. The action or 'stunt' sequences, comic interludes and even the melodramatic episodes could be seen as having a similar, though not identical, narrative function—each of them signifying as seemingly independent narrative units or texts. Moreover, most mainstream Indian films cannot easily be classified into any clearly identifiable Western genres as they invariably contain melodramatic episodes, action and special effect sequences, comic interludes, fantasies, songs and dances, suspenseful moments, and so on—all packed into the logic of a fragmented narrative which Ravi Vasudevan prefers to describe as 'non-continuous', instead of 'discontinuous'. Vasudevan considers this characteristic structure as typical of narrative forms in 'transitional' societies, pointing out that the problem of transition poses a cultural politics centred on the way local forms reinvent themselves to establish dialogue with and assert difference from universal models of narration and subjectivity (2000: 131). As a merchandise striving to trade pleasure, contemporary mainstream Indian cinema should be seen as an ensemble of a series of audio-visual spectacles. Such a conceptualisation of the cinematic narrative also calls for a fresh understanding of the process of reception, as the 'non-continuous' narrative offers the spectator a rather unstable location to occupy. Thus mainstream Indian cinema ends up making a mixed address, leading to a relationship of reception very different from that of classic Hollywood realism. It relays a series of views and sensations to its audience rather than following a linear narrative logic, thereby facilitating a mediated relationship to processes of identification (ibid.: 161).

The signification of these semi-autonomous narrative units in Indian films has, in recent years, been further complicated by the multiplication and spread of television channels. The most popular programmes aired at prime time by our ever-multiplying channels are assortments of dramatic, comic or song sequences, harvested from various popular films. Such programmes thus provide these sequences with an extended life that transcends the narrative logic of the film texts in which they were earlier embedded, further highlighting their autonomous potential to signify and 'entertain'. Thus the 'queer' sequence from a film—be it a song, dramatic or comic sequence—

when telecast separately, its 'queerness' is no more erased by the heterosexist narrative resolutions within which it was encased while within the film text. Many people, who never saw the original film, would end up seeing and 'enjoying' these sequences as they are telecast again and again for a long period of time. A striking example is the 'Ponne, Ponnambili' song from *Harikrishnans* (1999)which presents Mohanlal and Mamooty jointly parenting and pampering Baby Shamili. The sequence is reminiscent of myriads of similar songs in earlier Malayalam films that presented a heterosexual pair with a child, replaced here by two male parents. The 'Mane, Malaramban valarthunna pulli mane...' song of *Ayal Kathayezhuthukayanu* (*He is writing a story!*) (1998) presents a more misogynist version of male pairing that concludes with both Srinivasan and Mohanlal getting into bed together.[18]

That brings me back to the narrative significance of the heterosexual closures in such films, which I would like to describe as the 'heterosexual fixtures' as they seem to fix the identities of these characters and the signification of narrative from slipping into any nameable 'identities' or even 'acts' that could undermine the normative order. Such tropes, in most of these films, are scantily etched when compared to the much more detailed enunciation of the same-gender intimacies. In films like *Asuravamsam* (1995) there is no such closure.[19] In films like *Manichitrathazhu* (1994) and *Hariskrishnans* (1999) it is very tentative and ambiguous. In some other films, the heterosexual resolution remains fragmented or open-ended thereby undermining its very significance as a closure. A striking example is *Thacholi Verghese Chekavar* in which the superstar hero remains sincerely attentive to his male friend and indifferent towards the heroine throughout the film but, in an unexpected twist, decides to marry the woman in the concluding sequence. The newly constituted heterosexual couple then float out of a church where they are promptly joined by the hero's male friend (Vineet) and the three pose together for a very 'queer' concluding snapshot.[20] A final happy family tableau is a common trope of conclusion in Indian cinema, but what complicates the picture in this film is a continuing display of male intimacy that renders ambiguous the heterosexual resolution.[21] Some of these films could more aptly be described as 'hetero-social', since the eventual constitution of the heterosexual bond is tragically devoid of desire and prompted by gendered responsibilities, preceded by a long narrative celebration of same-sex desire.

POLITICS OF THE FIXTURES

I would like to argue that one of the functions of these heterosexual fixtures is to exile the same-gender desires and pleasures actively appropriated by these films into a realm prior to nomenclature and, subsequently, beyond knowledge—to a virtual 'no *man's* land' (pun intended) where they could remain forever nameless and hence pleasurable. In other words they are processes of 'un-naming' that inscribe same-sex desire as 'invisible' visual pleasures—where the very act of 'not seeing' becomes a source of pleasure. In the process, these fixtures end up enhancing the same-gender pleasures, which they try to render invisible.

Yet the fixtures also seem to have an important political function in the consolidation and maintenance of the discursive link between 'male' and 'masculine'.[22] Within the discursive logic of patriarchy, masculine represents phallic power, i.e., the power of domination/penetration. As a result, a body signifying as male could retain its masculine credential only as long as it does NOT subject itself to penetration. This includes even symbolic castration by occupying the 'object' position of another male's desire. Any male body that forsakes this responsibility becomes a traitor in the empire of virility. This is exemplified by the male triangle in *Thenkasi Pattanam* (2000). The film presents two men (Suresh Gopi and Lal) within an alternate domestic structure, having even an adopted child-sister, Devu (Kavya Madhavan). Yet they are stationed securely within the new *lakshman rekha* of masculinity by the subjugation of mutual desire that, albeit, pops up occasionally, as when Dasan (Lal) gazes at Kannan (Suresh Gopi) adoringly and quips, 'You are too good looking!' (*Nee apara glamourada*!). This discovery of the 'attractive' looks of one male by another is safely routed through the agency of a female, Sangeetha (Geetu Mohandas), thereby rendering the masculinities non-penetrable.[23] A crisis in this world of cautiously 'sanitised' masculinity appears as Shatru (enemy?) (Dileep) who arrives with a love letter for Kannan. In a flight of fancy Kannan then imagines Shatru, in an unexpected performance of *camp*, declaring explicit desire for him.[24] Kannan enacts complete ignorance of emasculating same-sex desire in males by asking Shatru if he is 'mad'. Yet, this very 'non-masculine' performance of Shatru is a figment of Kannan's imagination, as the former believes that what he handed over is an appointment letter. Thus it contradicts Kannan's 'pretended' ignorance of the possibility of 'effeminacy' or same-sex desire in a male. The discursive locating of the (male) spectator appropriated by this sequence deserves a detailed discussion, which I resist due to limitations of space and time. Incidentally, the sequence became so popular that it continues to appear in the television programmes regularly, in a structurally different incarnation of autonomous signification. The mindless (ostensibly humorous) physical torture that both Dasan and Kannan inflict on Shatru's emasculated body, both before and after this sequence, could be read as a process of masculinisation, a rite of passage for Shatru that could eventually entitle him to Devu's hand.[25] At the same time it could also be read as a ritual of self-purification for Kannan and Dasan—to sustain and consolidate their endangered phallic power.

There is another important aspect to the crisis of masculinity that these films portray, perhaps providing a crucial motivation to the final flight to the heterosexual fixtures. This is an encounter with a form of female 'masculinity',—i.e., the appearance of desire and autonomy within a 'female' form. In *Thenkasipatanam*, Meenakshi (Samyukta) dares to express her 'desire' for Kannan in a language of clarity, while Sangeetha (Geetu) does the same in addition to asserting her autonomy by rejecting Dasan's overtures.[26] Versions of such a pattern could be seen in most of the other films about male bonds. For example, both Ganga (Sobhana) and Sridevi (Vinaya Prasad) in *Manichitrathazhu* are phallic women posing different strains of threat to masculine power. Both Jagan Thampuran and Verghese Chekavar also encounter desiring women, whom they subsequently reject and banish totally from narrative existence.[27] Even Unnimaya (Manju) displays a sense of autonomy till Jagan domesticates her. The relinquishing of same-sex desire is integral to this heroic project of countering a female appropriation of the power to desire. The autonomous women (whatever helplessness has prompted their self-reliance) will have to be re-inscribed into feminine subordination; the desiring women are either to be summarily rejected or at least 'tamed'. If they ever qualify to get their men, it is only after 'purging' their corporeal desire and resuming the status as 'feminine' subjects in perpetual need of protection and domination.

MASCULINITY IN CRISIS

I would like to read the male friendship films as reflecting a crisis in masculinity that manifests in the context of ongoing economic and social transformations in contemporary India, particularly in the non-metropolitan regions, and the subsequent redefining of gendered desires and performances. Due to limitations of time and space I have confined this essay to an examination of the reception and signification of such films in the specific context of Kerala, and looked only at the strands of same-gender desire woven into the evolving fabric of cinematic pleasure.[28] I do not wish to suggest that identities have, till now, been evolving without similar traumatic restructuring. Yet the density of social changes in the post-feudal scenario of Kerala and the unnerving momentum they gathered after the 1970s certainly seem to have contributed considerably to this present crisis. The narrative (re?)elaboration of the 'male' body as an object of erotic desire, manifested in the Kamalahasan and Jayan phases of Malayalam cinema, seems to represent the first tremors of this crisis. Apart from crystallising 'masculine' desires for such bodies, it also seems to have aroused simultaneous anxieties about a female embodying of these desires. Within a cultural context that frames 'desire' as phallic, violent and hence emasculating, the eroticisation of the male body engenders paranoia about castration or, at least, a symbolic loss of power. Hence the 'masculine' desire for the 'male' has to be rendered nameless, if its pleasure is to be sustained and relished. As an 'unimagined' mischief scattered amidst the visual splendour of the cinematic spectacle it, forever, remains embedded within reassuring heterosexual fixtures that enhance a pleasure recurrently disavowed.

What I have attempted so far is a quick, cursory glance at the transforming structure of masculinities in the visual imagination of Kerala during the last three decades, rendered conspicuous by the most powerful medium of the twentieth century. This is a visibility made possible by a critically queer perspective, a deconstructive point of view that dismantles binarisms of thought and signification. It demonstrates that Indian cinema, especially contemporary cinema, is not addressing a fundamentally 'straight' audience, precisely because such an absolutely gendered and sexualised viewer is a mere conceptual fiction. What cinema accomplishes is a negotiation with multiplicities of desires, seeking their rehabilitation within viewing contexts deemed pleasurable.

I do not in any way claim this to be an exhaustive analysis of the evolution of masculinities in Kerala, or even its representation in cinema. Perhaps I have tried just to touch upon one strand of the complex conceptual weave that produces endless reams of prosaic gender designs in the social fabric of this region. I shall be more than excited if this could motivate a process of naming and knowing that dares to confront prevailing phallic structures, and clears a little space where less rigid textures of bodies, desires and pleasures could be generated.

Notes

1. Corporeal refers to the perishable, organic body.
2. Foucault has demonstrated that all forms of knowledges are 'fictions' constructed through discourses—frameworks of ideas, assumptions and social practices through which 'meanings' and hence 'realities' are created. He has also argued that the 'creation' of 'knowledge' is a way of establishing/consolidating power. Butler uses Foucault to question the presumed symbiotic relation

between gender and body. For her, not just masculinity and femininity but even 'male/female bodies' are the products of socially constructed performances. These performances then constitute the 'reality of bodies' towards which desire is deployed.

3. There was a prelude to this in the actor Anandan who starred in some of the 'forest films' (early 1960s) of Neela Productions, directed by K. Subramaniam and inspired by the Tarzan genre of Hollywood. *Kattumaina* (1963), *Aana Valarthiya Vanampadi* (1964), and so on are some of the best-known films of this genre. But Anandan never achieved any star status and the genre did not survive amidst, perhaps, the overwhelming demand raging at that time to indegenise Malayalam cinema.

4. The 'desiring women' were invariably widowed, abandoned or 'old and unmarried'—which underscored the crucial location of marriage in the constitution of 'female desire.' And these women never attained their object of desire, but lost him either to a young, virginal 'non-desiring' woman or to death. In Vishuvijayam he surrenders to the police, but WITHOUT a promise to return to the woman.

5. There are still many 'star' Kathakali (male) dancers who specialise in female roles, for instance, Kalamandalam Gopi. In the early decades of the twentieth century, in the absence of more modern arts like the realist drama or cinema, Kathakali was a popular form of entertainment, and many oral narratives refer to the 'alluringly sensual' performances of some of these (male) stars as Draupadi, Damayanti, and so on.

6. The diegetic space is the space within a cinematic frame, i.e., all that appears within the screen space. Early formal studies of cinema were focused on the signification of the components within this space. But more recent studies underscore the crucial function of elements outside this space (for instance, the cultural or historical contexts, categories of viewership, references to local or global events, objects or characters outside the screen whose presence is evoked, and so on) in cinematic signification.

7. I am sure that alternate discursive traditions which feature the 'masculine' as the object of desire could be traced in Kerala and elsewhere, especially among marginalised cultural formations and practices. I consider the phase initiated by cinema significant because of the discursive hegemony engendered by its prime location within the cartography of modernity.

8. Another, more 'Western,' version of existentialism was manifesting in the *art cinema* movement of the same period.

9. For detailed discussions, see Kumar (2002) and Radhakrishnan (2002).

10. Publicity posters of films like *Harikrishnans* (1998), *Dost* (2001), *Swapnam Kondu Thulabharam* (2003), etc., could be cited as examples. Though 'male friendship' films had become popular in Hindi from the late 1960s, it became a trend in Malayalam a few decades later.

11. That is, each of the texts contributing to and thus modifying the signification of the other.

12. One of the locations where we could explore the reasons for the apparent absence of a discernible public discourse on non-heterosexualities in India is in the nationalist appropriations of morality in the early half of the 20th century.

13. It is to be noted that film viewing as a public activity is increasingly becoming a male endeavour in Kerala, with the female enthusiasm confined to a few films that are publicised as exclusively for women. This also tells a lot about the condition inside the cinema houses in Kerala which, with the increasing reluctance of the middle class to participate in public cinema viewing, are becoming male domains from which females are excluded by a variety of social and cultural tactics. On the one hand, the increasing patriarchal and violent machismo in Kerala makes it an uneasy experience for a woman to go anywhere alone, and the worst of it could be a cinema house where she has to remain in darkness and in close proximity of males for a duration of two hours. This is not to say that women do not go to the cinema houses any more. But the precautions they have to take make it a tedious exercise and help consolidate the cinema house as a male world.

14. Khushboo in Tamil and Vijayashanti in Telugu seem to be the most recent female stars who had fan associations devoted to them. Both the actresses are now well past their prime and in semi-retirement. Moreover even during their most glorious days, they had not generated the kind of euphoria that the prominent male stars continue to give rise to.

15. For a detailed discussion on the scene, see Muraleedharan (2001: 65–75).

16. Among the many offers he makes, is one to get some women, but uttered in a language devoid of any desire and classified with others like gambling in a Casino in Las Vegas—thereby emphasising an attitude of extravagance mixed with indifference.

17. His possession of wealth makes the businessman 'powerful' and hence 'masculine'. It makes him the 'provider' who could pamper his friend with expensive gifts—an act that consolidates his 'masculinity'. Jagan, on the other hand, is the physically powerful 'protector' who safeguards his rich friend and his wealth. This helps to retain his 'masculinity' as well. Thus, the two men remain within shifting significations of 'masculine power' which prevents the desire relayed between them from becoming 'disempowering'/castrating.

18. The sequence presents the two men harassing and thus disempowering a 'haughty' woman, while displaying considerable mutual affection and physical intimacy.

19. In Tamil films like *Thiruda, Thiruda* and *Kathal Desam*, the feminine/female intervention that disrupts the flow of desire between the men eventually bows out or is edged out to reinvigorate the male bond.

20. Thus, the conclusion is reminiscent of Ang Lee's Taiwanese-American gay comedy *A Wedding Banquet* (1993). The film presents a gay Chinese immigrant in the United States, living with a white male partner, who procures a temporary wife to please his visiting mother.

21. For a detailed discussion see Muraleedharan (2001).

22. I use the term 'male' to refer to a gendered signification of the body and 'masculine' to denote an imagined identity of power.

23. Sangeetha rejects Dasan's proposal by saying that she is attracted to Kannan. This prompts Dasan to 'discover' that Kannan is very handsome. The expression used by the drunken Dasan became popular among the young men in the campuses in Kerala, as a convenient refrain to flatter each other and consolidate 'masculine camaraderie'.

24. Camp is the exaggerated performance of femininity by a male person. Initially considered a sign of homosexuality, camp has subsequently been refashioned by queer activists as a deliberate political act that undermines the normative façades of the masculine and its presumed 'natural' location in a male body.

25. This is elaborated in a song sequence which celebrates the violence as a plea-surable spectacle, justified by the emasculated appearance of Shatru.

26. This is NOT to suggest that the representation of these two women reflects any feminist politics.

27. See my discussion in 'Disrupted Desires: Male Bonds in Mohanlal Films' (2001).

28. The desirable male body featuring through all these transformation has always been marked as 'upper-caste', middle-class and Hindu, even when the characters did not officially represent such an identity. This is another aspect of the restructuring of desire that deserves detailed examination.

REFERENCES

Butler, Judith. 1990, Gender Trouble: Feminism and the Subversion of Identity. New York: Routledge.

Butler, Judith. 2000, 'Critically Queer', in Anna Trip (ed.), Gender. New York: Palgrave, pp. 154–67.

Corber, Robert J. and Stephen Valocchi (eds). 2003, 'Introduction', Queer Studies: An Interdisciplinary Reader. Oxford: Blackwell.

Gledhill, Christine and Linda Williams (eds). 2000, Reinventing Film Studies. London: Arnold.

Gopinath, Gayatri. 2000, 'Queering Bollywood: Alternative Sexualities in Popular Indian Cinema', Journal of Homosexuality, Vol. 39, Nos 3–4.

Halperin, David M. 1993, 'Is There a History of Sexuality?', in H. Abelove, D. Halperin and M. Barale (eds), The Lesbian and Gay Studies Reader. New York: Routledge, pp. 416–31.

———. 2002, How to Do the History of Homosexuality? Chicago: University Of Chicago Press.

Kazmi, Fareed. 1999, The Politics of India's Conventional Cinema. New Delhi: Sage Publications.

Kumar, Sanoj K. 2002, 'Jayanesque—Communication Perspectives on Body Politics: An Analysis of the Jayan Phenomenon', Unpublished Dissertation, Department of Journalism and Communication, Calicut University.

Muraleedharan T. 2001, 'Disrupted Desires: Male Bonds in Mohanlal Films', *Deep Focus*, Vol. 9, No. 1, pp. 65–75.

Osella, Caroline and Filipo Osella. 'Malayali Young Men and Their Movie Heroes', Unpublished Paper, SOAS and University of Sussex.

Radhakrishnan, Ratheesh. 2002, 'Stable and Unstable Masculinities in Malyalam Cinema: Some Pointers towards a Methodology', Unpublished Paper Presented at CSCS, Bangalore.

Rubin, Gayle. 1975, 'The Traffic in Women: Notes on the Political Economy of Sex', in R.R. Reiter (ed.), *Towards an Anthropology on Women*. New York: Monthly Review Press.

Trip, Anna (ed.). 2000, *Gender*. New York: Palgrave.

Vasudevan, Ravi. 2000, 'The Politics of Cultural Address in a "Transitional" Cinema: A Case Study of Indian Popular Cinema', in Gledhill and Williams (eds), *Reinventing Film Studies*.

5

Beyond 'Sexuality' (?)

Akshay Khanna

Identity can fuck itself (really well)

my red eyes are
scary
to me
what i see through
wisps
of dead hair

there was a war on, that night
(a
story of a little
person
sure the world was mad
'cos it wanted trousers
on these legs
and girls to
giggle about

mother father brother sister
saw it all
saw the flight
shied away and shunned
her
out)

the mirror spoke through red eyes
gay? straight? boy? woman? man? all?
nobody explains transgendered bisexuals

cells (atoms sound too determined) depart and meet
four five six dimensions
all the time

capture a moment
(ignoring a couple of uncomfortable dimensions)
and i'm
gay
man
who shaves
and smokes shit

lose a grip on one
(they're just so easy to lose when you interact with people)
and it's all gone

capture another
(will i ever give up?)
and i'm actually
bisexual
experimenting with
who i am

for a bit

the lucidity of chaos
is scary to me
what i see through
wisps
of dead hair

New Delhi, sometime in the summer of 2000.

 I am sitting in my sister's room, on the outskirts of Bangalore where my biological family affords a place on rent. The breeze is titillating, just the sound of a few dogs who live on these streets interrupting this picture of serenity. My Italian lover is gently licking my ear, sneaking furtive glances at the computer screen. Years ago, I chose to leave this house because I 'refused to compromise' my sexual desires. 'You cannot have sex before getting married.' 'What if I choose not to get married?' I had asked. 'That is your problem.'

By then, I had told my mother, my father and my grandmother that I was having sex with other men. 'You can live with us only if you live by our rules,'

the patriarch said. Empowered with a law degree, I had walked out, to find a life in another city.

It has been some years now. I have found other cities, other communities, other lives. I live in all of them, intermittently, including this one. I have found ways of negotiating space in all of them. Unlike what I had thought my life would be like, of being a hetero-normative son in one, a gainfully employed lawyer in another and a raving queen in a third, I now live all these lives with long hair tied in a bun, loud clinking bangles and the occasional nail polish to match my *dupattas*.

I have a penis that I love, she's called a pussy in some circles. My Italian lover has a pussy too, sometimes.

Am I straight? Am I gay? Am I bisexual?

When I had just started moving around in definedly non-heterosexual circles (maybe I should call them 'gay'), this question tortured every moment of self-reflection. Tormented by 'you're just in denial that you are gay', and alternatively, 'face it, you are straight, but you say you're not just because its cool', I spent many nights staring at myself in the mirror asking myself, what am I? This was probably the painful moment journalists at protests today ask about—'When did you find out that you were gay?' 'How did you feel?' 'How did you come to terms with the fact?'

Unfortunately for them, and perhaps for the heart-wrenching story that could be written about homophobia in Indian culture, I never did come to terms with 'the fact' that I was gay. Or bisexual. I decided not to. I decided, privileged as I was, that I did not need to name myself on the basis of my desires. There was something wrong if whom I fucked said everything about what I was. To me, this was the beginning of my questioning. Not just of what we collectively started calling hetero-normativity a little later, but of 'sexuality', of 'sexual identity'. A little excavation of the short history of the idea of 'sexuality' has gotten me engaged in a politics where I find myself opposing the processes through which I am called upon to name myself, and more importantly, called upon to understand the world around me in terms of 'sexuality'. In this essay, instead of naming myself, I try to name 'sexuality'. I try to name it as an effect of our post-colonial condition, where the options we have, to understand and address our realities are regulated by our colonial histories and our imperialist presents. In order to do this I shall first briefly historicise the term sexuality, then look at the other key framework in the queer movement—the human rights framework and briefly examine its history. I shall then articulate what I see as the problems with what has emerged as a sexuality rights framework. Finally, I shall turn against my argument and try and suggest ways forward.

(RE) LOCATING THE IDENTITY DEBATE

In the recent past a group of queer activists have been engaging in a particular debate. The debate arises from a discomfort with a rigid 'identity-based' activism. It has been and continues to be an emotionally charged and intense debate for all of us. It relates to the very basis on which we relate to our 'selves', to each other and to the political field that we hope to impact. To provide a flavour of how this debate has changed, in its focus and its location, I refer to an interesting process that has come about in Delhi—'Voices against Section 377'.

'Voices against Section 377', or 'Voices' as it may come to be called in the future, is a broad coalition of queer groups, women's groups, child rights groups, groups concerned with the HIV/AIDS epidemic and human rights organisations in Delhi, who have come together to protest against the violence engendered by the anti-sodomy law of India, i.e., Section 377 of the Indian Penal Code. This group is interesting in that it marks the convergence of different perspectives and concerns—a convergence on an issue that until recently has been resisted in many 'progressive' circles. Recently, this group had a day of conversation about 'the basics of sexuality'. The invitation to the event, sent out by PRISM, a forum and advocacy group that came to be formally set up in the background of the famous Lucknow case,[1] paints a new picture of the debate I have referred to above. An excerpt:

> Voices is a unique forum in that it consists of groups engaged with a wide range of issues—and sexuality is not the 'main focus' of the work of most of the member organizations. Inherent in this broad based coalition is a recognition of human rights violations which stem from the marginalization and criminalization of same sex desire.
>
> But how do we view same sex desire? Do we locate it in the framework of majority–minority—i.e. are we talking about the rights of a clearly defined section of the population which some refer to as sexual minorities? Are we talking only about people who identify as lesbian, gay, bisexual, transgender, hijra etc. or are we talking about all those who practise same sex desire, whether they label themselves on the basis of their sexual orientation or not? Or are we talking about the role ideas and politics around sex play in distribution of resources, power, pleasure, suffering...? This raises the larger question of what we mean by sexual orientation? And in fact of what we mean by sexuality itself. Is sexuality an aspect of our personhood—i.e. are bisexuals, heterosexuals and homosexuals particular types of persons?
>
> These questions are not just theoretical. The answers impact the way in which we 'do' activism on issues of sexuality. Every parcha that we write, every press release we issue is part of the creating of a certain kind of discourse on sexuality.

In a context in which this discourse is emerging it becomes critical to examine how we are shaping it. Last, and not the least, is the issue of how issues of sexuality relate to other aspects of our work—whether it be women's rights, human rights, child rights, anti-communalism, anti-war.... Are rights related to sexuality important but separate, or are there fundamental connections between these various dimensions of our work and activism?

The interesting thing about the above articulation is that it shows that the earlier concern with the 'way we identify' (or not) has given way to the question of how we carry out our activism—how does the way we 'name ourselves' impact the way in which we participate in political processes?

The 'day of conversation' started with a card game. The questions 'what does sexuality mean to you' and 'what is sexuality' were put to the participants. In turn, participants wrote down their responses and stuck them up on a wall for all to read. A discussion was then facilitated on the responses. Of the range of responses, ranging from 'sexuality is all that I am', to 'sexuality is my desires', the overwhelming number related the term to an idea of the self. 'Sexuality' emerged as a concept that enables people to relate their desires and sexual behaviour to their 'selves'. In simple terms, the idea of sexuality seems to make the link between our desires and 'what we are'—*whom* I fuck says something about *what* I am. This is the essence of the term 'sexuality' in bio-medicine,[2] and, perhaps not surprisingly, in queer activism.[3] As such, 'sexuality' refers, in these contexts, to *an aspect of personhood*.

WHY HISTORICISE 'SEXUALITY'?

In queer circles today, it is almost absurd to question the idea that each person simply *has* a sexuality—one that is somehow within the person, that is repressed by society and that needs to be expressed. In other words, the idea of 'sexuality' has come to be naturalised, that is, the relationship between the idea and 'reality' has been placed beyond question. In turn this has meant that we now imagine our sexual universes in terms of types of people, who have different types of sexuality. This also means that we are driven to translate diverse sexual behaviours, desires and politics into language that finds its base in the idea of sexuality as personhood. For example, the Hindi word 'yonikta', which crudely translates to 'sexualness' was created by activists in order to translate 'Indian' experiences of desire and sexual behaviour into a language compatible with the understanding of the sexual universe being constituted in terms of 'sexuality'. As the PRISM invitation suggests, we are in the business of creating discourse. A recent protest against Section 377 in

Delhi, which was widely covered by the Hindi media, was the first time that the framework of identity came to be articluated in Hindi, in a positive manner.[4] We are in the process of setting out the terms within which we shall be able to address the politics of sex. This places a responsibility on us to pause, historicise and recognise the potential and limitations of our discursive moves. Do people outside of the urban, largely English-speaking and relatively privileged queer movement think of themselves in terms of 'sexuality'? If not, what does this mean—are 'they' the less privileged to not have the benefit of this conceptualisation? Or is it about different ways in which desire plays a role in framing subjectivity in different contexts? Either way, the drive to deploy the framework of sexuality, to bring about its 'recognition' in law and policy by the state, to establish it as a framework for the redistribution of resources, power, suffering, pleasure and control over discourse in 'civil society' places the differences worldviews in a relationship of power, of dynamism. Surely, we must then examine closely the implications of the framework of sexuality.

For a moment, let me digress to the history of colonialism to emphasise the need to examine the framework. What was colonialism about? Was it merely about the size of the British army? The number of cannons and guns? Historians of colonialism suggest not. David Arnold, a subaltern historian, considers medicine as an 'authoritative vehicle' for the transmission of Western ideas and practices to India, the generation and propagation of Western ideas about India and, ultimately, of Indians' ideas about themselves. He ascribes a role to the rise of an Indian middle class and nationalist ideologues in the establishment of bio-medicine as a mechanism of regulation. In simple terms, the process of colonisation was one through which 'Indians' of the emerging middle class came to understand themselves, their bodies, their relationship with their environment, health and illness in bio-medical terms, in contrast with local health practices. Bio-medicine came to be the desirable system of health care and the disinterest that the colonial administrators showed in ensuring access to bio-medicine to colonial subjects came to be an issue of protest and resistance (Arnold 1993). As such, colonial rule was possible for the large part, not because of coercion, but rather, by the adoption of certain colonial frameworks through which to 'understand the self'. This adoption was the action of a relatively privileged middle class, of ideologues, of the creators of what we now consider 'India', the likes of Bal Gangadhar Tilak (ibid.).

The emergence of the idea of sexuality as the framework of understanding our sexual universes echoes this process in more ways than one. An uncritical espousal implicates us in a process through which certain ordering of experiences and certain mechanisms of regulation, of post-colonial regulation, come to manifest.

One significant clarification needs to be made at this point. My argument is not that the frameworks that were adopted by élite Indians were in any way *pre-formed* and *'Western'*. They were, instead, frameworks that came to be constituted in the colonial context. One may find, for example, the way in which colonialism was the context within which 'Western' subjectivity was as well-constituted. For example, if we take a look at the 'major milestones' in the establishment of bio-medical explanatory model(s)—syphilis, cholera and plague—conditions drenched in metaphor and epidemiology of colonisation, contamination and army, appear on an increasingly regular basis (Khanna, forthcoming). Second, in more tangible terms, sciences of the self emerged through interaction between peoples and practices. Vaccination, for example, was conceptualised in relation to 'native' practices of 'variolation'[5] (ibid.). The significance of this clarification for the purposes of the present essay is this—my argument against the application of the idea of 'sexuality' is not that it is 'Western'. My argument is that it arises out of a certain politics of regulation—a point where the human condition came to be 'captured' in positivist discourse in terms such as 'population', 'tradition' and 'modern'.

A second point of significance to this clarification is that the adoption of colonial frameworks was not merely a 'movement' of a framework or ideas from the 'West' to India. Bio-medicine in rural India is different from what it is and means in urban India, which is different from what it means in the United Kingdom or Europe. Similarly, the practice of Ayurveda in Kerala is different from that in London. In some sense, an idea gets *reconstituted* through the play of local discourses. The significance of this argument will hopefully become clear later in this essay when I consider ways forward.

THE HISTORY OF SEXUALITY

Section 377 of the Indian Penal Code, enacted in 1860, before the emergence of the idea of 'sexuality' as personhood, is concerned with sexual acts and not 'types' of people. It defines a particular act 'referred to in a limited legalese, not a criminal, medical or psychological type of person' (Katz 1990: 10). That is to say, the idea of sexuality as an aspect of personhood comes after the enactment of this law, which takes up most queer activist energy in India. When, then, do we see the emergence of the idea and in what context?

The articulation of sexuality as personhood is best located in the emergence of the homosexual, and simultaneously, the heterosexual in Euro-American discourses of medicine and criminology. This history has been examined in depth and framed in political terms by the likes of Michel Foucault, Jefferey Weeks and Jonathan Ned Katz.[6] Simplistically put, the idea of sexuality arose in a context where bio-medicine ascribed itself the authority to exclusively speak the 'truth' about sex and desire. This is around the time when the body became something that could be mapped and through which disease became subject to new rules of classification. Foucault (broadly speaking) identifies at least three processes at work in this period (Rabinow 1984).

First is the emergence of 'dividing practices'—where the 'normal' and 'abnormal' were categorised and separated. This was not just in conceptual terms, but often very physically, for example, by the identification of the 'insane' and the creation of asylums (Foucault 1988b), the creation of clinics for the diseased (Foucault 1994) and the creation of prisons for the criminal (Foucault 1995). In the context of sexuality, this division came to be in terms of a normal heterosexual and an abnormal homosexual.

The second process was the emergence of authoritative discourses and 'pseudo-sciences' such as bio-medicine, psychiatry and criminology. As such, here is the delineation of *who* may speak the truth about the human condition, and from what location.

Finally, and this is perhaps the most significant for our purposes, is the emergence of processes through which people are called upon to recognise themselves in terms set by such discourses. This 'call to recognise one*self*' (Foucault 1988a) is an essential part of the way in which populations came to be regulated in the modern nation-state. This is to say, once a person thinks of herself as being subject to a given norm, she starts regulating herself—there is no more need for a coercive state or society to stand with a whip to get her to behave in a certain way, to play a certain role in the economy. She does it to herself. For example, bio-medicine came to be a powerful vehicle for regulation in India because élite Indians began to think of health, illness and the body through the framework of bio-medicine. This has been understood as the unique aspect of power in the modern nation-state.[7] In a nutshell, this is a time in the history of Euro-American societies, and by extension to European colonies, is when a 'self', i.e., what it means to be a person, comes to be defined. But how did this self come to be eroticised? How did 'sexuality' become one aspect of this 'self'.

Katz suggests that this eroticisation of consciousness, behaviour, emotion and identity took place through the convergence of several social factors:

...the transformation of the family from producer to consumer unit resulted in a change in family members' relation to their own bodies; from being an instrument primarily of work, the human body was integrated into a new economy, and began more commonly to be perceived as a means of consumption and pleasure (Katz 1990: 10).

It is in this context, argues Katz, that doctors (unpwardly mobile professionals, reaping the benefits of a rise in power and prestige) prescribed a new sexual ethic as if it were a morally neutral, medical description of health.

I do not intend to get into a detailed critique of these formulations, but simply to emphasise that the idea of sexuality as an aspect of personhood, as a mode of subjectivity, a mode of consciousness, arises in a very particular historical moment, a particular political context, a particular shift in economic modes of production and demands made on human self-consciousness. It is part of the larger process through which the 'modern subject' came to be.

At the same time, the process of colonisation was in no way uniform, or as simple as I have portrayed it above. It is not as though the sites of resistance, of conflict between 'modern' frames of self-consciousness and local worldviews were finally and completely settled. These interactions continue to date—Ayurveda, 'witch-doctors', 'grandmothers' remedies' continue to compete with and interact with bio-medicine as frameworks of explanation of health and illness. And, 'sexuality' as a mode of consciousness is perhaps yet to move beyond a small number of us, largely urban, middle-class, English-speaking 'Indians'.

VIOLENCE AND THE POLITICS OF DIFFERENCE

What then, have been the processes through which queer activism has come to be constituted in terms of this historically particular idea of 'sexuality'? There are two aspects that I see as relevant in this regard.

First is the fact that queer activism has arisen in response to violence, in response to 'discrimination' and what, perhaps inaccurately, is being seen today as an all-pervasive 'homophobia' in Indian society.[8] Per force, it is focused on a framework of violence. But the reason for this is not limited simply to the fact that the movement is galvanised by experiences of exclusion and of violence. It has something to do with the way in which power is addressed in 'progressive' circles in India today.

I remember when a group of us that finally came to call itself PRISM, started a dialogue with women's groups politically affiliated with the Left, around 2000, we were given a patient hearing and finally told that 'our issues' would be taken up if we could articulate them in terms of violence, in terms of a tangible political lobbying point. Perhaps we can understand something about 'progressive' Indian politics from this. I would hazard a suggestion that we can learn something about post-colonial politics in general from this example—that for the working of power to be recognised and addressed, it must be manifested as violence, or it should be capable of being understood in terms of 'discrimination'. The subtle and 'everyday' processes through which we are gendered and sexualised normatively simply cannot be the basis of a 'movement'. My point is not to suggest that violence does not need to be addressed. The issue to me is—to what extent does the framework we adopt limit or enable us to understand and address the context that enables violence?

This leads me to the second relevant aspect. Queer activism is for the large part 'human rights activism'. The only framework available to us, to address violence, apparently, is the 'human rights' framework, a framework essentially based on a politics of difference, on an understanding of the politics of sex in terms of types of people. This has a history as well and a significant one at that. A little historicisation is in order here.

The human rights framework is a significant milestone in the process of the legal conceptualisations of entitlements, bodies and personhood. It is a framework of justice obtained from a particular configuration of liberal democratic politics in the post-World War II context. It represents an attempt to restore legitimacy to modernity, after its failure where 'modern' societies, and not 'uncivilised savages', were responsible for brutal acts. It is also the framework through which post-colonial states may be evaluated and the scope for the exercise of a particular form of 'human agency' may be measured.

Historically, the human rights regime is located in the relationship between the body and the state and where the body is conceptualised as sacred and 'vested' with inalienable entitlements. As such, the idea of 'human rights' is based on a certain understanding of personhood (one that, significantly, corresponds with the understanding of the body in bio-medicine). At the risk of oversimplification, human rights is an articulation of the imagination of the world in terms of 'subjects'—it is a culmination of a long colonial history and the creation of mechanisms through which the post-colonial world is to be regulated. Most significantly, it enables the framing of complex power dynamics in the body, in terms of individual experiences. This often means that we understand and address power without the examination of social, cultural, economic and political processes through which power imbalances are maintained. Where these processes *are* brought into activism and analysis, they are understood in terms of how they affect the individual or community.

'Human rights' is perhaps more naturalised in queer activism than 'sexuality'. Just as every person simply *has* a sexuality (even 'asexuality' is a 'sexuality'), every person *has* human rights. 'Discrimination' on the basis of sex, gender (caste, race, and so on) and sexual orientation cannot be permitted in 'civilised societies'.

There is another aspect to this history—it relates to the mechanisms of colonial administration. The understanding of 'Indian society' for the purposes of colonial administration, for example, was based on the imagination that it is divided into neat and pre-existing, natural 'communities', that each 'community' has a natural 'leadership', which represents the community's interests, and which, therefore, can be the basis for liberal politics (Spencer 1997). This imagination seems to be the basis of 'human rights', of postcolonial Constitutions and of progressive politics in India. The main implication of such a framework is that in participating in politics, we simply *must* imagine the existence of pre-existent 'communities', and types of people. We simply *must* participate in a politics of difference. This is to say, it is through our participation in politics that the idea of types of people gets naturalised.

ARREY BABA, SO WHAT?

What are the implications of this politics of difference, of using the framework of 'sexuality' and 'human rights'? The first is that we have to imagine our situation as though the categories of people—'straight', 'gay', 'lesbian' and the like already exist—we are not in a position to address the ways in which we are called upon to recognise ourselves within certain frameworks. To do so would be to question the very location from which we speak. To suggest that 'sexuality' is a historical category would be to open up the possibility that it is an anomaly that can be changed. This is to say, our self-essentialisation seems to be basic to our 'legitimate' political activism.

This renders us unable to address the social, cultural, economic and political processes through which hetero-normativity, and the violence it engenders, work. We stop ourselves from addressing the manner in which the 'hetero-normative' system and person come to be. We restrict ourselves to addressing the manifestations of hetero-normativity that can be construed as 'violence' against those of us who may be recognised as fitting the categories of the 'gay', 'lesbian', and so on. This, in some sense, is a way in which we exclude those who do not identify, including those who choose not to identify.

But can hetero-normativity be understood in terms of denial and violation of rights of certain types of people? Talking about 'sexuality' becomes about talking about 'homosexuals', about queer people, with no apparent implications for 'other' people. As such, it is possible for progressive women's groups to offer support to 'our cause', rather than enable queer experiences to feed into their analyses of hetero-normativity. For example, the 'lesbian suicide' becomes about a certain type of women rather than about the workings of hetero-patriarchy, as though 'lesbians' in Kerala are unaffected by the workings of class, caste, religion, gender and other frameworks of difference. The way this issue has come to be articulated recently is that this politics of difference enables 'coalition' rather than 'intersectionality'. In the context of a history of the refusal by women's groups to acknowledge same-sex desire, the possibility of 'coalition' effectively makes neutral any disruptive potential for hetero-normativity within the women's movement. Sexuality becomes the 'other's' issue, which can be engaged with safely from a distance, in a rather antiseptic manner.

WAYS FORWARD?

The above arguments have been problematised very incisively in the debates I refer to in the queer community. First, having historicised 'sexuality' and 'human rights', is one not trivialising the 'emancipatory potential' of the sexuality rights framework? Second, how do we ensure that the framework of intersectionality does not eventually amount to invisibilisation of same-sex desire and violence faced by people on its basis? Third, how does one ensure that this historicisation of 'sexuality' does not feed into an 'Indian/traditional versus Western/modern' debate which would lend weight to a nationalism discourse such as *Hindutva*?

These are very live questions and I do not intend to 'answer' them—I do not think the issue is of an 'either–or' type, either we use the framework of sexuality rights or we don't. The sexuality-rights framework is an aspect of our living history and there are complex reasons for its existence. The challenge perhaps is to disable hegemony of this framework over our understandings of our condition, of our sexual universes. Perhaps it is about ensuring that we allow frameworks and imaginations other than those relating desire and entitlement to personhood to speak, to participate in the framing of discourse. At the very last is the subtle but important difference between 'empowering sexual minorities' and enabling resistance to hetero-normativity. I take two examples of what this difference means.

The first is the sexual minorities support group. One of the rituals in this new form of collectivisation is the round of introductions. At a support group meeting one announces one's name, and one's 'sexuality'. Two observations

I make with respect to this ritual—one, that many clearly state that 'before coming to this support group I did not 'know' that I was a kothi or a bisexual'. The support group *is* about the naming of oneself, recognising oneself within certain terms, 'identifying' oneself—the exact process that I have been so critical of in this essay. The second observation, however, shakes the foundations of the critique—often one finds that in one support group meeting a person identifies with one category. Two weeks later the person has changed to another category, only to perhaps revert to the first in another few weeks. This often evokes laughter in the group, as though identification were a joke. Perhaps it is. The point here is that this 'identity' *means* something different to different people. The idea of 'identity' is being reconstituted through local discourses. A critique that says 'identity is wrong because it is Western' then means nothing. Similarly, 'human rights', and 'human rights activism' are different things in Europe as compared to the United States, as compared to Delhi, as compared to Bangalore. In some uses of these terms, the 'problem' is squarely located in an individual experience, the 'right' is vested in the individual. In others, 'human rights' refers to marginalisation of 'communities'. In yet others, human rights merely means the absence of state aggression.

To me it seems that the problem lies in the hegemony over the use and meaning of these terms. I think we need to recognise the mechanisms through which this growing hegemony takes place—systematically and through power dynamics within organisations, within groups. For example, to what extent do 'advocacy' documents—parchas and the like, brought out by 'sexual minorities groups' convey the temporality of the idea of identity when they say 'we are kothis, hijras, lesbians, men who have sex with men...'? Similarly, to what extent do policy advocacy and lobbying at the international level, in Geneva, express the diverse existences of 'human rights'? Perhaps some amount of our energy needs to go towards understanding and addressing the processes through which the disjunctures brought about by the reconstitution of ideas is regulated and managed.

Notes

1. Where people from two NGOs doing outreach with 'men who have sex with men' were arrested under charges of abetment of the offence under Section 377, amongst other things. The people arrested were refused bail on the ground that they were a 'threat to Indian Society'. The Hindi media spoke of the group largely as a 'gay club' that was polluting Indian society.
2. By 'bio-medicine' I mean medical practices and understandings of the 'body' typical of 'Western' medicine, based on a dichotomy between 'mind' and 'body'.

This makes the body available to understanding, explanation and intervention by positivist discourse.

3. Over the last few years a range of terms have been used to describe 'alternative sexuality', 'lesbian gay bisexual transgender KQJH...', 'sexual minorities', 'marginalised sexualities'. I use the term 'queer' as a broad reference to all these formulations and identities, as, to my understanding the term does justice to most of these understandings.

4. Previous coverage of 'sexuality'-related issues revolved around the famous Lucknow case, where the term 'gay' was used to describe a certain Western phenomenon polluting the purity of Indian culture. Similarly, the coverage during *Fire* protests and the recent *Girlfriend* controversy revolved around such an exclusionary framing of sexuality identities, placing their existence outside 'Indian culture'.

5. Variolation is the bio-medical term for 'native' practices similar to inoculation, where smallpox from earlier epidemics was used to infect people so as to enable immunity against stronger strains. This practice was observed in large parts of Africa and Asia.

6. Not to be confused with Jonathan D. Katz of Yale University, who intends to work on 'MSM' in India.

7. Foucault calls this particular mechanism of power 'panopticism', based on an analysis of an architectural design used for prisons and hospitals—the panopticon. The design is a semicircle of cells where prisoners are kept separated from each other. Each cell is illuminated by a small window at the periphery and the inmates cannot see each other. At the centre of the semicircle is a high watchtower from where each cell can be clearly seen, but an inmate cannot make out whether or not the tower is occupied. As such, inmates believe themselves to be watched all the time and regulate their own behaviour at all times. This is the basis of Benthamite jurisprudence, which is the philosophy behind the Indian Penal Code.

8. 'Homophobia' relates to fear of and violence against homosexuals and homosexuality. This presumes that those being violent think about sex in terms of personhood, an assumption that I feel is unjustified. My suggestion in this regard is that we need to find other languages to understand and speak about violence relating to sexuality. For an interesting argument about 'homophobia' in this regard, see Seabrook (2004).

REFERENCES

Arnold, David. 1993, *Colonizing the Body: State, Medicine and Epidemic Disease in Nineteenth-century India*. Berkeley: University of California Press.

Foucault, Michel. 1988a, *History of Sexuality*, Vol. I. London: Penguin.

———. 1988b, *Madness and Civilization*. London: Vintage Books.

———. 1994, *The Birth of the Clinic*. London: Vintage Books.

————. 1995, *Discipline and Punish*. London: Vintage Books.

Katz, Jonathan. 1990, 'The Invention of Homosexuality', *Socialist Review*, Vol. 20, No. 7, pp. 7–34.

Khanna, A. Forthcoming, 'Us, "Sexuality Types"—A Critical Engagement with the Postcoloniality of the Sexuality Rights Movement in India', in Brinda Bose and Subhabrata Bhattacharyya (eds), *Queering the Pitch: The Politics of Sexualities in Contemporary India*. Kolkata: Seagull Publications.

Rabinow, P. (ed.). 1984, *The Foucault Reader*. London: Random House.

Seabrook, Jeremy. 2004, *Love in a Different Climate*, Verso Science, Technology and Medicine in Colonial India. London: Verso.

Spencer, Jonathan. 1997, 'Post Colonialism and the Political Imagination', *Journal of the Royal Anthropological Institute*, Vol. 3, No. 1, March 1997, pp. 1–19.

II

Stories of Struggle

6

Many People, Many Sexualities
A Personal Journey

Elavarthi Manohar

MY GENDER MY RIGHT I was born in 1971 into a middle-class farming family in a small village near Chittoor, Andhra Pradesh. Till the seventh standard I studied in and around my native place. After that I went to a boys residential school about 100 kilometers from my village. By the time I finished SSLC, I was fairly clear about my attraction towards people of my own sex. I had a few sexual encounters in those three years, mostly with my classmates—always in the darkness, without any talk or discussion. The next morning we would pretend as if nothing had happened.

In 1986, at the age of 15, I went to Hyderabad to do a Special Diploma in Electronics. In 1988, I was watching a movie in a theatre when a middle-aged man made a pass at me. I was scared, excited, confused about how to react. After the movie it took at least 30 minutes before I could speak to him. This incident opened up a new world for me, a world where lovers meet only under the cover of darkness. It also introduced me to cruising (men meeting other men for sex)—maybe in a dark corner of a public park or playground, or a public toilet, in a bus or railway station. You meet someone, talk and maybe decide to go somewhere to have sex (though this happens very rarely). Sometimes, even after having met a person several times, you may not know his real name, let alone his address and occupation.

By the time I was 18, I used to frequent these areas quite regularly (at least two evenings/nights a week) in search of friendship and love. I must have met over 200 people in this way, without knowing the barest details about a single one of them (their work, residence/office address/phone number). Often, I never saw them again, though many promised further meetings at a particular place and time. I was very lonely and had no one I could talk to, or discuss and share my feelings with. I was seeking to understand my sexuality and visited the cruising areas in the hope of meeting people like me (homosexual). But no one was interested in talking about these issues, particularly with a social activist (I was active in the Students Federation of India at the time). The experience only increased my loneliness. Being vulnerable to blackmail, the people who frequent these areas are usually too scared to reveal their identities. These are people who literally survive on the margins of society. I lost hope of meeting anyone with whom I could share my confusions and doubts.

Cruising areas are not safe either. Occasionally, someone would be caught by a policeman who would steal all his money and valuables (like a wristwatch). He would threaten to take him to the police station, inform his parents, relatives, and so on. There is also the risk of being physically or even sexually abused. Many *goondas* and hustlers take advantage of this situation by posing as homosexuals. Once you admit that you are also gay, they verbally abuse and beat you up, threatening to haul you off to the police station unless you hand over all your money and possessions to them. Whenever this happens, you feel like committing suicide and leaving this unfair and violent world. You hate yourself for being homosexual and vulnerable to abuse and resolve never to venture into these cruising areas again. But you don't really have a choice. You go again and again and get abused again and again. You live under the constant threat of being blackmailed by the police, hustlers and others. You can't even shout when you get raped.

HELPLESS AND ASHAMED

I began to dislike myself for being a homosexual and felt ashamed that I had to hide my sexuality all the time. Many questions haunted me: 'Why did I become a homosexual? Did someone convert me? Am I not a man (enough)? Why am I so sensitive? Is it because I am feminine?' My body would jolt with fear every time I thought... 'What if someone (classmate, friend, fellow social activist) discovers that I am gay? Would I be able to live the rest of my life with shame?' I felt awful whenever I had to pretend that I was heterosexual. I could own my sexuality only under the cover of darkness, in a world peopled by anonymous individuals; everywhere else, I had to suppress it. Leading a double life was tearing me apart. Suppressing my sexuality did not help either.

As a gay adolescent, you go through so many doubts and confusions about your sexuality, sexual identity, sexual desires/attractions and so on. The turmoil that one goes through is further intensified because there is so little information and very few people whom one can confide in or talk with openly on these issues. Many people who appear to be liberal and progressive in other areas of life are very prejudiced when it comes to sexuality. They include communists, socialists, trade unionists, environmentalists, Gandhians, Dalit activists and even some human rights activists and women's activists. I never dared to reveal my sexuality to any of my co-workers in my four years of active association with the left students movement. Any discussion about sex and sexuality—leave alone homosexuality—was taboo in these organisations.

In 1990, I joined a leading computer company in Baroda as a hardware engineer. I worked there for around 18 months. I used to frequently visit a cruising area and regularly meet a group of four to five people. Of these, I managed to discover the place of work of only two. They generally restricted their conversation to whom they had sex with or whom they wanted to have sex with, who was new to that cruising area, what precautions they could take in order to avoid being caught by a policeman or a hustler. Most of them were married. None dared to live/lead a gay life without the cover of marriage.

However, being able to meet a few people on a regular basis helped me feel a little comfortable with my homosexuality. I wanted to have a lover; I wanted to lead my life without having to marry a woman.

In 1992, I read an article about *Bombay Dost*, a gay magazine from Mumbai, in *Andhra Jyothi*—a Telugu newspaper. The article, however, did not mention the magazine's address. I was thrilled to discover that there was a gay magazine. I took a job in Mumbai in a month's time. Since contacting *Bombay Dost* was my one-point agenda for living in Mumbai, I asked every individual I met in the cruising areas about it. But it took at least three months of rigorous effort to get in touch with *Bombay Dost*.

Positive Change

My life went through a major positive change in Mumbai. I made a few gay friends with whom I could discuss my sexuality. It was great to meet so many homosexual men who were very comfortable with their sexuality, who didn't want to live their lives under the cover of marriage. Some of them were living alone. It took me hardly any time at all to come to terms with my homo-sexuality. Within three months I was able to find a lover/boyfriend. We started living together in February 1993.

I was thrilled when I found a box-file full of newspaper clippings on alternative sexuality at the Centre for Education and Documentation (CED),

Mumbai. As I had worked with student/youth/left/environmental movements, it took very little effort to understand the oppression faced by homosexuals. I was instrumental in starting the Khush Club with my lover and five other gay men. We wanted to document information on homosexuality that would help gay people to come to terms with their sexuality, counsel people who were confused and uncomfortable with their sexuality and spread awareness about HIV/AIDS among the gay community. We organised several social gatherings, providing opportunities for gay people to meet in a safe space. During this process I got in touch with a few lesbian activists who were also active in the women's movement. Their group, however, only survived for around 18 months. Differences over what direction the group should take and whether it should become more political or remain social led to its break-up.

Lesbian women have very little space in this society. Gay men had access to many cruising areas (over 50) in Mumbai but lesbians had no place to meet other lesbians. At that time, there were no combined gay and lesbian groups in India. There were at least five or six groups for gay men in cities like Delhi, Kolkata, Mumbai, Bangalore and Lucknow. One or two of them were open to lesbian women but they didn't feel comfortable in these groups. Like their heterosexual counterparts in our male-dominated society, many gay men—even activists—are sexist and make anti-women statements. While gay and bisexual men who are married can go out and have their sexual needs fulfilled—at least in towns and cities, married lesbians cannot refuse to have sex with their husbands. On the other hand, many gay men do not feel obliged to fulfil the sexual needs of their wives. These women suffer in silence and visit psychiatrists with problems like 'I am unable to arouse my husband'. Most gay groups in India still haven't taken a stand on the issue of gay men getting married to women. For these and other reasons, it was difficult for lesbian women to be part of gay groups.

In 1994, a few lesbian women, (gender-sensitive) gay men and I tried to form a 'gay and lesbian' forum—Khush Manch—in Mumbai. Since we wanted to keep sexist and communal people out of it, we called it an anti-communal, anti-sexist, democratic, gay and lesbian forum. We wanted to have co-chairs (a man and a woman) so that the women would have an equal say in the forum. While the group died a natural death after a few months, its members decided to work openly as gay and lesbian people in other social activist and voluntary organisations.

In Mumbai, I was active in the Narmada Bachao Andolan (anti-Narmada Dam movement) and Nirbhay Bano Andolan (a forum formed to fight communalism and fundamentalism after Mumbai's communal riots). I was

OUT (open about my homosexuality) to many social activists. It was a conscious decision taken in Khush Manch to make homosexuality visible among social activists. Many women (mostly from women's groups) were supportive. Some people behaved as if they didn't know about my sexuality or hadn't heard about it. Some men stopped coming near me—perhaps they thought homosexuality is contagious. Some even stopped speaking to me. Together with a few lesbian friends who were associated with Khush Manch, I tried to influence social action groups to support 'gay and lesbian' rights, to look at these people as oppressed people. This was very important for me, as some leading gay activists were communal and active proponents of Hindutva.

ACCEPTING BISEXUALITY

It was a shock for me when my best friend (a woman) and I realised that we were in love. I didn't believe that I could be bisexual. It was very difficult for me to accept the heterosexual aspect of my sexuality. For the first time, I realised that I had lots of negative feelings towards heterosexual people/ heterosexuality—an inheritance from the gay community/culture/groups. I needed help from my friends in order to come to terms with my bisexuality. Most of my gay friends (including activists) were cold, unsupportive and insensitive. I suddenly realised that as a bisexual, I did not have space in the existing gay groups. It was my feminist women friends from the Forum Against Oppression of Women who gave me the support that proved crucial in coming to terms with my bisexuality.

In 1994, I moved into Bangalore where I started attending the meetings of a local gay group, 'Good As You', held once a week. I was the only man identified as bisexual in the group. A couple of women also attended the meetings, but very rarely. It was difficult to raise issues related to bisexuality because of the anti-bisexual feelings of a few group members. Many gay men (including those who were married) were very anti-bisexuality. I was asked to decide whether I wanted to be gay or straight. Bisexuals are regarded as people who are unstable and confused about their sexuality or people who don't have the guts or courage to accept that they are homosexual and so use bisexuality as a mask in order to gain acceptance in society. They face discrimination not only from heterosexuals but also from gay men. I decided to be open about my bisexuality in the group and face the ensuing conse-quences.

I have attended most of the Good As You meetings in the last four years, but because of my bisexuality I have often felt alienated from the rest of the group. It took around three years for some more men in the group to openly assert and identify themselves as bisexuals. Today we have around 10 men who openly identify themselves as bisexual—even though only a few of them attend meetings regularly. Bisexuals are unwelcome in a vast majority of gay groups in India. Other than Good As You, there are very few groups in India which allow them space. There are almost no bisexual men among the known gay activists in India. Bisexuality as an issue is rarely discussed, even among gay and lesbian groups/initiatives/rights discourse. Although Good As You is a safe social space for gay and bisexual men, there is no political or serious thinking even on issues affecting the LesBiGays (lesbians, bisexuals and gays). A majority of the members don't see this group as an activist space.

A few students of the National Law School of India University (NLSIU), Bangalore, organised a symposium on gay rights in their campus in September 1997. Sanjay Bavikatte, the main force behind this symposium, got in touch with me through Good As You. Many of the organisers were heterosexual people. They wanted to support gay rights because they felt that gay people are oppressed. The initiative, which was part of their study circle effort on gender, inspired me to start a group with LesBiGays and others (who are sensitive towards LesBiGays) to support LesBiGay rights. I discussed this with a few of my friends (both LesBiGay and heterosexual) and called for a meeting. A few people from Good As You, a few heterosexual friends, and many organisers of the NLSIU symposium attended the meeting and all of us felt that there is a need for such a group, which was formed a few days before the symposium was held.

We began meeting once every two weeks. Many issues related to LesBiGays are discussed at these meetings. The group has realised that there is a paucity of information not only about homosexuality but about heterosexuality as well and that there are several issues relating to heterosexuality which still need to be addressed. Since patriarchy oppresses both women and LesBiGays, we decided to call ourselves 'Sabrang' (all colours),[1] indicating that our group has space for all sexualities—gay, lesbian. bisexual, heterosexual, transsexual and others. Sabrang believes in a plural, anti-sexist, anti-communal political ideology. Like other issues, we wanted to bring sexuality into public discourse and to fight myths and misinformation about sexuality in general and about LesBiGays in particular. We wanted to document, publish and disseminate information on issues relating to sexuality and to resist any form of discrimination based on one's sexuality. But Sabrang also sees itself as an activist group which supports the rights of all people who face discrimination on the basis of their gender, caste, class, religion, ethnicity, language, and so on.

With the agenda of making sexuality a developmental and human rights issue, Sabrang is working towards building a coalition of all oppressed groups. It believes that LesBiGay activism should support other social movements, for it cannot achieve success without the support of other groups. It also strives to reach out to people from non-English backgrounds and from the lower strata of society who are doubly disadvantaged.

I feel more safe, secure and comfortable in Sabrang than I did in any other group working on LesBiGay issues. This is one space where I feel bisexuals and lesbians are not oppressed by gay men, where people think not only about LesBiGays but also about the parents, spouses, children, friends and co-workers of LesBiGays.

Many people deny the existence of LesBiGays in India, dismissing their sexuality as Western and an upper-class phenomena. Others see sexuality as a concern that is too individualistic to warrant attention in a poor country like ours. Some label it as a disease to be cured, an abnormality to be set right or a crime to be punished. This denial, backed by an enforced invisibility, exposes LesBiGays to abuse and discrimination. Physical attacks, sexual abuse, emotional and social alienation, psychological trauma become the everyday lived reality of many LesBiGays. Self-acceptance in such a disabling environment is difficult, leading to low self-esteem, depression and sometimes even suicide.

Sexuality issues are considered irrelevant and élitist and hence routinely excluded from the human rights agenda in the Indian context. The social system and archaic laws (Section 377 of the Indian Penal Code, which criminalises sodomy and is interpreted as an anti-homosexual law, is frequently used by the police to extort money from gay/bisexual men) stigmatise, discriminate against and oppress LesBiGay people. A culture of silence pervades the issue of sexuality and invisibility is the inevitable fallout of this enforced silence. LesBiGays and adolescents are the ones who are seriously affected in this process. By not accepting LesBiGays, society also places many other people in a troubling dilemma—their spouses, children and so on. Every effort to bring sexuality, homosexuality and bisexuality into public/rights discourse will help LesBiGay people to get in touch with other people like themselves. It will help them to understand the oppression that they face due to their sexuality. It will give them courage to raise their voices and oppose these prejudices and intolerance. It will give many of them the courage to come out and to assert their sexuality publicly (as I am doing with this article for the first time in my life). It is easy for LesBiGays to face the world once they are comfortable and positive about their sexuality.

The moment LesBiGays become aware of their situation, a major change will come through in their situation. I would like to end this article with a quotation by a Black, gay, American writer: 'The victim who is able to articulate the situation of the victim has ceased to be a victim; he or she has become a threat.'

NOTES

1. Though referred to in the present tense in the article, Sabrang is no longer a functional group.

7

Solitary Cruiser

Pawan Dhall

 This had to happen. It was destined that I would one day agonise over meeting deadlines for a piece on the politics of sexuality. I should have anticipated this much earlier by putting together some of my mother's remarks. One of them being that I am short-tempered because I was born during the Naxalite Movement. And another being a privileged nugget of information I can share in the context of politics of sexuality without blushing—that I was an outcome of coitus interruptus not getting interrupted in time!

My mother, sociologists and perhaps environmentalists might be best able to figure out how I could have absorbed the anti-establishment fervour as a toddler. However, I think the signs were there in childhood itself. For as my mother would tell you, I once slapped one of her friends when she took liberties with my cheeks while I was trying to pontificate on graver things in my pram car on a sunny winter afternoon.

Not just baby rights, but circumstances seem to have made me conscious about socio-economic equity early on. This was when I was only a couple of years into primary school. My father was working as a labour welfare officer in one of the private temples of the then modern India. His boss' wife was supposed to have been an imperious, class- and status-conscious woman. But one day when she insisted (half jesting with me) that she and her husband would not allow my father entry into the colony club because he was a lowly officer, I ticked her off by saying that god would make sure my father would get an entry.

This made my parents rather proud of me, but I am sure a trifle panicky too. For the lady was known to take things to heart. However, my remark seemed to have touched off on the god-fearing side of her. I was rewarded with a visit to her house and all of an éclair, quite a luxury in those days (and probably today too). Whether this was appeasement or appropriation, I am not sure, but it did not seem to work. The taste of the rich melting éclair did not quite replace the distaste of her remarks, which lingers on till date.

While the timing and circumstances of my birth and certain childhood incidents might have done their bit to shape my politics as a human being, my 'accidental' birth, I am sure, contributed quite significantly to my politics as a sexual being. Going by the belief that life is full of circles (both over-lapping and concentric ones), it is no wonder that my entire adult life has been (and is being) spent working on sex, sexuality, sexual health and, of course, reproductive health issues.

In fact, while it is my sexuality and struggles around its expression that have been the immediate provocation for the writing of this essay, I see this act of writing also being inspired by a less visible motivation. As I try to make a case for sexual choices, I also want to thank my parents for having borne me with much love and care though I was not quite 'expected'. After all not only does coitus interruptus seem rather stifling, reliance on it as a means of family planning (even today) also takes away the choice to not have a child (particularly for the woman). It can also kill a woman (and her child) if she is not in a position to become pregnant. Thankfully, both my mother and I were lucky, much more than millions of other women and children in India. And so was my father, for he too, like many other men, was functioning within the choices made available to him by his (sex) education and society at large.

Perhaps if there had been freer discourse on matters sexual (along with greater availability and use of slicker condoms), I might not have been born. Or even if I were, my sexuality might not have been an issue. But those are conjectures. In the here and now it is much more funny to pull a fast one on friends when I tell them that I was born on the same day as my parents got married (even if 14 years later). And it is positively more exciting to be part of efforts and movements that seek to make sex life-saving and life-nurturing and not just merely life-giving.

It is also bittersweet to look back at how events and people have influenced my search for greater sexual and emotional fulfilment, the very basis of sexuality politics. While I have not been alone in this search, I have often found myself straying and cruising away from the high roads where sex and its expressions always seem to be after one fashion or the other, but rarely after a passion. Where sex is often a means to desperate rather than dignified survival. Where the promised destination turns out to be just another sexual ghetto.

One of the most abiding memories is of the days I was just stepping into Kolkata's queer[1] networks. Not that I had not known or networked with queer men in Kolkata or elsewhere before this. My earliest mentors who had helped me come to terms with my sexuality were not even in Kolkata and I had already known them for nearly five years. But getting to know my home city's queer scene was one of the most exhilarating periods of my life.

It was 1990, my second year in college. Things were happening to me—emotionally, intellectually and numerically! One contact led to another and before long I had known more queer people in the space of a year than I had in all my life (and without the blessings of the Internet, e-mail or e-groups).

These contacts were not just in the city but all over the country and way beyond, thanks to a couple of personal advertisements in queer publications. The fun part was getting to know *probasi* queer Bengalis in the United States, some of whom were stunned that I had put my home address in the advertisements. They thought I had been brave, but it was easier than braving the Indian postal department in trying to get a post box!

In any case I did not want to hide. It was the end of my isolation and lonely evenings at home, and I desperately wanted to connect with people of my kind as myself, and not with a fictitious name or identity. Having come out as gay to a couple of my favourite nieces who were in the same age group, having braved their questions about my genitalia and signed a mutual boyfriend hunt pact with one of them, I was raring to fly

My flight, however, hit an air pocket early on. My stepping into Kolkata's queer world did not create any sexual history, but the buzz went around fast that a new face had been sighted. I soon realised that I was not going to make very many friends in town, because friends in my definition do not force you to have sex in a certain way. They do not insist on checking out what they have heard about your skills at fellatio from the grapevine, more so when you are in the middle of one of your first few sexual encounters, feeling vulnerable and in need of guidance. And they do not advise you to start looking for other friends once they have had you in a certain way.

The succour I was looking for was certainly not in being touted as a new kid on the block. But I did find it in many other ways: in a painful second coming out to my parents, the first having been a hurriedly dismissed affair in my high school days when all parties involved were at a loss with how to deal with it, including myself who had initiated it. It had been put down to the workings of an adolescent mind without much of a second thought.

However, there had to be a second time. With tears and sleepless nights but also deep introspection on part of my parents and myself. There were also glorious conversations with my mother during after-dinner walks, when I first learnt to argue about issues I had been reading about. Sex, sexuality, gender, equality, diversity were never distant abstract issues to me. Now they had become all the more lived realities for me.

At this point I cannot but thank my parents again for not having denied me the right to express myself—my mother for listening to me, my father for listening to me through my mother and both for drawing upon all their wisdom and courage to deal with the situation. I must also thank the hundreds of queer folk, particularly those in India and the South Asian diaspora, who had set up support groups, brought out publications and made themselves visible in the media. I could not connect with all, but there was great comfort in knowing that there were so many others like me in every corner of the globe. Some of them not only gave me information and support, but also energised me into joining the queer movement.

I made a start with contributing articles to queer publications like *Freedom* (published from Gulbarga), *Shakti Khabar* (London) and *Bombay Dost* (Mumbai). Most were rejected but the writing bug had already bitten me. I tried my hand at short stories and while none were published, I used one of them to come out to my English professor in college when I asked him to certify it as an original piece for a contest I was participating in. I was far more successful with letters to the editors of newspapers and magazines. After having commented on a range of issues like sati, India's economic policies and the state of Kolkata's roads, I finally got an opportunity to further come out with a couple of letters in support of homosexuality.

I sincerely hoped that such a coming out in the media would seriously damage my marriage prospects in the eyes of my extended family. This hope gets belied to this day, but in those days I managed to pull off a great wedding of my own. A typewriter gifted by my parents to me on my 23rd birthday helped me wed my festering desire to put Kolkata on the queer activism map with my career choice of journalism. The outcome was a newsletter called *Pravartak*, typed out secretly in the dead of the night, photocopied at a shop that was fortunately too busy for anybody to notice the contents, later stapled and distributed discreetly through a growing queer network.

Pravartak is no longer published but it set me on a journey during which I have often looked back, but never to change my course. I tried my parents' patience some more when I dropped out of university to join a newspaper, and later when they saw me getting involved with queer activism. But after my having been involved with several queer and other development initiatives and connected with a vast network of queer and non-queer people, through 15 years, they probably no longer find queer so queer.

A gay accountant friend of mine, who helps my father with some of his accounts, is first my friend and an accountant, only then gay. When my mother baked a cake for the birthday bash of Counsel Club, a Kolkata-based queer support group that functioned between 1993 and 2002, the appreciation that she received and enjoyed was anything but queer. Perhaps it would have helped my parents if they had looked at themselves as activists too in the first place. As a labour welfare officer and mechanical engineer in several factories, my father felt strongly about the interests of labourers and acted on them too. My mother too was a homegrown activist. In the early 1990s, when Yugoslavia was breaking up, a Croatian friend of one my aunts wanted to donate her savings to the poor in India as she feared losing it all in the civil war. My mother convinced her to donate the money to people not covered by well-known charitable institutions. With help from our domestic help, my mother took up the responsibility of giving the money to families in neighbourhood slums, particularly to cover the school tuition fee for their children.

I find that in my work I am following in the footsteps of my parents. I also see my work as inspired by other social movements that have apparently nothing to do with sexuality. One of them took birth some years before I was even thinking about coming out a second time to my parents. The Narmada Bachao Andolan inspired me to conduct a signature campaign in high school in support of the movement and against the construction of the Sardar Sarovar dam. The signatures collected were sent to the Prime Minister's Office, which responded months later with a thank you note for our comments.

Having spent my early childhood in a Kolkata suburb resplendent with flora and fauna (at least the kind that can survive in a semi-urban setting), it took me a long time to overcome a sense of having been uprooted when my father's job brought us to Kolkata proper. A few apologetic trees in our lane were all that I could see from the window. Since then Kolkata has turned much greener thanks to a strong green movement in and around the city. But currently it is at its sootiest worst because of roads being widened, flyovers being built and even landmark trees being felled without a thought.

While I have not been proactively involved in either the Narmada Bachao Andolan in particular or the green movement in general, I see myself as turning a queer green in the future. It took me some time to articulate the connection between green and queer issues clearly to myself. Today I firmly believe that all queer sexualities have as much a right to bloom, blossom and thrive as the forests (and the communities dependent on them). Love and desire of all kinds have always drawn sustenance from the elements and protecting one should mean protecting the other too.

Somehow this equation lands me in trouble with queer friends, colleagues and others who love to cruise in public parks but think nothing of littering it with plastic. Or others for whom queer liberation lies in pubs, parties and saunas and no more. I have nothing against these as long as they do not drown out the sounds, fragrances, drama and eroticism of nature.

I feel it is a long time since I was isolated as a queer person. But there have been several other isolations all along to deal with. Being ridiculed for seeing the reflection of handsome men in *neem* and *shirish* trees has not been the only one. At one point of time being the only one in Counsel Club arguing in favour of non-queer people attending the group's meetings was a painful experience. This happened much after all other founding members had left the group and the newer members felt that the group would not be a safe space if non-queer people were to attend its meetings. It took an exhausting walk through the then five-year history of the group to convince most members that it was precisely the open nature of the group (for queer people, by all people) that had helped it become one of the strongest and safest for queer people in India. The participation of supportive non-queer people had brought in valuable perspectives and experience, and putting an end to that would have only been regressive.

In many ways this experience in Counsel Club was more unnerving than the days when I used to be a member of Fun Club, one of the earliest queer initiatives of Kolkata (1990–91). Initially Fun Club had had the image of a strictly fun spot for queer men. Later the key members felt the club needed to grow like its counterparts in other parts of India and some friends insisted I attend its meetings. The meetings essentially turned out to be men waiting in one room for the action to end in the other so that they could have their turn, and I was requested to speak about HIV/AIDS issues and answer related questions while they waited!

Speak I did and answered questions too but soon found out that I was the only one in the room really concerned about taking HIV/AIDS information into the adjoining room. I was both amused and irritated in warding away hands creeping up my thighs as I explained HIV and AIDS. But I gave it my best shot.

I never made it to the adjoining room. Fun Club too never made it after 1991 and I got busy with working on *Pravartak* to keep the flag flying in Kolkata, which for quite some time was a lonely affair. These isolations were difficult to deal with but gave strength and direction.

In another instance in 1991, I found myself isolated in an AIDS seminar where some key speakers insisted that India's culture would prevent AIDS from spreading much. There were not many convincing arguments made against this line. I was in the audience and still without the guts to get up and say that Fun Club or the Sonagachi red light area was not far away from the seminar venue, and that many men were visiting them probably right at that point of time and were later going to have unprotected sex with other sexual partners (which could be their wives or even other men). Clearly the speakers and the audience at the seminar had been cultured into denial and silence by their culture, which was probably a mish-mash of Indian and Victorian cultures. Many would argue that Indian culture in the ancient days gone by was less cussed about sex than the Victorian one, and that the advent of Victorian values through the British influenced the Indian mindset against sexual openness. To some extent I agree with these arguments, but also feel colonisation by your own culture is worse if it prevents you from questioning and thinking anew.

In certain sections of the Indian queer scene, for instance, it seems impossible to remain a 'complete man' if you get into a saree, or to remain an 'ideal woman' without getting into one. How you identify is not important, others have a label for you. You cannot identify as a man, not even as a different kind of a man, if you even as much as tend to throw your hands while talking. In these sections it is only natural if feminine men stitch, but masculine men must tear clothes apart if they are to be considered 'husband material'. What's more, feminine men are not supposed to lift heavy objects, but masculine men are supposed to lift feminine men. Jhansi ki Rani rest in peace! But Lord Vishnu should put in an appearance as Mohini because there is work to be done in yet other queer circles where even a hint of what is considered femininity evokes demonisation if found in men.

Lord Vishnu should have been around also when I, in my first two-way queer romantic relationship, found fault with my partner for not being masculine enough. Or when I used to eagerly lap up what a youth career and personality development magazine had to say about how men should and should not move their wrists. I suppose Lord Vishnu did come around when I later fell in love with a man who was truly versatile in sexual knowledge, attitude, behaviour and practice but should have taken some dressing and make-up tips from me!

Today I am often on my own. Not just because I am still single, but also because it is useful and healing at times to distance oneself from the politics of the queer scene and look at it and myself more objectively. A walk under a canopy of trees is almost always reassuring and helps to clear cobwebs. These walks are often filled with thoughts of the people I love and admire. Parents, old and new friends, colleagues, fellow activists and lovers, yes, but also others who when it came to it had the guts to tell others, go take a walk.

A cousin sister who refused to marry till she was ready for marriage, another cousin who married a Muslim man, a late human rights activist friend's mother who decided to turn activist herself against family norms. All these people and many more have and still are shaping my politics as a sexual being and as a human being, the two of course being inseparable. Their actions encourage me to look at myself in new ways, even if for a hearty laugh. For instance, I am beginning to consider identifying as 'a gay man who is straight, curious and sometimes thrilled with frills'!

I would recommend a solitary cruise once in a while to all readers. An opportunity for introspection apart, there would always be the chance of your meeting someone you might want to spend time with in the 4 o'clock evening sunlight, preferably under a tree. But there is no need to despair if you do not meet anyone. In terms of company at least, trust me, just the tree would do!

Notes

1. The word 'queer' has been used as an umbrella term for people who in one way or the other break 'heterosexual' norms of sex and its expression. As an umbrella term I prefer it to terms like 'sexual minorities' and 'LGBT people' for this particular writing. But the word 'queer' literally translates into 'odd' in many Indian languages, which can be politically tricky!

8

Englishpur ki Kothi
Class Dynamics in the Queer Movement in India

Alok Gupta

INTRODUCTION

 One rainy Sunday evening, in the middle of the notorious Mumbai monsoon, I decided to discover a lesser-known (to me) part of gay life in the city. Leaving behind the GayBombay meeting—a support group of gay and bisexual men that meets every alternate Sunday and which I have been attending for over 5 years—I took the train to Matunga station. I climbed a narrow over-bridge and was soon transported into the Tamil heartland of the city. After a good long walk through this dense and parochial suburb, in this most unlikely space, I found my destination.

I was heading for Maheshwari Udyan (Maheshwari Gardens or MGs) a long-established meeting ground for the city's homosexual community. Amidst the bustling crowd of Sunday family outings (the breeders we call them) in this very picture-perfect 'family' park, gay, bisexual, kothis and hijras have been meeting, socialising, cruising and running condom campaigns from days that pre-date any of the much talked about Internet rage or the current spirit of queer activism.

With a sense of thrill, excitement and slight nervousness, I stepped into the park. There were all kinds of people walking in the park—kothis, panthis, married gay men, and those-still-unmarried-but-not-so-determined-to-fight-the-marriage-pressure. My attention was suddenly caught by a whole bunch of hearing-impaired kothis bundled together in a group, communicating with amazing histrionics and affectations: a visually inspiring combination of sign language and camp. Did the straight people in the park know what was going on? Or had they, over the years, arrived at some unspoken consensus, and delineated some portions of the park as gay and some as straight?

Suddenly from behind me I heard a voice call out to me: '*Ye Englishpur ki kothi kahan se aayee....*' (Where did this kothi of the English land come from?) And wow, there it was! I may share a forbidden sexual orientation with the crowd, but I was still very different from them because of my class background. The way I dressed and carried myself revealed my class more than anything else could. I may also be a homosexual, but I was different. I was a cunning Ambassador of the English-speaking people. Not just that, I was from an exclusive, inaccessible-to-all and English-speaking domain called '*Englishpur*'.

It would be too dramatic and foolish for me to pretend that this walk in MGs really opened my eyes to the issue of class. But it would be fair to add that my interactions, like of many others, with the gay community, allowed me for the first time to confront and not just overlook the issue of class. A friend once said that it was through coming out and accessing gay spaces that he was, for the first time, interacting with people from lower classes on an equal platform. It sounded fine until he qualified that by saying that: 'Gosh, if my mother were to see this she would not be scandalised by the gay thing, but the kind of people I am hanging out with.' I am not sympathetic to my friend's feelings but I appreciate them for their clear honesty. It is in this honest, not always politically correct (although not bigoted either) spirit that I have set out to write this essay, an attempt to look at the issue of class in the queer community more critically.[1]

'PEOPLE LIKE US'

We live in a deeply class-ridden society. The class-based divisions that exist in urban India have clear parallels in the queer community. We all know that, and we also know that none of us can actually do anything about it.

Class undeniably plays a very crucial role in our experiences as queer people, in that it dictates our access to the resources of society. I came out through the Friday meetings held weekly at the Humsafar office in Mumbai. A welcome space, where gay men—largely from the middle- and upper-middle-class, English-speaking backgrounds—gathered every week and talked about being gay. The discussions were in English, of course, and shuttled between the social, the political, or sometimes something that was fun and frivolous. I also used the Internet, and read gay books in English from the Humsafar library. This led to an immediate identification with the global gay identity.

The regulars at the Friday meetings were keen on a different space, away from activism and Humsafar's primary focus on health and HIV. Thus a parallel social support group called GayBombay was formed. As GayBombay (GB) began its work through the Internet (a mailing list and a website) its patrons held the same profile as those at Humsafar: middle-class, English-speaking, urban men.

In fact I have spent most of my out queer life with people from very similar backgrounds to mine. The similarity of class seemed so natural, that in reaching out to people in the closet the catchphrase became, 'come for the meetings, it's only people-like-us', 'us' being the catchword, which meant three things: English-speaking; middle- or upper-middle-class; and non-effeminate.

It is the last factor that complicates my own simple analysis. In queer male spaces, the distinction of class is further complicated by gender. The gay community is further divided into those of us who may be more effeminate tossed against those who are not. As a fellow activist remarked: 'Its simple really, the less effeminate you are the more you are able to conceal yourself, and vice versa.' A pseudo-macho understanding has evolved, partly as respite to paranoid gay men in the closet, of a 'normal' gay man who is not effeminate, as opposed to the 'abnormal', effeminate fag who is ready to go and shout it out from the rooftop.

The kothi community, being both overtly effeminate and working-class, is the best candidate for this prejudice. So in this drama where class meets gender, the queer male community may roughly be divided into:

• kothis, who come mostly from the working or lower middle classes, and identify (although not always exclusively) as passive sexual partners;
• hijras;
• working-class, non-kothi-identified gay and bisexual men;
• middle- and upper middle-class gay- and bisexual-identified men; and
• everyone else who identifies under MSM.

BIRDS OF A FEATHER: A SKETCHY HISTORY OF QUEER SPACES

Through the mid-1990s a clandestine explosion of queer spaces was taking place all over the country:

• the Thursday meetings of Good As You (GAY) in Bangalore that began in 1994, which have now completed a decade;
• the Humsafar Friday meetings which started around 1995;

- the GayBombay space that began in 1998;
- the Humraahi meetings at the Naz office in Delhi from 1997 (a continuation of the lapsed Red-Rose meetings); and
- the Counsel Club meetings in Kolkata which started in the early 1990s.

There was a certain similar trend that dominated these meetings. They were
all frequented largely by the urban, middle-class, gay- and bisexual-identified
crowd.[2] The language of the meetings was predominantly English. These
meetings would discuss diverse issues ranging from being gay, the social
compulsions to marry, and being out in the workplace and family. Slowly and
gradually an HIV-focused discourse also became part of these discussions,
but only at the level of safe-sex awareness. These were nascent and self-
conscious gay spaces, uncertain at that stage of the direction in which the
gay movement was moving. These were also exclusively gay male spaces with
little or no discussion on kothis, hijras and lesbians or even bisexuals.

In retrospect, these meetings served multiple purposes. They were primarily looked upon as sites of support, where gay and bisexual men could meet
others like themselves and find support. With no other social avenues, they
were also at the same time the only social spaces[3] that provided a weekly
opportunity to catch up with friends and hopefully find a date. Somewhere
in the support and social sphere, politics would also play a role either through
discussions on Section 377, police abuse or some sensational media outing
or rumour.

Since then, these spaces have branched out, and several new social spaces
have emerged including regular parties, film festivals and other events. But
the extent to which these original spaces translated into any political initiatives, or the extent to which they reached beyond their self-selecting members
is very difficult to assess. Yet it cannot be denied that these spaces, though
they might not have led directly to political initiatives, did serve as locations
where gay and bisexual men could meet as themselves, thereby raising their
level of confidence in themselves and in an emerging community. Some have
argued that, at this stage, the gay community was creating or establishing a
critical mass of people who would then come out and embark on a political
journey towards greater visibility, equality and empowerment.

Today, almost 10 years after one of these first spaces was set up, we have
come to a stage where there is a much more visibility, a greater degree of
openness and many more queer spaces. At the same time, we have failed to
encourage or motivate gay men to have the confidence and feel the political
need to come out and support the queer movement. There may be enough
reason for us to be happy now, but there is also much cause for reflection.

A Different View

In the early stages, the success of these gay spaces, in reaching out to those belonging to the lower middle and working classes was next to negligible. The predominantly middle-class focus and environment of these informal networks alienated people from the working and lower middle classes at the time of the initial organising.

Ironically, the HIV epidemic served as a watershed for the movement. For the first time, systems of formal organising emerged. The desperate need to reach out to men-having-sex-with-men gave validation, legitimacy and structure to previously informal gay spaces, in the process giving gay men places to conduct meetings, hang out, socialise and organise, all for free. It immediately kick-started support systems, magazines, help-lines, counselling, meetings, libraries, and so on, which benefited people like me. But even this did not immediately translate into a greater participation by the lower and working class gay men. The focus was still on the middle classes. A fellow activist remarked:

> How could it change that easily? These were spaces started by brave and well meaning, but at the same time middle or upper middle class men and women. Queer they may have been, but like any middle and upper middle class people they were best at reaching out to their own.

The real change came with the outreach work on HIV. To broaden the base of their campaign against HIV, gay groups had to reach out to people who both could not afford condoms and were out of the mainstream information loops. This necessitated outreach to the cruising areas to tap the floating population of MSM, hoping to put the message of condom-use in their minds as they furtively navigated the railway stations and public parks. But the second and more crucial question was: who would do this kind of work? In the words of Goda who co-founded Udaan:[4] 'No gay man would go and distribute condoms at the toilets at railway stations. You needed kothis to do that.' This saw the employment in large numbers by MSM-focused organisations all over the country of kothis and hijras, as, in NGO-jargon, 'peer-educators' and 'outreach workers'. The movement at this stage was only beginning to remodel itself on the global wisdom of LGBT politics, although it rarely had representation. The refusal of kothi and hijra communities to be bracketed within this gay, bisexual and transgender framework caused the first official rifts in the larger queer community.

Kothis and hijras demanded independent recognition both as bona fide sexual minorities and partners in the movement. At the same time a whole new field of study was evolving beyond the middle-class and urban motifs of gay, bisexual and transgender. Along with this came a very distinct and refreshing voice for the rights of kothis and hijras. The very notion of kothi became both an affirming indigenous homosexual identity and a threat to the urban conception of 'gay'. Even today, there is a sense of resentment towards kothis amidst urban gay men, with the latter often insisting that there is no difference between gay and kothi identities. As a gay man remarked: 'A kothi is just a passive gay man who is also very effeminate. Why do you need a separate identity for that?' The response from the kothi community is: why not? The kothi groups continue to see 'gay' as an exclusive and unwelcoming space of upper-class and English-speaking homosexual men.

Seshadri and Ramakrishnan (1999) predicted:

> We expect conflicts between new identities and old ones resulting from a combination of transphobia and classism: individuals with homegrown identities such as kothis tend to perceive themselves as differently gendered and are of lower socio-economic strata than those with access to gay, lesbian or bisexual identities and discourse.

The concern expressed by Seshadri and Ramakrishnan was soon vindicated with the erstwhile gay spaces splintering one after the other on lines of class. As more and more kothis and Hindi- and Marathi-speaking men began to participate in the Friday meetings at Humsafar, the numbers of previous regulars (read: middle- or upper-middle-class, English-speaking gay men) in the meetings declined. There was almost an exodus of middle- and upper-middle-class gay men from the Humsafar Friday meetings to GayBombay, when neither was meant to compete with the other.

The Friday meetings still continue but have undergone a major face-lift. They are now conducted in Hindi and Marathi. They are attended mostly by kothis, hijras and gay and MSM-identified men from more working-class and non-English-speaking backgrounds. And the overall attendance is much larger than ever before.

Humsafar's was not an isolated experience. Shaleen Rakesh, the coordinator of Naz India Trust, which provides the space for the Humraahi meetings in Delhi, says that:

> The Humraahi meetings continued for a long while. Then gradually kothis who were employed and working at Naz for outreach work on HIV began attending these meetings. After a while some of them came and complained to me that they felt extremely alienated in the meetings because they could not speak in English and stood out as different in the way they dressed and behaved.

Naz India then helped start a separate group for kothis and hijras called Humjoli, which began weekly meetings on Tuesdays. Shaleen explains that the reasons for creating different support groups through Naz was their very different worldview and a different understanding of the issues that were important to them, which meant that the needs of the two groups were different as well. It was a supply-and-demand model, so if a group of people wanted a different space, they created it.

This still left a gap. With the overwhelming gender roles that dominated Humjoli a large proportion of men who did not identify as kothis or hijras, but were also not comfortable in the slightly upper-class Humraahi meetings, started a third group called Humnawaaz for gay, bisexual or just MSM-identified men, who came from relatively lower-income-class and non-English-speaking backgrounds. So in the same physical space of the Naz India Office, three completely separate groups, all dealing with homosexual men, met on different days and almost never interacted with each other.

'UNFORTUNATELY THERE IS CLASS'
HOW INCLUSIVE IS THE GAY IDENTITY?

The notion of class in India is complex and has been studied and explained through several models within the social sciences. I prefer to look at it simply through two essential factors: access to money and the ability to speak in English.

The frustration felt by Goda, a kothi-identified queer activist from a relatively lower middle-class background, who came out in the early 1990s and got involved with the informal networks of gay activists, captures the dual pinch of money and English:

> At the age of 21, I learned that gay people regularly meet at Gokul's in Colaba over the weekend. I started going to Gokul's, made friends and started hanging out with these people. But it was not easy at all, they spoke in English all the time, which I was not at all comfortable with. They could easily order a drink or food and sit in restaurants, for which I had no money. It was all dutch, you pay for yourself.

The availability of safe spaces like NGO offices and drop-in centres, may have made it easier for people like Goda to participate in the meetings, but the English language continued to be an excluding and extremely difficult hurdle to cross even when the meetings tried to be inclusive.

Good As You (GAY) is a group of gay men that meets every Thursday in Bangalore. Self-conscious of their middle-class and English-speaking environment and afraid to seem exclusive, GAY members have repeatedly tried to ensure that their discussions be translated into Kannada and Urdu. However, according to Arvind Narrain, a long-term member of GAY, 'There never would be people from non-English speaking backgrounds in the meetings to require translations. So in the absence of people from Kannada-speaking backgrounds, it ended up being an empty political gesture.'

Does the GAY experience allude to the inevitability of class? Is it simply neither easy nor practical to expect people from different class backgrounds to associate with one another even if they are gay? Pawan Dhall, a long-term queer activist and now a member of SAATHI in Kolkata, shares a completely different experience through an anecdote of the early years at Counsel Club:

> It was possible in Counsel Club during its peak phase for car-owning English-speaking rich men to sit next to suburban unemployed Bengali youth, dhoti-clad businessmen from Kolkata's traditional business district and sociology or software guys and for them to all talk about marriage, sex or Section 377. I wish there was a TV camera to document all this!

One explanation could be that Kolkata is a relatively linguistically homogenous city with most people across the class spectrum speaking primarily in Bengali, even when they might also be fluent in English. In more linguistically diverse cities like Mumbai and Bangalore this link is lost, with English being touted as a link language—but one that automatically exacerbates the class divide. Activists have made many attempts to bridge such divides. Pawan Dhall proposes deliberate but gentle methods: 'A universal space may not attract numbers in the beginning, but the most progressive action will come from such a space because it's like cross-fertilisation.'

Something to this effect was attempted by Naz India in Delhi. In response to a need to create an exclusive space for queer men to drop in and hang out, Naz in Delhi helped create a separate space under the Milan Project in 2000. According to Shaleen Rakesh its aim was to provide an opportunity for gay men to interact with kothis. It was the exclusivity of the space as a queer-male-only drop-in centre that made it more attractive for men to drop in, as opposed to the Naz office, which was an NGO also working on larger issues of HIV and public health. But due to an unfortunate incident when a bunch of local goons beat up the kothis who were visiting the project, it was forced to shut down.

It was not only local goons who disliked the presence of kothis in their territory. Such cross-cultural initiatives have also faced resistance from within the gay community. Shaleen's attempts did not cease with the collapse of the

Milan Project. He had long been trying to open the city's nightclubs to the gay community, and he now tried to make them more inclusive as well.

I wanted the club scene to be more accessible to people from lower class backgrounds, especially kothis. I let the word go at a party once that through Naz I would encourage more and more kothis to come to the nightclub. The next day I was flooded with emails, calls and SMSs from the Delhi gay community, threatening to boycott the club if the kothis land up.

This Delhi experience may not speak for the attitude of the entire gay community, but just the fact that sentiments like these exist speaks of the challenges ahead for the movement. As an activist remarked rather angrily when I shared the above anecdote with him:

More than the bigotry in this incident, what's annoying is the absolute lack of recognition that it is the kothis and hijras who are marching for the queer recognition that allows the rich sons of privilege to dance away till the wee hours of the morning.

The social/party scene is already getting more diversified. In response to the expensive ticket for the GayBombay New Year's Eve party, Humsafar organised a parallel party at a more affordable price.

On the political front, people from different class backgrounds do gather and attend discussions, seminars and conferences on queer rights, where passionate accounts are shared. But in the end despite all that political bonding, they self-select their companions, people with their own class backgrounds, and retreat to spaces that belong to their independent classes. To share a personal example, at the recent conference on Masculinities and Sexualities in Bangalore (June 2004), three young kothi activists who came from a new group called Humsaaya, Mumbai, complained of the sense of isolation they felt. They were glad that they were included in the conference, but felt disappointed that for a lot of middle-class English-speaking activists, the interaction ceased once a session was over. They never interacted with them after the sessions or even during breaks. They never got any opportunity to even get to know anyone. 'No one speaks to us', they said, 'or if they do we can't understand them. We don't know English.'

A recent documentary titled *Many People Many Desires* brought together by Sangama,[5] very movingly depicts different queer lives in the city of Bangalore. The camera navigates from an interview with an out gay man in a fancy Café Coffee Day on MG road to the story of an ageing hijra in the modest suburb of Ulsoor. I asked Shravana, a kothi, what he felt about the movie. Shravana works as an outreach worker and supervisor for an MSM HIV/AIDS project in Bangalore. He is in his thirties now and was married off under family pressure. But he left his work in the temple where he assisted his father and joined this NGO, because he wanted in some way to be associated with the queer community.

> Both kothis and gays have similar problems, they need to just understand each other. I see a gay man I find him attractive...or am just curious. But if I approach them, they just run away, literally retrace their steps. Why do they do that? Gay guys go to clubs or parties, it's only for gay men. Kothis see gay men as people from big families. That is the main distinction that we come from small families. He [a gay man] takes it behind his arse and so do we, but money still makes all the difference.

Both kothis and gay men may have similar problems, but largely they inhabit very different worlds. According to Mario D'Penha, who is part of a queer student group in Jawahalal Nehru University (JNU), New Delhi, 'We have no idea of the experiences of other queer people and we need to take deliberate measures to bridge this gap.'

Would the end of Section 377 of the Indian Penal Code mean the same thing for both kothis and gay men? A gay man would now just have more access to clubs, bars, an openly queer social life, and may subsequently acquire political and civil recognition of his sexuality, all of which at a cost that he may be able to afford. But what will it mean for a kothi or a working-class homosexual, who will have the right, but not the money to enjoy it? If the issues facing the gay community largely concern themselves with sexuality, for the kothis the predominant issues are of class. Gauri, while articulating the real need and issues that affect kothis, says matter-of-factly: 'Sexuality *se jyada khana, pet bharna aur ghar bahut mayne rakhta hai'* (shelter and food are more important than sexuality).

The larger concerns of the working and lower classes prevail, even if you are queer. How will you feed yourself and your family by the end of the day? How will supporting any queer struggle contribute to that need? It is this very understanding that is completely absent. Maya Sharma, a long-time labour and lesbian rights activist, puts is wisely:

> We have to acknowledge the silence between the urban and rural contexts, between activists with class privilege and those from the working class, between our own varying levels of Westernisation and use of English, and the grassroots reality we were trying to understand. The fact remains that the lives of... [many queer people]... are equally distant and alienated from upper-class, urban Indian as well as all Western representations of homosexuality, and their personal struggles, which cannot be separated from their socioeconomic struggles and traditional contexts, are largely unmirrored and therefore remain largely unknown.[6]

SOCIAL VERSUS THE POLITICAL

Is it actually possible for us to transcend these differences? We as queer people exist as part of the larger Indian society with all its myriad class and community distinctions and the current class-based trend of diversification of the queer community is only a reflection of that. An optimistic view might be that being queer might actually be something that helps people transcend these differences. Most queer people would acknowledge having a much more diverse range of acquaintances than their straight peers. So why does this inclusiveness stop short of really crossing class boundaries?

One of the few real and contemporary parallels is with the women's movement, which has its own class and caste issues. Maya Sharma argues that the old feminist slogan of 'Hum Sab Ek Hain' is absolutely superficial and the women's movement in India has realised that and accepted the fact that it exists in different spaces that are differentiated along lines of class, caste and religion. However, she notes the need for ways of communicating with each other across these differences.

The problem with the queer community starts with acknowledging that these differences exist at all. Most middle-class or upper middle-class activists that I met in the course of my research either felt that class was not such a big issue, while others recognised it but did not think of it as a problem. Only a few felt that something should be done about it. On the other hand, obvious as it may sound, almost everyone that I spoke to from lower-class backgrounds felt class to be one of the major barriers facing the community at large. This was the most interesting feature: the movement from class being 'an' issue, to 'the' issue. A basic consensus that emerged from these discussions was that it is okay to have different social spaces but we should have interactions, if not on purely social occasions then through political compulsions. Thus a distinction has been drawn between social spaces and political spaces—social spaces allow us time with our own and political spaces bring us together on a common platform.

In fact there is a strong queer contingent in favour of this argument. After all we do live in a society that consists of strong and indissoluble class differences which the queer community which, at its best, only mirrors, and at its worst, exacerbates. There are benefits too, just by the greater number of queer men who are accessing these spaces, even though they don't all use the same spaces. This may have not only increased the numbers in the movement but also provided a stronger queer leadership from working-class backgrounds, activists from the kothi and hijra communities who run their own independent NGOs. If it wasn't for the current diversification, the over-representation of upper-class men in the queer movement would never have been questioned.

This view is not without opposition either. Most activists are appalled at the idea that class can actually segregate us. They argue that we, as queer and therefore marginalised people, should naturally be able to question other forms of discrimination, class being on top of the list. So they argue that the queer community itself should be a site for change, to address the more difficult questions of class, along with sexuality and gender.

However, somewhere between these two polarised viewpoints lies an interesting justification that borrows from none other than the experiences of the feminist movement. It is the distinction between 'exclusionary' and 'autonomous' spaces.[7] An exclusionary space by definition keeps people out with little or no justification. So the nature of an exclusionary space is of discrimination and violation of a valid entitlement. On the other hand an autonomous space may also keep people out, but with reason and justification. For example, a Muslim women's group that chooses to be autonomous, is not exclusionary by not allowing non-Muslims to participate in it. If it did, it would lose its identity. Such an exclusionary identity is acceptable as long as these different autonomous spaces come together in support of each other for larger political interests.

Does a group like GayBombay then qualify as an exclusionary or an autonomous space? The distinction between autonomous and exclusionary blurs specifically in cases of groups like GayBombay. The distinction derives from the relative strength of the groups vis-à-vis those they seek to exclude. A relatively strong group might find it more comfortable or convenient to keep out certain people, but its very existence is not threatened by their inclusion. A weaker group may need to keep out people because their inclusion would vitiate the purpose of the group. The first is exclusionary, the second autonomous.

This distinction is easy to see with a group of hijras getting together and starting a group, which they may want to keep open only to hijras. Expecting gay men to join the group would completely alter its purpose. On the other hand a gay group that doesn't allow kothis into its meetings would be exclusionary, simply because they are operating from a stronger basis than the kothis. Upper classes, even when they are gay, enjoy very strong privileges. In the interest of the larger queer community, the upper-class queer spaces do have a greater responsibility towards the lower-class queer spaces. Having said that, there are practical constraints that may not be impossible to deal with, but are real enough to deserve a mention.

GayBombay's experiences have at some level been fraught with such practical limitations. The club/party scene that the GayBombay group pioneered is worth a mention here. The club scene began as a response to the horrific police raid at the White Party, in 1999, which ended an era of farmhouse parties in the outskirts of Mumbai. For an entire year after that there were no parties at all. Members of the GayBombay group then got together and decided to remedy the lack of parties. They looked at exactly what went wrong in the White Party, where the police selectively targeted men who were in drag, and the ones who were found indulging in any sexual activity in dark corners.

GayBombay went to nightclubs, which were doing bad business and got them to give out a weekday night for gay parties. The nightclubs, initially hesitant, but lured by the prospect of profits, agreed to let the faggots in. But there were concessions involved, in fact two important ones. First, 'no drag' was the rule of the hour—not, arguably, due to any transphobia—but as a purely cautious strategy based on the experience at the White Party.[8] And second, the decision of a cover charge being fixed by the nightclub, was taken out of the hands of GayBombay and this left out many who couldn't afford to pay between Rs 300 and Rs 500 to enter.

Such an initiative led to a huge influx of gay men accessing these social spaces, perhaps more than ever before. A regular GayBombay party attracts 300 to 400 men on an average. But it still ends up excluding several more. GayBombay has increasingly been criticised for its 'no drag' rule and expensive tickets. The 'no drag' rule has now been scrapped, thanks to opposition from within the group, and the parties now alternate between expensive and cheaper venues.[9]

However, this too does not mean that the issue of class has been resolved. The cheaper parties may reach out to more people, but never enough. As Sopan, a co-convener of the GayBombay group, remarks about the quarterly GayBombay film screenings: 'The film screenings are completely free, but they are not cross class.' Somehow money is still not the only problem. According to Goda, 'I know people who want to go for the GB parties and can afford it, but when they go they feel out of place and complain. So we organise cheaper picnics and sometimes parties too.' Should groups like GayBombay deserve no respect for the phenomenal work that they are doing, even if it is limited to a certain class of gay men? To note the frustration of Sopan, 'Unfortunately if you do something for the middle class, it's nothing, it's ignored, and not valued, but if you do something for the working classes you are looked on as a Messiah.'

It is clear that there is a need to examine the distinction between exclusionary versus autonomous within the reality in which class operates.

WE ARE HERE, WE ARE QUEER: A DISTANT ECHO!

As part of my research I spoke to many hijras and kothis, enough to gather a whole new definition of the gay identity. From the perspective of the hijra or kothi community the gay identity could very well be redefined. A gay man would then be someone, 'who is emotionally and sexually attracted to someone of the same sex, and is deeply paranoid about anyone discovering his identity, and would never openly stand up for who he is, and will always stay in the closet'. Frivolous as this may sound, it does carry a grain of truth. Let's look at this in conjunction with something that Jeremy Seabrook has to say in his book *Love in a Different Climate*:

> On the other hand, the openly gay, the sons of privilege, tend to meet in the more up-market areas, at parties and in each other's houses. They are likely to be more discreet; and although some of their families may know and accept their sexual orientation, many will still maintain a careful concealment and, publicly at least, live out a life of impeccable heterosexual orthodoxy (Seabrook 1999).

Now Seabrook may be a bit harsh, but once again it is true that the gay community is largely built around, especially in India, the culture of concealment.[10]

Gay men argue that they have careers, families and status in the society, which can be jeopardised by coming out. For example, Bala, in *Many People Many Desires*, says that: 'The gay men have more at stake by being out.' This is an argument made in opposition to kothis or hijras who may not on the other hand have that much to lose by being out. Gauri, who co-founded and runs Sakhi Char Chowghi, a support group for kothis in Bombay, does not agree. According to her, 'Kothis come from lower socio-economic backgrounds, they also have families, they live in neighbourhoods where they have little or no privacy, they have more at stake if they lose their jobs, but they will still be the one to come and march with you.'

The GayBombay website,[11] which I repeatedly use as a benchmark for a middle-class queer voice, proudly proclaims the *raison d'être* for its inception: the need to create a simple basic support group that would not intimidate middle-class gay men, who of course come from respectable families. According to Vikram, a convenor and member of GayBombay,

> At the stage of coming out and confronting their sexuality gay men are highly insecure and vulnerable, and they are super sensitive to issues like class or effeminacy. We have to try to put them at their ease, without necessarily agreeing with or condoning sentiments they have about such issues.

This can be combined with the fear of the transgender which really is a reflection of the phobias of most gay men about their own gender and sexuality. This phobia results in them distancing themselves from the perverse, i.e., the camp, gender-bending, limp-wrist fag. So while these middle-class gay spaces encourage men to embrace their forbidden sexuality, they also reinforce, or do not do much to challenge their other prejudices.

On the other hand, groups working with kothis and hijras embrace the very trans, or camp behaviour. Gender becomes the face of class. Nitin Karani, a convenor of Sunday High, an alternate Sunday meeting space at Humsafar, and a member of *Bombay Dost*, calls it the 'prudery' of the middle classes. The aspirations of the upper middle classes are about complacency, which also translates into an apolitical sphere where you don't want to meddle with the authorities and live your life as peacefully as possible. Whereas life for the working classes is essentially about a constant struggle for survival, which is why it is not surprising to see the eagerness and enthusiasm with which most kothis have embraced the political aspect of the queer movement.

As middle-class spaces are retreating into a non-political zone, it is spaces like Udaan that are uncovering a whole new political zeal for themselves even if it is largely centred around their work on HIV/AIDS prevention. Udaan began as a support group for kothis, and MSM, in Maheshwari gardens. According to Goda:

> The real change came when one of our friends was very sick with AIDS and we had to struggle to get him admitted in a Government Hospital. We finally managed to get a bed for him. The doctors would come with an entourage of students and make my friend get up and bend like a dog, and put his pants down. The Doctor would point a stick at his ass, and declare, 'Look at the asshole of a homosexual.' That was the most humiliating experience for us all. We decided that Udaan had new challenges ahead of it, and the discrimination we faced was going to be a major issue.

If we look even briefly at the history of public protest and marches in the last 10 years, there is an overwhelming support, commitment and presence of kothis and hijras who have been at the forefront of protests and demonstrations. This has been the case right from the time of the protests that took place all over the country after the arrest of gay outreach workers in Lucknow, to protests organised by Vividha and Sangama against police atrocities in Bangalore and of course the Kolkata Pride March that took place for the third time in 2004. It is always hijras and kothis marching with banners, out there, with a smattering of gay men, who represent the entire community of sexual minorities. According to Vikram: 'You have to encourage guys to come into the community first, and once they do that, they might become more political.'

Something seems to have gone wrong with the initial support spaces for gay men. They were designed for support and were, for most, weekly social soirées, till something better came along. It was the political aspect that was the hardest to establish. For example the Humraahi meetings suffered a setback after alternative social spaces like weekly parties began. The attendance on Fridays at the Naz office dropped significantly. The lure of this space was only for its social value and once better alternatives emerged people moved on. With the need for support behind them, gay people seem happiest in the social spaces and are almost blasé about the political arena.

The Internet revolution broke all records for the gay movement, just by the large numbers of men who accessed gay spaces through the web and came in touch with the community. GayBombay is the best example of a space that has, no doubt because of the Internet, reached out to thousands of men in the city of Mumbai, through its three-pronged approach: a website and a mailing list; bi-weekly meetings, and now parties and film festivals. Admittedly, the Internet has its limitations. Nevertheless, it has done a fantastic job.

The regular GayBombay parties in the city of Bombay attract 300 to 400 gay men. But in 2001 during a protest against the arrests of gay activists in Lucknow barely a handful of gay men showed up. It was only hijras, kothis, lesbians and women's activists who came in large numbers. Somewhere down the line, the assumption that the availability of support and social spaces, as well as the medium of the Internet, will push (if not all, then at least a few) gay men into the politics of the movement, has been proven wrong. Gay men are only retreating further into invisibility, not least because of the safety and anonymity provided by the Internet. As Sandip Roy Chowdhary (2002) notes, 'Some activists fear that even as it allows men to find friends, boyfriends or tricks, the Internet will put them all in a giant virtual closet.' Chowdhary raises an important issue. In attempting to provide safe spaces for the gay community are we pushing the community back into the closet? Have we crossed some thin, invisible line between being supportive and being overprotective to the detriment of any visibility at all?

There are several reasons why the gay community desists from a larger political commitment, let alone association with the larger queer community:

- There is the Bala view, where he talks of the greater risk involved for gay men by coming out and openly supporting the queer cause. Bala's

comments are fairly representative of large sections of the gay community.
- There is, on the other hand, caution from sectors of the community that feel it is too early to push the gay community into a political space. The community still needs time to develop confidence to make that kind of a commitment.
- At a trivial, but important level, especially in India, the constant infighting between different queer communities and organisations has contributed tremendously to both the inability of the movement to present a united front, and for younger queer people to actually show any active interest in joining it.
- We also haven't been able to find a more inclusive queer political voice. Queer people are diverse, also in their political views. So far the political aspect of the movement is chaired by groups and members inspired by politics of the Left. It is not a bad thing by itself, but it does end up excluding a lot of others. As a young gay man remarked to me: 'Just because I am gay, and identify as queer, and am interested in supporting the movement, I don't want to have the same commitment for people being displaced by unruly dams or bashing America during tea and lunch breaks.'

Ultimately, however, the strongest barrier seems to be the one of class. Gay men are simply uncomfortable marching alongside hijras and kothis. There is absolutely no recognition of similar struggles and aspirations, at least in the context of sexuality, between hijras, kothis and gay and bisexual men. There is still a strong push towards understanding gay as fundamentally different from hijra and kothi, where the fundamental difference may actually not be as strong as the superficial ones of class and gender have become.

We have failed to make a case to the gay community as to why one needs to support the larger queer movement. This will happen only when we, as gay people, realise that we only have a lot to gain by playing a more proactive role in this movement. This will require both supporting and sustaining the movement in conjunction with the other communities like the lesbian movement, the kothi and the hijra communities. There are ample reasons why the gay community desperately needs to look beyond itself. It is not always going to be in the secure position it imagines itself to be in presently. As visibility increases, so will threats, risks and above all, homophobia. The Shiv Sena attacks on the screening of *Girlfriend*, not to mention the extremely homophobic content of the movie, were a chilly reminder of the protests around *Fire* and the signs of intolerance to come.

The issue of police harassment and violence has for long been confined to working-class queers, thus creating a false sense of safety within the gay community. But even this might be changing through the rise of extortionist gangs and blackmailers that have infiltrated gay spaces, in parties, cruising spots and the Internet, luring gay men into promises of a sexual encounter that leads to abuse, harassment, shame and, of course, an empty wallet. The GayBombay website reports cases where gay men in the city of Mumbai have been blackmailed for long periods for amounts as high as over Rs 100,000. The unexpected attack by over 50 policemen and women at the White Party revealed the fragile position of the gay community. The problem is that the gay community itself seems to not take this seriously enough.

For the first time gay men got together at a Humsafar Sunday High meeting to plan and strategise on how to deal with the rising incidents of blackmailing. Of course the biggest limitation in such an incident is that no gay men would come out and lodge a police complaint. But the very fact that such a meeting took place speaks of a new recognition of the need to organise around political issues. Vikram agrees that the apathy of the gay community towards political activism may be changing: 'As more and more people are coming out they are realising the need for support. There are many more people who are living together as partners, who are coming out in their workplace. All this raises anticipations of discrimination, violence and the need for safeguards.'

It is in our hands to extend this need and connect it to the larger political movement.

Conclusion: Where is the Political?

As a sidetrack, there is an interesting parallel with Singapore, which has suddenly found itself winning gay acceptance but within limits. The government has raised no objections to the rising numbers of gay bars and saunas in Singapore, as long as the gay community does not make any political demands. An article on a popular Singapore gay website laments the disappearance of politics in the Singapore (Sal) gay scene and feels the need for it to come back:

> But just how long can sex and partying last, before we discover that we cannot do many, many other things that straight people can do? For example, marry legally the person we love, adopt kids and even hold a high-flying government job with an open conscience that you're gay? After everybody's got his share of fucking and dancing, it's these basic rights that count in defining human dignity and self respect.

We need to understand that the need to be political is already out there, whether we like it or not. It starts with everyday experiences, like the black-mailing or the police harassment, which links to larger struggles like Section 377, and so on. We need to organise politically not only to take the movement and our demands ahead but also to plan against backlashes that often result in such increasing levels of visibility on queer issues. When the need to be political reasserts itself, it is inevitable that we will run into class issues, so it is best that we start debating them right away.

NOTES

1. This is not an academic study. The essay is based on interviews and discussions with many people involved or working with or who are part of different gay, lesbian, kothi, hijra, transgender and men-having-sex-with-men (MSM) spaces. The essay will also limit its analysis to the identities that fall under the umbrella of queer male spaces. Finally, the essay does not aim to offer solutions or answers. Its main purpose is to document and articulate certain concerns and debates, and place them in the context of the reality of people interviewed.
2. However, Counsel Club meetings stand as an exception. According to Pawan Dhall, one of the group members, these meetings never took a defined class line and were never predominantly English-speaking.
3. There would be occasional gay parties, but not in every city, and not always easily accessible or affordable for all.
4. Udaan, which means a flight, in the hope of liberty, was co-founded by Goda in 1992 as a support and advocacy group for the kothi and other MSM-identified men.
5. Sangama is an organisation that works for the rights of sexual minorities, sex workers, and PLWHAs in Bangalore. See www.sangama.org for more information.
6. Maya Sharma is involved with Maanjal Women's Empowerment Society. This quote is from an unpublished paper that brings together Maya's personal narrative as an activist, and her oral history documentation of working-class women, with same-sex desires, in the Hindi belt.
7. I am very grateful to Shalini Mahajan from LABIA and FORUM, for making this point to me.
8. This was also combined with a strictly enforced 'no sex' rule, in case undercover policemen and women enter the party, as was the case with the White Party. Finally parties in established nightclubs took care of other problems, like alcohol and catering licenses, which established nightclubs already have, but were impossible to attain in the old farmhouse parties. The White Party, for example, was finally nailed for lack of appropriate licenses.
9. By 'cheap' I mean as low a cover as Rs 200 per person.

10. The only criticism I have of Seabrook is that he seems to assume that lower-class gay, kothi or MSM-identified men are necessarily always out, or never marry.
11. The website can be accessed at www.gaybombay.cc.

References

Chowdhary, Sandip Roy. 2 December 2002, 'GayBombay', http://www.salon.com/tech/feature/2002/12/02/gay-india.

Sal. 'To the Death of Gay Activism in Singapore', http://www.sgboy.com/st/fecoaO2.htm. Accessed online 24 July 2004.

Seabrook, Jeremy. 1999, *Love in a Different Climate*. London: Verso.

Seshadri, P. and L. Ramakrishnan. 1999, 'Queering Gender: Trans Liberation and Our Lesbigay Movements', *Trikone*, Vol. 14, No. 3, pp. 6–8, 18.

9

The Roads that E/Merged
Feminist Activism and Queer Understanding

Chayanika Shah

 International Women's Day, 8 March 2004. While attending the Joint Women's Groups celebrations, some of us sit with bated breath as the names of the groups organising the programme are read out. One of the activists from a 'mainstream' women's group reads out the names one after the other and then, without any fumbling or any kind of hesitation, she reads the name of our newly renamed collective, 'Lesbians and Bisexuals in Action'[1] (LABIA), and we are elated at hearing her pronounce the *L**** word.

Why that anxiety? Why were we almost certain that she would fumble? Why the happiness at a name being read out? Why was it important for us to rename ourselves and be addressed as such? Were we being paranoid? Were we not living in March of 2004? There is a small story to each of these questions and I sit here trying to trace the story from a very subjective position. I am sure there shall be a number of ways to see it all—maybe more exhaustive, more theoretical, more factual.... But I shall do my bit of living two decades of activism within the women's movement and almost a decade within the queer movement.

CLAIMING WOMEN'S SPACES

I joined the urban women's movement as part of the Mumbai-based collective, Forum Against Oppression of Women,[2] more than two decades ago and have stayed with it all these years. The early years of the 1980s were a heady time. It was a time for street actions and also a time for staking our claim as women. It was wonderful to ascribe words to ideas that I did not know existed inside my head. My political understanding of why society was the way it was grew with a composite understanding of how gender, class and caste affected its institutions and structures. I learnt ways to define myself as a woman, learnt to claim rights over my body, learnt to like it and make friends with it, alongside learning to love others like myself.

We critiqued the family and, many of us, in our personal lives questioned the institution of marriage (even though many of us entered it with the hope of bending its rules backward and forward). In intimate conversations we spoke of openness of all kinds in relationships and of all the kinds of relationships that people experienced. Some of us, even then, were keen to identify and speak of ourselves as lesbian or bisexual while others were happy to lead the kind of life that we led. After all, 'what was there in how I called myself, my relationship was the important thing'. We thought we were very radical. In the few attempts made to classify the Indian women's groups with the Western classification terminology, we, in the Forum, were often branded as the 'radical feminists' (although we were sure we were the 'Marxist feminists').

We were active in the campaigns against rape that demanded that rape be understood as the use of patriarchal power against women's bodies, thus reclaiming new definitions of being women. We fought against all violence, particularly within the marital family, and set up spaces for women to talk about their abuse and deal with their horrifyingly violent daily lives. Though we worked towards unmasking the institutions of family and marriage we did not take the analysis or actions to the extent of questioning their very right to exist. Our demands were for basic minimum human dignity and the recognition of rights for women within these institutions.

In Mumbai, as independent working women wanting to own the city, its roads, its public spaces and its public transport in particular. One of the most proactive and energising campaigns was towards making the women's compartments in the local trains free of men (and hence abuse) for all the 24 hours of the day.[3] Travelling in late-night trains, throwing off the men who tried to enter the compartments and the constant negotiations with the authorities gave many of us the arrogance and the courage to walk the streets of the city at any hour of the day and night. This, like the 'take back the night' campaigns, gave us freedom in the city as well as a sense of ownership of public spaces and that in turn helped us to experience a definite sense of independence.

Later came the struggles and campaigns against hazardous contraceptives and, in the process of fighting them, the need to define birth control for ourselves, new understandings of and friendships with our bodies and once again a look at intimate relationships, particularly with men. Alongside this, were the struggles for gender-just laws governing intimate relationships within which the institutions of marriage and family were under scrutiny yet again.

FACING HIDDEN REALITIES

In between all this, our radical group, which met for its weekly meetings in a lesbian household, was shaken out of its complacency by two women far away in a small town in Madhya Pradesh. Two women constables decided to get married to each other and this resulted in their losing their jobs and other victimisations.[4] We were forced to acknowledge other realities—of lives outside cities and violent marriages, of violence that was so invisible that it did not even get a name or mention until it crossed a 'limit', and also the reality of our groups and campaigns that had not taken such realities into account and when faced with them could not really figure out a way of dealing with them. We tried a human rights approach at that time—no person should lose her job on such grounds, the state cannot violate the rights of its citizens in this manner, and so on.

For those two women maybe we were not able to do anything. But the discussions that we had as a group changed something for us permanently. Since then, at least in our urban, English-speaking group, lives and realities of homosexual women kept coming up in everything that we took up. Be it the discussion on gender-just laws for looking at intimate relationships, topics to be discussed at National Conferences, or our discussions about our body. Slowly and steadily, these thus far excluded lives were being included and finding a space. In fact, these lives started forcing a space within the larger women's movements as well thanks to the persistence of a few women and groups like ours.

The journey has not been smooth. There was a decent share of opposition but there was support as well. This pattern was repeated at every level. In our group, amongst other similar autonomous women's groups, and within the larger women's movements, there was a fair share of support and opposition. Many times the constituents of each section were unexpected, surprising us by not conforming to the general trend of their politics.

I suddenly note a change in the 'we' that I am using and so I think it is important to pause and track my own personal journey as well. I sit pondering over the keyboard for a long time trying to figure out where did I change and when and why? For I was one of those who thought that relationships were important, identities were restricting and soon I found myself in the category willing to identify as lesbian, wanting to stand up and say that I exist and have existed, slowly becoming a part of that small group that wanted space for lesbian and bisexual women, identified thus, within the larger women's movements. It would be nice to be able to give neat little causality statements like you know this happened and so then I changed and so on. But life does not give us such clear indicators of cause and effect and so I venture to mention what to me in hindsight seem to be the possible reasons.

I think it was mainly the fatigue of leading a hidden life, for even if I was open to an extent, this openness meant a lot of untruths and hiding. It was painful to hide the importance of my relationships from those that mattered and I soon realised that as this was an integral part of who I was, when people did not know it, they did not know a large part of me. Besides this, there was the experience of coming out to 'near and dear' ones, to parts of the family, to comrades and friends, to others in the women's movements. The reaction was expected and yet the intensity of hatred and discomfort expressed at times was unexpected. It was not easy and somewhere it made me resolve that things had to change. Coming out, becoming visible and claiming spaces became an important agenda.

At this point, a few women got together and set up Stree Sangam, a lesbian and bisexual women's collective in Mumbai in 1995. Soon I became part of it. The idea for all of us was to not remain hidden all the time, to be more visible and at the same time to create spaces where women could feel safe and comfortable with other women like themselves, and to prepare society to accept people like us, women like us.

It was around the same time, in the mid-1990s, when suddenly the overall scenario in society also changed. Sexuality itself became something that people started talking about a lot. Partly it was the presence of the HIV/AIDS epidemic and the work that was being done around it by various agencies and also the pressures of the funding agencies with their West-driven agendas. Many groups of 'sexual minorities' came into being under the garb of the two kinds of organisations mentioned above.

The last 10 years have been very exciting and challenging in many ways for us, as women who identify themselves as lesbian and bisexual. We were trying to straddle the two worlds of women's organising and 'sexual minorities' organising. These worlds were very different and the experiences of both have informed each other in ways that have altered our individual and collective worldviews substantially. But before I discuss how this happened, I would like to talk a little about what was it that was typical of both these worlds.

LESBIANS ARE WOMEN TOO

We claimed space within the women's movements. We recognised from our own lives and those of other women who came in contact with Stree Sangam that women's groups could be the safe spaces in which women could open up, make contact and reach out. We pointed out that there was no such clear space and we demanded that this space be created. We laid claim over the women's movements and demanded that these movements in turn take up our struggle as part of the larger struggle of all women. In a sense, we recognised that we were one of those oppressed minorities who had been invisibilised by the larger women's movements.

As someone who considers herself totally a part of the women's movements, I know that we[5] have been guilty of neglecting and sidelining issues of many different sections of women. We were talking of all women but were concentrating on women from a certain class, caste, region, religion and sexuality. From time to time, Dalit women, tribal women, women from religious minorities, single women and now lesbian and bisexual women have pointed out that their issues do not have space or are not prioritised within the women's movements. The plural use of 'women's movements' instead of the singular is, in fact, an acknowledgement of this neglect and an honest attempt at saying, but also believing, that 'women' are no generic category. Their issues had to be raised in multiple ways through multiple strategies by several groups with diverse understandings.

Each of these sections of women and those advocating for their inclusion, have faced varying degrees of rejection and acceptance. So as far as lesbian and bisexual women go, active violence against them is of course condemned. At the same time, individual personal and collective group responses in different situations, have included statements like, 'It is not normal'; 'I do not approve'; 'Our women will not be able to identify with groups whose names contain words like Lesbian and so we cannot march with them for 8th March'; 'There are no lesbian women amongst the women that we work with'; 'This is alright for urban groups. We cannot raise it anywhere'; 'Women's friendships are so accepted within our society. If you start naming them like this you shall take away that anonymous space that women have today'; and many more—ranging from those expressing utter disgust to those trying to be politically correct but falling just short.

There was resistance expressed by not allowing a group campaigning for lesbian rights to march in a Women's Day rally along with other women's groups on 'regular women's' demands or active opposition to discussions on 'such' issues at National Conferences of Women's Movements. Passive opposition came in the form of groups just not prioritising issues of lesbian and bisexual women in their regular work. A few also actually believed that silence meant safety and anonymity for women in relationships. In their view, we would endanger the ways in which women live female friendships and hence we should not be too visible or 'aggressive'.

BEYOND INVISIBILITY

For those of us who identified as lesbian/bisexual and also identified with the women's movements, working with groups focusing on issues of 'sexual minorities' (or whatever was the right term) was also not easy. Finding women like us was the most difficult task. In a society that does not allow any public space for women, where and how were we going to be able to find women like us? In the absence of any known names with which we could identify ourselves proudly, how were we to ask someone we thought was like us, whether she was really 'like us'? If women identified their relationships as friendships, were we not imposing our understanding of the special character of this friendship by giving it a name which was not known or was much maligned? The shroud of invisibility did not make any space for any sort of interaction.

The newspapers continued to report on other women like the ones in Bhopal, those who got married, or were separated, or attempted suicide for fear of being separated from each other. These women were from all over the country. They were women and young girls from small villages and small towns. We managed to make contact with some of them but with many others we were too late. They were either no more or were under too much pressure to make contact. While we never stopped hearing from everyone that all of these were issues of urban, English-speaking women; isolated and lonely women who were apparently very unlike us, who allowed their lives and desires to succumb to marriage or suicide, often voicing their desire to live differently but not knowing that other ways of living were possible.

In the urban areas we could meet more women. These women were sometimes more aware of the language of women's desires for women, and some identified as lesbian or bisexual. But many were very closeted and although they wanted spaces to meet other women, they were afraid of being identified. They were concerned with issues of safety, security and loneliness and needed safe networks and safe spaces to meet other women.

Some of these women who came to Stree Sangam were looking for such social spaces. They found our kind of groups boring and not enough fun. They were usually not interested in any kind of political action. Visibility, organising, patriarchy, sexual politics, rights and fighting or struggling for them were alien concepts or at least they seemed like issues that they did not want to get involved in. Those of us who identified as lesbian feminists, were oscillating between wanting to connect with other women, grappling to find ways in which we could find them and reach out to them, and the utter exhaustion of being a support system to even a handful.

The absence of supportive families in many of our lives meant that there was tremendous demand and claim over a support system which was itself a toddler looking for support. The need for invisibility and the fear of being found out added to the confusion. And instances of families getting violent, of complaining to the police, of housing societies throwing women out of rented apartments on 'accidentally' finding out, did not help at all. We were trying to reach out as much as we could—when adult women were kept locked up in their homes, when they lost their housing or their jobs, or when they went through relationship troubles and break-ups. This small miniscule support system though inadequate, was all there was. There was an urgent need to create more spaces and to do something to make life more liveable for all those who were forced to remain silent and invisible.

Some of us tried to set up phone help lines and other safe, accessible spaces for all women who loved women. Others tried to look further into the structural inadequacies of the medical and legal systems that justify violence against lesbian and bisexual women, in fact against all those who challenge the predominant hetero-normativity in society. We worked with women's groups and supportive human rights groups and initiated dialogues and campaigns to work towards changes within law. We joined campaigns against Section 377 with them and other gay groups. We also had discussions on other existing laws and on defining our demands for a non-discriminating society in future.

We also tried consistently to ally and work with others in the extended 'sexual minorities' community (which was slowly emerging as the alphabet soup LGBTKQHE....)—the gays, the kothis, the hijras.... Many of their lives and realities were very different from ours. Their issues were more related to public spaces, ours were about invisibility. We were trying to find a community with them—a community which believed in looking at our collective issues and lives within the frameworks of a politics akin to ours. A politics that dealt with injustice, violence, discrimination across all divisions of society, that moved further with a vision of a new world. We were not always successful.

The patriarchal behaviour of the gay community sometimes really baffled us. Women were almost completely absent from many of their worlds. The absence of any understanding of 'gender' and patriarchy was extremely difficult to deal with, especially since their lives constantly challenged the mainstream notions in so many ways all the time. The absence of any dialogues and connections with other progressive movements and politics was frustrating.

It was a weird experience for someone like myself who had spent years in autonomous women-only spaces. The misogyny in the behaviour of some gay men was difficult to deal with. It was strange to see the multiple ways in which notions of femininity (that we had been constantly battling against) were being reinforced by the very acts that transgressed the borders of hetero-normativity as I understood it. The 'queens' were beautiful but at times they forced me to be more 'woman' than I felt and at other times they made me question my new feminist definitions of being a woman.[6] And yet, meeting them, seeing them and being with them made me see many more dimensions of my life as a person who questioned hetero-normativity of society. It expanded my understanding of society, of patriarchy, of gender.

OUT IN THE OPEN

Over the last 10 years within Stree Sangam/LABIA, within the Forum and amongst a few of us who have been reading on, thinking about and conducting workshops on sexuality with different groups of people, discussions on sex, gender and sexuality have become more complex. We have all changed, shifted and moved in our understandings, individually and collectively. We have discovered other like-minded allies across the country—people from lesbian groups, other 'sexual minority' groups, women's groups, human rights groups and many individuals too. It is due to the concerted efforts of all these people to raise issues and complicate discussions at all fora and in all possible progressive spaces that we were able to change Stree Sangam's name last year.

It is this collective work that has created a situation where we are officially a part of the women's movements. It is the outcome of many visible and not so visible battles and skirmishes that the person reading out our group's name on 8 March 2004, did not stop, pause and want to vanish when reading it. We are not hidden any more under innocuous sounding names like 'Stree Sangam' but we are out in the open, stating who we are. We are in a position today to identify ourselves as a politically active lesbian feminist group which plans to work with other groups towards breaking silences, towards making society more open to women's desires, towards finding names for ourselves and our loves, towards making this a safer space for all those, whether visible or invisible, to lead their lives in ways that they choose to live in. As we proudly said in one issue of *Scripts*, the magazine that we produce,

Stree Sangam has decided to reinvent itself, in name and in deed. Today we conceive of ourselves as a campaign and action group of queer women called Lesbian and Bisexual Women in Action. We choose to remain autonomous and non-funded. We choose to speak loudly and proudly of who we are and want to reclaim the space for political action and personal expression. We see oppression based on gender and sexuality as part of the same hetero-patriarchal norms that oppress other marginalised peoples as well. We wish to continue to ally with others, who, like us believe that working towards a society where all genders and sexualities would be respected and treated equally is necessary. Our strategies are multiple and complex, but our alliances are crucial. As are our politics and our lives (*Scripts* 2003: 13).

E/MERGING PATHS

This journey has helped me and those with me look at our feminisms with greater scrutiny. We do feel that by visibilising women's lived realities, we will help create a world where more women will have the space and support to live the lives that they want. Besides addressing the violence of silence around issues of lesbian and bisexual women's lives, this also helps open spaces for all those women who do not fit the world's definition of 'good' women.

So far as women's movements are concerned, we have, by and large, concentrated on the rights of those who lived by the norms laid down by society. Women who have relationships outside of marriage—monogamous or multiple, with whomever they wanted to; women who choose to acknowledge, express and act on their desire; women who choose to sell their bodies and look at sex work as a profession going beyond the notions of violence that prostitution was understood to be; women who challenge the very basic norms and structures of how society thinks that women should behave—talking of rights for all these women is a difficult task.

Acknowledging their existence could be interpreted as endangering the movements of and for the 'good' women. But feminism is not about maintaining status quo. It is about challenging all oppressive structures of society. Looking at 'bad' women will in fact help us voice exactly the nature of control over women's sexuality and to relook at all institutions anew. And these processes have begun in at least small sections of the women's movements that have started engaging with all those marginalised by mainstream society.

Understanding lives of women who question the whole notion of femininity in multiple ways has implications for the ways in which we have understood and worked with gender so far. 'Women' who pass as men—either because they do not have ways in which to understand their desire for women or because their bodies truly do not fit the gender 'woman'; 'persons' who go through immense pain and suffering to actually alter their bodies, who are willing to pay all the costs for it in every form merely because this world does not allow them the freedom to be who they are; 'men' who wish to cross-dress and not act as men; all those who find the generic terms 'men' and 'women' inadequate to define who they are—complicate our understandings of gender in ways that looking at the categories of 'women' and 'men' cannot!

Patriarchy is about inequality in relations, it is about power. Looking at the sex and gender divide, we did question the societal structures that gave rise to these unequal power relations. It is an understanding that helps us even today to recognise the structures of power in society. It helped us open up the notions of being men and women to an extent. Gender roles have been questioned and we have tried to open the watertight compartments of male and female to some limited extent. For many years, however, we lived with the complacency of sex as a biological reality and 'woman' as a given category. We lived without actually questioning whether all bodies had to necessarily fit into being male or female only.

Working with queer realities has, however, opened a whole new way of looking at sex and gender. People who do not identify as male or female clearly, or those who do not identify with the gender categories, or those that identify with one sex and gender but are not comfortable with the watertight definitions of these genders—there are many kinds of people and many kinds of realities. All these realities demand humanity, space and rights within this society. More importantly they raise questions for all of us. Why are there only two sexes? Why are there only two genders? Why is there a one-to-one correspondence between a particular sex and a particular gender?

And then comes the key question. Is compulsory heterosexuality only about controlling desire or is it also about dictating that the world can have only two kinds of people—women and men? Does it expand the meaning of hetero-normativity to an extent that we are just about beginning to comprehend? Does this not raise new ways of looking at the notion of family? And if we accept that there can be more ways in which people could define themselves, then what does this do to our understanding of feminism, to our recently reclaimed category of 'woman'? How are we going to be able to accept the privilege and power of the naturally born woman over all those who do not fit?

I must admit that raising these questions has not been easy. The first time in our discussions when I was asked to really answer the question, 'what is it that makes me a woman?', I resisted very hard. Being a woman and claiming this body and this identity as a positive identity was something that I and others like me had just recently learnt. The women's movement had helped us do this. To question it is not easy. In the kind of world that we live in, where even being a woman is so difficult and where the category 'woman' has constantly been under attack, it is not easy to let it go and accept the fluidity of gender. And yet as a lesbian woman, living, working and interacting with many women for whom these are not just theoretical questions— this understanding has given an insight into hetero-normativity that has made me understand many aspects of my life and the world around me much better.

The women's movements were the first to articulate concern over the control over sexuality and the societal constructions of gender and are hence the closest link and support for the nascent 'queer' movements in the country. Queer political movements also have to work within the feminist frameworks questioning patriarchy. We have to be together and in the forefront of the struggle against hetero-normativity and patriarchy. We have to learn to theorise and politicise together but strategise in ways that shall take into account our individual and specific realities in this vastly unequal and lop-sided world.

NOTES

1. A collective of lesbian and bisexual women formed in April 1995 and earlier known as Stree Sangam.
2. Forum Against Oppression of Women was formed in 1980 as the Forum Against Rape and has since functioned in Mumbai in its members' houses with voluntary work put in by numerous women over the years. It has chosen consciously to remain a non-registered, non-funded, autonomous collective, a breed of organisations that is fast becoming extinct with the pressures of a globalised society. It began as a campaign group and has worked on various issues in the last two-and-a-half decades of its existence.
3. Till 1982, while the local trains had 'ladies only' compartments it was so only till eight in the evening. It was after a sustained campaign by the Forum where we actually 'guarded' two trains twice a week against the entrance of men for a month and then negotiated with the authorities, that one compartment per train was made '24 hours for ladies only'.
4. During December 1987, there were a series of press reports covering the marriage of Leela and Urmila, two police constables in Bhopal, who were discharged from service for 'conduct unbecoming to public servants'. Several women's groups conducted a signature campaign for their reinstatement into service.
5. I must admit that I feel such a dual sense of belonging and separation from the larger women's movements that I cannot avoid this fluctuating use of 'we'.

Sometimes it is for all those who are perceived to belong and at other times for those perceived to not belong.

6. I must admit that meeting many women also did the same to my sensibilities. In the absence of a lexicon it was almost as if the roles of 'man' and 'woman' were both being played to the hilt. As we sometimes wondered, at times relationships between two women were more heterosexual than those between some women and men that we knew. There was a successful mangling of both notions of gender and sexuality—the mainstream and the newly emerging feminist one as well.

REFERENCES

Scripts, Vol. 3, October 2003, p. 3.

10

Voicing the Invisible
Violence Faced by Lesbian Women in India

Bina Fernandez and *Gomathy N.B.*

 Lesbians are vulnerable to the violence faced by all women—rape, battering, sexual harassment and child abuse. However, lesbians not only have to contend with violence *as women,* but also *as lesbians.*[1] This is comparable to the specific kinds of violence women face on the basis of their identities as Dalit or adivasi. There are significant differences though.

First, the epistemic root of the violence faced by lesbians is in the denial of their very existence in Indian society. Lesbianism is often decried as a 'Western import', and allegedly restricted to the urban élite of Indian society. However, the indisputable evidence of same-sex love in different historical contexts[2] in India (the *Kama Sutra* and Khajuraho temple carvings being two commonly cited examples), and the increasing number of news reports from small towns and rural locations of women attempting to marry other women, are facts that contradict these oft-repeated denials of lesbian existence.

Second, lesbian sexuality is not necessarily immediately apparent from the woman's name, physical features or social practices, and a woman can choose (or not) to reveal her sexual orientation. Some women might indicate their sexual orientation through subversion of gender by adopting 'masculine' clothes and behaviour. Other lesbian women may simply state that their relationship is more than a friendship. Many lesbian women may choose to *not* indicate their sexual orientation at all. In such instances, unlike in the case of caste or religion (where name, outward appearance and/or behaviour are often signifiers of identity), lesbian women are not 'identifiable'.

Third, the continued criminalisation of homosexuality in India under Section 377 of the Indian Penal Code can be read as an implicit sanction of violence against lesbians. This is in contrast to legal protections from violence available to Dalit and adivasi women under the Prevention of Atrocities Act.

Fourth, in a patriarchal society, where compulsory heterosexuality and control over a woman's sexuality are the norm, the position of lesbians is inextricably linked to the status of women in society. Regardless of sexual orientation, a woman's sexual freedom is often predicated on her economic independence. In India, women's sexual choices are already constricted. Recent studies (see Jaiswal 1999) have shown that women report a higher incidence of domestic violence resulting from issues relating to sexual relations, particularly their refusal of sexual contact.

In such a hetero-patriarchal context then, for a lesbian to assert her sexuality becomes difficult, even dangerous. A woman who has an intimate sexual relationship with another woman implicitly challenges male control over her sexual life, and is often the target of violent misogyny. This is not to say that other women do not face misogynist violence, but to state that when lesbian women 'transgress' the patriarchal boundaries on sexuality, the *reason* for violence differs.

The violence that lesbian women experience is gender violence—not only because they are women, but also because it is specifically directed towards controlling their sexual autonomy. Freedom from violence for lesbians is, therefore, inextricably linked to the issue of sexual autonomy for *all* women.

RESEARCH OBJECTIVES

The main objectives of the study on violence against lesbians were to:

1. Understand the nature of the violence (physical, emotional, mental and sexual) experienced by lesbian women, in domestic, institutional and social contexts.
2. Understand the impact of such violence on lesbians.
3. Explore the perceptions and knowledge of mental health practitioners (MHPs) about violence against lesbians
4. Understand the therapeutic interventions of MHPs with lesbians.

The decision to focus on the specific institutional context of mental health (objectives 3 and 4) was made with the intent, understanding the situations

in which lesbians sought mental health care and to understand the knowledge, attitudes and interventions of MHPs in such situations. In both cases,
the purpose was to examine the extent to which the situations and the
interventions were violent.

RESEARCH METHODOLOGY

In the Indian context of sexuality, when one considers that there is no
recognised language to talk about women's sexuality in general, let alone
lesbian sexuality, uncovering the textures, connections and the layers of
overlap between these arenas becomes an even more complex task.

The research methodology of this study is situated in a feminist standpoint epistemology. It is informed by the principle that who you are and
where you are situated makes a difference to your point of view and consequently the research or knowledge you produce. A primary principle of
feminist research is to make transparent all aspects of the research process—
the whys, hows and whos. Related to this is the principle of self-reflexivity,
that is, considering how the first decisions influenced the research process
itself.

So, we take the risk—not only 'public' (as professional researchers, liable
to be charged with 'bias'), but also 'personal'— when we state that we bring
to this research our identity as lesbian and bisexual activists. The choice and
design of the research itself was propelled by our own life-experiences, and
by our concern about the distress we have seen among women who were
attracted to women. In particular, the rising trend of lesbian couple suicides
evoked a strong response. This research is then part of our ongoing search
for a language and constructs to articulate a subjugated experience—first to
ourselves, but also to the 'public'.

As Violi (1992) argues:

> we need to produce for ourselves our own social and collective forms of self-
> representation, and to make visible a different, alternative, social and cultural
> order within which to define our identity and subjectivity. In that sense, we are
> seeking to transform private knowledge into a more publicly based resistance, or
> at least a diversification and undermining of hegemony. The challenge is to
> remain sensitive to the diversity, given the power of the hegemony (Patrizia Violi,
> cited in Edwards and Ribbens 1998: 13).

'Who' we are and 'why' we chose this research impacted on the 'how', both
in designing the methods and in the negotiation of the 'personal' and the

'public' in different components of the study. Central to the 'how' was the principle of self-reflexivity.

RESEARCH DESIGN

This study is part of a larger research project on violence against women in Maharashtra conducted at the Tata Institute of Social Sciences. In order to address the two sets of research questions on lesbians and MHPs, the research was designed with three components, and generated four data sets.

Research Component	Location	Data Set Generated
1 Semi-structured interviews of MHPs	Mumbai	1. MHP (22) views, knowledge and interventions 2. Lesbian client profiles (70)
2 Structured questionnaires for lesbians	Mumbai, Pune, Delhi, Kolkata	3. Quantitative data (50 women)
3 In-depth interviews of lesbians	Maharashtra	4. Narratives (8 women)

The semi-structured interviews of MHPs were expected to generate information about their views, knowledge and interventions; as well as secondary data about the experiences of violence by the larger universe of lesbian women. With the MHPs, the interviewer's self-presentation was as a professional researcher rather than as lesbian, since we thought it would make the MHPs more open in their responses. The other two components of the research had lesbian informants. The structured questionnaires were expected to illuminate questions about the nature and scale of violence experienced, while the in-depth interviews were expected to provide an insight into patterns of violence.

Our identity as lesbian activists was a point of entry with other lesbian women for the second and third research components, that is, the structured questionnaires and the in-depth interviews. We have been members of Stree Sangam (a collective for women who love women) and have been in contact with a network of lesbian organisations in Pune, Delhi and Kolkata. Our status as 'insiders' of the lesbian community enabled us to contact lesbian participants for the study from this network. To an 'outsider', the issues of confidentiality and trust would have rendered this group invisible and inaccessible. Therefore, a key issue was sensitivity to maintaining their confidentiality,[3] while simultaneously ensuring that the diversity of their experiences was represented (as the quote by Violi above recommends) without being exoticised or objectified.

EMERGENT ISSUES

Triangulating the inter-connections between the three components of this study, we identified the following key issues in understanding the nature of violence against lesbians.

Silence

Silence emerged as a central concept in defining violence faced by lesbian women. It represents the invisible bulk of the 'iceberg' of violence. The normative presumption of heterosexuality is an epistemic violence that ensures the absence of knowledge of the realities of lesbian existence.

For the lesbian woman, silence can reflect three different possibilities. First, she may not have acknowledged the possibility of being lesbian to her self. The two women who were identified as 'latent lesbians' by two of the MHPs would perhaps be examples of this. Second, women may experience internal conflict as they struggle to reconcile their desire with the social prohibitions on it. Third, they may acknowledge their identity to themselves, but choose to suppress the expression of sexual identity due to fear of violence. All possibilities reflect the socially inscribed absence of choice. In the third possibility, women may choose silence to maintain their privacy. This silence, however, can only be a meaningful 'individual choice' if it is made in a context of freedom from fear of violent consequences.

For the people she interacts with, silence could again reflect three possible types of interaction. The first possibility is their lack of knowledge about lesbian existence/sexuality. In the second, the person may know but tolerate (is silent about) the woman's sexuality. This may be because the relationship does not require further engagement on this issue, as reflected in one of the narratives about a work relationship. This form of silence needs to be differentiated from the third possibility, where the person denies or ignores the woman's expression because the person feels that such expression is 'wrong'. Categorising these acts of silent hostility as violence unpacks the grey area of silence masquerading as tolerance or acceptance. Both the narrative and the quantitative data clearly established a large terrain for silent hostility, which had severe emotional consequences for the women. In the survey, the maximum incidence of emotional violence in the family was in acts of denial/ silent hostility. The damage caused by silence is personal (internal conflicts, loss of self-esteem and loss of relationships) and, therefore, invisible. Indeed, the depth of this damage was only apparent through the detailed analysis of the narrative data. There was a strong convergence in all three data sets of suicidal ideation among lesbians. The research design, however, had not adequately probed the nature and extent of this ideation, that is, what the reasons were, and whether the ideation had led to suicide attempts.

Family

The arena of maximum violence (of all types) for women was the family. This was clearly established in all three components of the study. In the survey, 77 per cent of the women who experienced violence (30 out of 39) indicated the family as the domain for incidence of violence. This is not surprising, given the central role of the family in Indian society and the patriarchal familial control exerted on a woman's sexuality, mobility and access to resources. The form of control exerted by the family lies in a continuum between silent and punitive, and depends on the degree of disclosure and the nature of the existing relationship.

When a woman's lesbian identity is explicitly disclosed (forcibly or voluntarily), the family's reaction may be accepting or not. Emotional violence forms the foundation of the family's non-acceptance of the woman's lesbian identity and their attempt to control her. There is a convergence of all three data sets to indicate that the family would keep the fact that she is lesbian a secret from the outside world due to the associated shame and stigma.

Non-acceptance can extend to more directly physical violence, including beating, imprisonment, and even remedial action such as shock therapy. However, when the woman seeks external help to counter this physical violence, the family retaliates by entailing the support of social institutions— the police, mental health professionals, religious leaders, and so on. In many cases of explicit violence, the woman is forced to choose between her family/ home and her partner/orientation. The consequence of such a choice is a loss for the woman. In many cases, refusal to give up her orientation results in eviction from her family—physical and emotional. This is corroborated in both the questionnaire and the narrative reports, where the termination of abuse occurred with the woman compelled to leave her home and/or sever relations with her family.

Fear of the loss of family and fear of violent consequences underlay many of the choices that lesbian women made, particularly those related to suppressing identity, or disclosing it in non-explicit ways. In the latter case, actively violent engagements may not occur, but the family is silently hostile, which then enforces her silence, and erodes her sense of self.

Thus, this research clearly establishes the family as the critical domain for the enforcement of coercive control over a woman's sexuality. There are few instances where the family has accepted and supported the woman, evidenced in both the quantitative and narrative data.

Cycles of Violence

The transitions from violence to ignoring, tolerance or acceptance occur over a period, and can be tracked through cycles of violence. Within a domain, a woman constantly negotiates the disclosure of her sexuality and the violence (real or feared) experienced. The consequences of disclosure may start with violence and shift to silent hostility when the woman refuses to submit to the coercion. It is rare for a cycle that begins in violence to end in acceptance. None of the narratives indicated this, and only three of the 39 women in the survey who experienced abusive reactions indicated that the termination of abuse was due to acceptance. Reaction cycles may also start with silent hostility or denial and shift to acceptance, and in this process, acceptance can be facilitated by exposure to the reality of lesbian existence, as some of the narratives demonstrate. Also, a couple of MHPs have facilitated acceptance through family counselling to help parents come to terms with their daughter's lesbian identity.

Institutional Violence

The violent consequences of the prohibitions on homosexuality encoded in religious, legal and mental health institutions were clearly established in this study. Regardless of the woman's religious beliefs, some of the narratives clearly pointed to the use of religious prohibitions by others to justify their intolerant or hostile reactions to a woman's disclosure of lesbian identity.

Devout women from religious traditions (such as Islam and Christianity) with explicit condemnation of homosexuality might experience greater internal conflict than women who do not practise their religion. A significantly high proportion of the women (66 per cent) did not practise their religion. Of the nine women from Judeo-Christian traditions, only one practised her religion. However, the survey design did not probe further to establish if there was a connection between absence of religious practice and internal conflict about homosexuality and religion.

Violence and coercion that began in the family was often sought to be reinforced through referral to one or several of social institutions, particularly the police or mental health professionals. The role of the police has been more directly coercive as evidenced in the narrative data of four women. The family was responsible for invoking police assistance to control three women who were interviewed. In each instance, the police attempted to separate the woman from her partner by subjecting her to public ridicule, threats, taunts and even by the fabrication of a case under Section 377.

Mental health professionals are aware that homosexuality is no longer considered an abnormality, but there are grey areas of uneasiness and judgement about it that is reflected in the public awareness. Homosexuality is still seen as an abnormality and therapy is seen as a 'cure'. There was a strong convergence of all three data sets on this. In the lesbian client profiles, 21 per cent of the women had been forced by family to visit the MHPs in order to change their sexual orientation. In the survey, 11 women (22 per cent of the sample) were faced with allegations of abnormality, and five were forced into psychiatric treatment of abnormality. From the narrative data, there is one woman's narrative which recounts her mother's attempt to subject her to shock therapy while another woman had experienced several months of aversive shock therapy at a mental health institution. However, mental health interventions can, unlike the previous two institutional interventions, also be positive. Several of the MHPs interviewed had counselled their clients through their emotions of confusion, guilt, shame to greater self-acceptance, and as mentioned, a couple even engaged in counselling their families towards acceptance.

Transgender Issues

Gender Identity Disorder (GID) comprises an area of diagnostic classification where the internal conflict of lesbian women plays out with maximal dissonance. All the women in the lesbian client profiles who wanted sex reassignment surgery (SRS) were evaluated as not meeting the GID criteria. Two sets of narratives offer glimpses of the struggle women endure in order to accommodate their desire for women within the rigid demarcation of normative gender and (hetero) sexual roles. For one woman, the accommodation was through adopting a male gender identity without considering SRS. For the other, it was through adopting a transsexual identity and considering SRS. Both accommodations necessitate some degree of self-denial and violence towards their bodies. The MHP's lack of clarity on GID exclusion criteria implies that such women will perhaps be less likely to receive the support they need in order to reach self-acceptance of their lesbian identity.

Consequences and Resistance

The consequences of violence for lesbian women apparent in the narrative and quantitative data could be described at three levels:

Personal—although the incidence of physical battering, and incarceration was apparent in both data sets, it was in the narrative data set that it became clear that the emotional consequences of fear, guilt, shame, anxiety and depression were much more significant for the women, and could, in some cases, lead to suicidal ideation.

Social—women faced the loss of relationships with family and friends, public stigma and ridicule, and the censure of social institutions

Economic—eviction from the home, severance of family financial support, loss of job, and so on.

However, even women who experienced extremely adverse consequences of physical violence, eviction from family and home, or public shame and censure were persistent in their resistance, and their attempts to seek support and validation. Significantly, <u>none</u> of the women in the study expressed a wish to change their desire for women.

NOTES

1. For instance, the analytical frameworks for rape in Brownmiller (1975) or Lenore Walker's (1984) 'Cycle of Violence' framework for battered women would *not* be adequate or appropriate to examine the violence faced by lesbian women.
2. See Ruth Vanita and Saleem Kidwai (2000) for a rich documentation of these traditions.
3. All names and identifying information of participants have been changed to protect confidentiality.

REFERENCES

Brownmiller, S. 1975, *Against Our Will: Men, Women and Rape*. Harmondsworth: Penguin.

Edwards, Rosalind and Jane Ribbens. 1998, 'Living on the Edges—Public Knowledge, Private Lives, Personal Experience', in *Feminist Dilemmas in Qualitative Research*. London: Sage Publications.

Vanita, Ruth and Saleem Kidwai. 2000, *Same-sex Love in India: Readings from Literature and History*. Basingstoke: Macmillan.

Walker, Lenore. 1984, *The Battered Woman*. New York: Harper Colophon Books.

Jaiswal, Surinder. 1999, *Examining Health Records for Evidence of Domestic Violence: A Research Study in Maharashtra*. Mumbai: Department of MPSW, TISS, ICRW.

11

Complicating Gender
Rights of Transsexuals in India

Ashwini Sukthankar

 I began writing this article on transsexual rights inspired by the impulse to critique the elements of the campaign for achieving those rights, as we understood them. I proposed to write as a feminist, concerned that sex reassignment surgery reified the rigid definitions of gender—what it means to be a man or a woman—that feminists had always sought to question. I thought to write as a lesbian activist, worried that a transsexual rights movement in India would only aggravate the phenomenon where two women seeking to make a life together are encouraged to believe that one must metamorphose into a man in order for the relationship to be acceptable or recognisable to society.

I worried about the excessive importance given to the expertise of medical specialists who would have the right to decide whether those seeking the sex reassignment were 'man enough' or 'woman enough', subordinating the role of the individual self, and eroding the range of available modes of gender expression in this realm. And I worried about the ways in which the privilege of such expert opinions served the commercial interests of a medical and pharmaceutical establishment that stood to make a fortune from the sale of hormones and surgical procedures.

However, as a result of my conversations with Satya, who spoke from his perspective as a female-to-male (FTM) transsexual person currently living in Pune, and with Famila, a hijra person living in Bangalore, I was forced to acknowledge that the transsexual rights discourse that I had researched and read about in the abstract, and had sought to critique through this article, functioned as the proverbial straw man in terms of the struggles around sex assignment (and sex reassignment), in the specific contexts that either of these activists described. As a preliminary matter then, it must be stated that, at times, the roster of transsexual rights that I address here is portrayed as unfairly monolithic, and I rely heavily on the foregrounding of the voices of Famila and Satya to serve as the counterpoint.

Thus, even before I begin to discuss the pros and cons of a right to have either the state or private health insurance companies pay for sex reassignment surgery or a right to marry—central elements of the transsexual rights struggles in the West—it should be stated that both Satya and Famila have their own critiques of the privileging of such struggles in terms of their own lives and experiences. Both seem to share a conviction that it would be premature to engage in critique, however, given that there is nothing concrete to critique: not only is there no consensus within the community regarding such rights, but more importantly, 'the community' itself is still a fledgling and contentious proposition.

As Satya cautions:

> There is no community, no critical mass of trans people coming together. It's so nascent, there's no context for discussing transsexual rights. In Pune, we've put together a space called 'Sampurna', which is an informal network of trans people—there are three FTM and one MTF [male to female] who are a constant presence, and some other MTFs who float in and out. But even the connections between MTF and FTM people are initial. And the connections between hijra space and trans space are very initial. The hijra identity has a historicity, it's culturally located. Trans identity is urban, and has a strong class component. With respect to hijras, there are traditional ways and traditional rituals that are operative.

DEFINING COMMUNITY

Famila, a member of Vividha, a collective of sexuality minorities, expresses a similar point of view in terms of the difficulty of naming and defining a shared community with a shared agenda:

> The hijra discourse is very different from the discourse of transgender or transsexual persons. There are differences of class, of language, of the kinds of discrimination, harassment and violations faced. For me, when I think of transgender or transsexual persons, what comes to my mind is people who have greater access to information and have a very different class privilege. For hijras, that's not the case—lots of us are not English speaking. And, unlike many transsexuals who get expensive surgery and can pass as men or women, lots of hijras are very easily recognizable as hijras.

While there might not be commonality in terms of identity, Famila asserted that allegiances could and should happen:

> Vividha [a shared space for all sexuality minorities] is one way of doing it. Originally, among the hijra community, talking about LGBT issues, our elders would say, 'what is all this rubbish?' But that is changing. More and more, we can tell our elders: just as we have our sexuality, our gender expression, they have theirs.

Both Satya and Famila were very clear about limiting the scope of their analysis to their particular geographic locations in Pune and Bangalore respectively. A nationwide campaign for rights demanded from the state, such as those common in the West, is still a distant prospect. That is not to say that certain rights claims, such as demands for anti-discrimination legislation or protections against hate crimes, do not have a visceral appeal across geographic context or identity category. In Washington, D.C., where I currently live, an MTF transsexual was recently murdered. One of her clients shot her, after she had performed oral sex on him in exchange for money, in what he claimed was a moment of blind panic and disgust at the discovery that she was genetically male (Chibarro 2003: 1). In Bangalore in 2004, a hijra named Chandni burned to death. The man widely acknowledged by her friends and family as her husband claimed that she had killed herself when he discovered that she was genetically male and rejected her; local activists assert that he murdered her (*Deccan Herald*, 8 December 2002).

As a testament to the ease with which certain sexualities can be construed as exploitable and disposable in very different cultural contexts, or, in at least one of the two cases as a comment on the state's general sympathy for criminal defendants who use 'gay panic' or 'trans panic' as an excuse after acts of extreme violence on marginal bodies, the stories tend to provoke empathy and familiarity, or even identification among all of us whose sexual expression places us outside a given mainstream.

Famila's proposal in terms of a common agenda with lesbians, gays, bisexuals and others—'anti-discriminatory laws, a committee set up by the state to look specifically at sexuality minorities and not just hijras to look at violations of our human rights by the state'—recognised this. 'In spite of our differences, there are some commonalities. And I still believe that a shared movement is the only way out, whatever may happen, with all of us coming together.' Satya agreed that discrimination and violence were the primary areas of overlap.

Both acknowledged, however, that appeals to the state are not devoid of risk. Neither subscribed to the crude distinction between negative rights (roughly defined as freedom from state intervention) and positive rights (equally roughly defined as demands for state intervention). Rather, they recognised that, as Satya noted, whether the issue was one of seeking the decriminalisation of sodomy or, on the other hand, active involvement by the state to enhance the social and political representation of sexual minorities through mechanisms such as reservation, 'the control of the nation-state over the body is what must be addressed'. This did not lead, analytically, to the assertion that the state should take no position on gender identity—a policy that would merely serve to reinforce a highly unequal status quo. On the contrary, what Satya called 'the practicality issues like reservation, the purpose of which is to give voice to what has been silenced', made it imperative that 'the law [...] elaborate on the question of what it means to be subordinated through the man/woman binary'.

WOMEN VIS-À-VIS TRANSSEXUALS?

While claims for reservation for transsexuals and/or hijras in various realms of the social and political process are still in their infancy, I imagine that women will not be unanimous in their support of such a proposal. Some lesbians in the Indian context have been (or are) reluctant to open up their space to either FTMs or MTFs who relate to women, citing, for example, that the former have male privilege and a certain freedom from discrimination in public space and in their relationships, and noting that the latter, socialised as men, cannot understand the experience of growing up female. Transsexuals, MTF and hijras may be accused of certain opportunism, of enjoying the pleasures of feminine gender and sexual expression while continuing to assert their 'birthright' as men in terms of the inheritance of family property, for example.

While such suspicions may be overcome over time, the more material obstacle—the issue of whether the claims of hijras and/or transsexual people to reservations will mean a further drain on resources already spread thin among women may well linger, and Famila's tentative proposal for reservations for hijras as 'a percentage within the category of women' has the potential to cause conflict. Women's groups were divided in their response to the case of Kamla Jaan, former mayor of Katni, Madhya Pradesh, who was removed from office by the High Court in January on the logic that the position was reserved for a woman, and she was not a woman (BBC World Online, 29 August 2002).

The resistance to alliances between transsexual people/hijras and the women's movement will not be entirely from the side of the latter, as Famila admits: 'The hijra community is a reflection of the heterosexual, patriarchal system, whether we like to admit it or not. We have to work to break those patterns. I, and some others, are trying to do that, but it is a very difficult task.'

For both Satya and Famila, the issue of state control over bodies and choices created common ground beyond the women's movement as a whole. As Satya pointed out, 'this is an area of commonality not just with LGBTMNOPQRST people, but also with sex workers: state intervention in the issue of what I choose to do with my body is the larger issue.' For Famila, the connection between the struggle of hijras and that of women sex workers was not just a philosophical one, but very material. She says:

> The major allies for us here are women sex workers. It is about the choice to do whatever you want, but it is also about economic struggle—for most hijras in Bangalore, it is our only source of income. Many don't possess the skills to go into the mainstream and take up mainstream jobs, and there is also discrimination and lack of opportunity.

From this perspective, then, it would be useful to approach the priorities of transsexual rights struggles in the West. One of the efforts that has been receiving significant press coverage recently is the United Kingdom's Gender Recognition Bill. Urged on Parliament in part because of a British case that was brought to the European Court of Human Rights, the Bill gives transsexuals the right to re-register their gender on birth certificates and other documents predating their gender transition, and gives them the right to marry in their 'true gender'.

SEARCHING FOR GENDER IDENTITY

The notion of transsexuals as subject to an authentic, immutable and externally imposed gender identity which underlies this proposal was in discussions sponsored by, for example, the Lord Chancellor's Department, which supported the Bill by dissociating transsexual people both from gender performance and from notions of choice. The statement, tellingly stated, in part, 'It [transsexualism] has nothing to do with drag queens [...] Transsexual people do not choose their gender identity. Transsexualism is an overpowering sense of different gender identity' (The Lord Chancellor's Department). The resistance to a language of choice, or even of gender identity as something in flux over an individual's lifetime, is a central element of the strategy adopted by many activist groups in the United States as well.

The International Conference on Transgender Law and Employment Policy asserted that:

There is a broad consensus among medical researchers that transgenderism is rooted in complex biological factors that are fixed at birth. This research confirms what transgendered people know and experience on a much more personal basis: being transgendered is not a choice nor a 'lifestyle,' but a difficult, uninvited challenge (International Conference on Transgender Law and Employment Policy 1997: 1).

There are three central themes here that each deserved to be addressed—the statement that gender identity is fixed at birth; the assertion of a right to marry based on 'true' gender identity; the deference to medical professionals in determining the realities of a community and of the individuals within it.

Both Satya and Famila were critical of arguments denying the instability of gender identity and of gender categories. As Satya pointed out, 'gender identity, even within the reality of one person, can shift all the time within a lifetime. The question should be, how should the law reflect that lived reality?' Given this, campaigns to allow for the change of an individual's birth certificate to reflect post-operative gender appear somewhat disingenuous: 'This is invisibilising the reality of what was at a certain point in time. While there is some sense of security to be gained from this, I still believe the change should be a transparent process.' For Famila, the proposal ran counter to her sense of gender categories as multiple and fluid. 'Among hijras, not everyone wants to be recognised as a woman,' she pointed out. 'Many want to be recognised as a third gender category.' According to Famila, relying on an argument linking a claim for rights to the assertion that the individual's condition is involuntary is often symptomatic of political naïveté, or merely the lack of information or access to a community:

I believe there should be a right of free choice, though not many in the hijra community would agree with me. But a few years ago, I too would argue that way: I was born like this, and it is not my fault. But I have changed: knowing about different issues, knowing other people and their struggles added up to this, and now I say, this is who I choose to be. The argument that we are 'born that way' makes us weak: I felt it was not coming from me, but fear made me say that. Even today, it is not easy. When I would say I was born this way, automatically I would get sympathy. But when I say I choose to be this way, people comment, 'Today you choose to be this, tomorrow what will come next?'

The issue of the medicalisation of transsexual identities is a more fraught one, for a number of reasons that follow analytically from the preceding discussion. Campaigns that seek to have the state or private health insurance companies cover the costs of surgery tend to posit that birth status is a medical disability to be corrected through cosmetic, surgical and chemical interventions. This is problematic for me on multiple levels.

From a philosophical perspective, what would it mean to support an agenda that understands gender identity as comfort and discomfort along the axis of normal and abnormal, and prioritises the correction of the 'problem' through expensive and time-consuming medical processes? Should we not consider the possibility that a more appropriate approach might be to question the prevalent understanding of gender-deviant bodies as a problem, to be addressed through group political action rather than individual surgery? Granted, there is something both paternalistic and condescending about the question when posed that way and in the abstract, and that is nowhere more clear than when the question is placed in the context of the lives and experiences of Satya or Famila, whose perspective on surgical alternatives clearly anticipates such critique, as we shall see. However, it would be worth remembering that the right, when stated in the abstract, is as over-inclusive and under-inclusive as its critique: to state, as the International Bill of Gender Rights does, that 'All human beings have the right to control their bodies, which includes the right to change their bodies cosmetically, chemically, or surgically, so as to express a self-defined gender identity' (Inernational Conference on Transgender Law and Employment Policy 1995), is to deny that public policy might have any role to play in the shaping or limiting of such an absolute right.

As a secondary step, even if one were to consider that regulation as appropriate, whether the gatekeepers to sex reassignment are private entities seeking profit and/or recognition, such as doctors and psychiatrists, or the state with its own agenda of control, or hijra community elders who might not represent the dynamic and varied interests of the individuals within the collective, it seems fair to say that caution is still warranted. From a materialist perspective, I question demands in the West that the state (or private health insurance) pay for the cost of sex reassignment, from the perspective of the allocation of resources. It is a zero-sum game, and without a sustained situation-specific analysis of which projects in the realm of sexuality, health and gender will have to be cut back to pay for these measures. It is for these reasons that I experience reluctance in supporting the struggle in the abstract.

Without a perspective on how the discourse of disability/normalcy that sustains these claims affects the claims of other people attempting to navigate non-mainstream paths through the terrain of gender, the campaign can seem narrow in its appeal. For example, an article posted on the website of the

British transsexual rights group Press for Change explains how the author persuaded his health authority to pay for genital surgery in the following terms:

> I have wanted to have lower surgery for quite a while now, mainly so that I can pee standing up. I don't feel complete without being able to function in this way. I also feel sad and frustrated that I cannot show my 3 year old son how to stand and pee ('How I Challenged my Health Authority's Policy on Funding Surgery').

For the lesbian parents or single mothers of male children, this argument could feel distinctly self-indulgent.

As noted before, however, Satya and Famila anticipate many of these critiques in framing a perspective on medical intervention. To begin with, many of the critiques seem premature, since the primary concern, on the part of both activists, is the issue of information. Satya argues:

> There is a need for an interface with the medical community. There is no information, and there is no accountability. The medical community won't divulge any information, and won't discuss any international code of conduct, such as that put forward by the Harry Benjamin Institute [The Harry Benjamin International Gender Dysphoria Association, February 2001] There are no gender clinics, even in teaching hospitals—we have to coordinate between the various departments ourselves.

Ultimately, for Satya, supporting the transsexual right to surgery means supporting the feminist principle that 'biology is not destiny'. For me, in terms of this debate, the principle would stand for the proposition that just as the equation of female bodies with femininity, motherhood and so on was open to challenge, it should be as much of a goal for us to assert that femininity can be claimed in spite of the body. Satya, however, noted with respect to the principle:

> It's very interesting from the trans perspective—because no one, whether FTM or MTF, can achieve the kind of manhood or womanhood, respectively, that comes from hetero-patriarchy. In the most tangible sense, as an FTM, you can never produce your own sperm! What would it take away from a genetic man, in terms of manhood, if that were the case? And for an MTF, you can never be childbearing—and that's a central definition of the hetero-normative definition of 'woman'.

It is noteworthy that a 1980 law in Germany governing the recognition of transsexuals requires that post-operative transsexuals seeking rights under the law be non-reproductive—in terms of capacity, not choice!

Famila locates her response to the critique that transsexuals and hijras are forced to buy into mainstream definitions of gender by pointing to the example of beauty pageants which, she argues, function very differently in the hijra context:

> I think the whole concept of beauty is very fine. For one thing, everybody should be allowed to beautify themselves; secondly, I very much oppose the standardisation of beauty. This year in hijra *habba* [a festival held in Bangalore on 3 September 2003], there is such an event, but we're calling it a self-expression event, not a pageant.

Through events such as these, Famila asserted, people at large, not just hijras, would have to engage with the notion that there is a difference between the celebration of beauty and the proposition that there can only be a single definition of what it is.

The right to marry, for transsexuals, is probably the issue that has threatened to divide lesbian, gay and bisexual rights activists and transsexual rights activists in the West. Whether the latter are opposed to LGBT marriage as a campaign, expressing resistance to any that would replicate hetero-patriarchal structures, or whether they have a deep commitment to same-sex marriage as a goal, they will nevertheless be disturbed by the recognition that most legislators who are willing to support 'right to marry' laws for transsexuals are, as Stephen Wittle notes, terrified about 'inadvertently opening the way to same-sex marriage' (Wittle 1996), and are determined to frame the argument in a way that would preclude that possibility. It is not that simple, of course. As activists in the West have pointed out, positions on the same-sex marriage debate will be complicated and challenged, not only by the 'same-sex marriage' between 'Tom and "Sam, formerly known as Susie"' (the category of marriages that the right-to-marry legislation is designed to promote) but by the marriage of 'Tom and "Susie, born as Sam"' which the legislation can do nothing to prevent (Coombs 1997: 4). While Satya does take a position:

> state privileges should be available to anyone who wants them. . . . There are many problems with marriage, but even if one has a critique of monogamy and hetero-patriarchy, an individual should be able to function as a free agent. Why should some have access and others not?

He is also left with questions:

> Marriage as an institution is constructed in a very strategic way—it entails commitments where, if you violate them, there are consequences. If things break

down, there is recourse to a third party. Should there be a third party? Should it be the state? The community? Which community? We have to acknowledge that relationships are intertwined with the real world, and that there are questions of insurance, joint loans, child custody that need to be resolved when a relationship ends.

Ultimately, this essay ends as a question also. Transsexual rights could be located at any conceivable point on a spectrum. We could experience and express panic that a stated right to medical intervention, to surgery, to the refashioning of the self and of the body, can only lead relentlessly down a slippery slope to the validation of claims in favour of voluntary amputation, for example, where individuals with healthy limbs seek to have them removed because they have always imagined themselves absent a left leg or a right arm. Or, on the other hand, we could acknowledge that everyone wrestles with gender to some degree, and frame gender rights as 'universal rights which can be claimed and exercised by every human being', rather than 'special rights applicable to a particular interest group', as stated in the Prologue of the International Bill of Gender Rights Conference on Transgender Law and Employment Policy. The debate requires that we all accept that we have a stake in the outcome.

REFERENCES

Chibarro, Lou. 2003, 'District Man Arrested in Second Trans Murder', *Washington Blade*, 29 August.

Deccan Herald. 2002, 'Impartial Probe into Hijra's Death Sought', 8 December.

BBC World Online. 2002, 'India's First Eunuch Mayor Unseated', 29 August, Hyperlink: 'http://news.bbc.co.uk/2/hi/south_asia/2224164.stm'.

The Lord Chancellor's Department. 'Government Policy towards Transsexual', No. 6, Hyperlink: 'http://www.lcd.gov.uk/constitution/transsex/policy.htm'.

International Conference on Transgender Law and Employment Policy. 1995, 'The Right to Control and Change One's Body', In the International Bill of Gender Rights, Formulated by the International Conference on Transgender Law and Employment Policy, 17 June, Hyperlink: 'http://www.altsex.org/transgender/ibgr.html'.

————. 1997, 'Discrimination Against Transgendered People in America', *National Journal of Sexual Orientation Law*, Vol. 3, No. 1.

'How I Challenged my Health Authority's Policy on Funding Surgery', Hyperlink: 'http://www.pfc.org.uk/medical/fundlng.htm'.

The Harry Benjamin International Gender Dysphoria Association. 2001, 'Standards of Care for Gender Identity Disorders, Sixth Version', Hyperlink: http://www.hbigda.org/socv6.html.

Wittle, Stephen. 1996, 'Legislating for Transsexual Rights: A Prescriptive Form', 17 May, Hyperlink: 'http://www.pfc.org.uk/legal/whittle3.htm'.

Coombs, Mary. 1997, 'Transgenderism and Sexual Orientation: More than a Marriage of Convenience', *The National Journal of Sexual Orientation Law*, Vol. 3, No. 1. Available at http://www.ibiblio.org/gaylaw.

12
Queering Kerala*†
Reflections on Sahayatrika

Deepa V.N.

MY GENDER MY RIGHT *At the time of writing this essay, two women's photos have been widely publicised in the Kerala media. They have been described as lesbians and accused of involvement in drug deals and sex trafficking. Although these women deny a romantic relationship, and vehemently oppose the other accusations, they fight for the right to live together as companions in the face of opposition from their families. Recently an activist friend lost her flat for sheltering these women, partly as a result of the media publicity; and the women themselves struggle to find the housing and employment they require to live together independently.*

As I reflect upon Sahayatrika, as an attempt to develop a support network for lesbian and bisexual women in Kerala, I grapple with questions about the advantages and pitfalls of visibility. The increasing media representations and visibility on the subjects of lesbians and other sexuality minorities exists alongside deep-rooted prejudice and social hostility; and for those of us trying to develop a sexual minority politics in this state (and for those who are not, but are still affected by its consequences) we must think about how to negotiate the future. As someone who was fundamentally involved in designing and implementing this project, I propose in this essay to reflect upon what Sahayatrika was and was not, what it achieved in such a situation and what it did not. It is hoped that the experience of Sahayatrika might provide some lessons and points to ponder for further struggles and endeavours.

* This essay was completed in March 2004. The situation in Kerala is somewhat different now.
† Special thanks to Reshma Bharadwaraj, Aryan Krishnan and Dr Jayasree for their many debates and discussions, which contributed to some of the ideas in this essay.

The Sahayatrika Project was problematic by almost every index of political correctness. It was a political initiative that was made possible through foreign funding—in our most active period, we operated through a 10-month grant from an international agency concerned specifically with sexuality minority issues. It was coordinated by a non-resident Indian (myself) whose major life experiences and political experiences were with gay/lesbian communities in the West—a profoundly different scenario from both the emerging sexuality minority activism in India and the cultural specificities of 'queer' life in Kerala. Sahayatrika itself came to be perceived as representing a community and a movement (one tabloid newspaper estimated our organisation membership as being 1,000-women strong!) when in fact our contacts with women were sometimes tenuous and fleeting. This tenuous community had an invisible spokeswoman with a fake name and dubious identity—'Devaki Menon'—a pseudonym which sometimes represents myself and sometimes Sahayatrika workers collectively.

If at all Sahayatrika has been successful in its efforts to support women-loving-women in Kerala and to raise awareness about their marginalisation, this is above all because it sought to address the needs of a real and living—though mostly hidden—population. In this essay, I use terms like 'lesbian and bisexual', 'women-loving-women' and 'women with same-sex attractions' to cover a whole range of existences, from those who call themselves 'lesbian' to those who have still never heard of the word. There are women who maintain relationships, women who suppress their orientations and get married, and women who live in isolation from others who are like them. There are women who commit suicide, and there are women who survive.

My own involvement with Sahayatrika was rooted in my experiences as a sexuality minority in another country, and in my consciousness of friends in Kerala who were struggling. And maybe Kerala itself was ripe for another social experiment. Newspaper stories about lesbian suicides had been reported in the press for several years and a handful of people sought to draw attention to this. Some renegade feminists and social activists were also, controversially, supporting marginalised sexuality issues like sex workers' rights and were committed to assisting any emerging sexuality minority movement. Moreover, all over India, especially in the urban centres, there was increased activism and visibility by queer groups who sought for the recognition of sexuality minority rights as legitimate social issues. The cynical might say that the publicity that Sahayatrika has received has also been propelled by the commodification and hyper-sexualisation of lesbian identity, especially as it has been constructed by tabloid papers, internet porn, blue films, and other aspects of popular culture and media. And this is also true. Actually any sexuality minority group (or individual) in Kerala will be subjected to a certain type of sexualisation and harassment upon entry into the public sphere—and in the case of women-loving-women, this tends to collude with already existing gender dynamics of violence and control. In this essay, as I suggested earlier, I hope to explore how those of us trying to develop a lesbian politics or sexuality minority politics can negotiate these tensions, as we strive to become social, political, and sexual subjects and defy our own objectification.

PARADOXES OF VISIBILITY AND IDENTITY

The major goals of Sahayatrika were (a) to create a support network for women with same-sex attractions and to ensure that counselling and advocacy were available to them, (b) to document the marginalisation of lesbian/bisexual women in Kerala, through incidents of suicide and other human rights abuses, and (c) to raise public awareness about the issues faced by women-loving-women and other sexuality minorities, through talks, workshops and media publicity.

We offered support services to women who contacted us through letter writing, e-mail and a telephone helpline; and we are at present conducting a series of fact-findings based on reports of lesbian suicide that have been appearing in local newspapers for the past few years.

The experience of working for Sahayatrika in Kerala has been very different from that of lesbian groups in the urban centres of India. Sahayatrika is not a lesbian group in its own right, unlike some groups in other cities; instead it is a helping organisation that tries to facilitate the development of a loose network of women. But we have contacts with a diversity of women which may differ from the largely urban, middle-class/upper-class make-up of lesbian groups in other parts. Our Sahayatrikas come from Hindu, Muslim, Christian, dalit and adivasi communities, in occupations ranging from school teachers to rubber tappers, from businesswomen to housewives. Our core support team is comprised of women claiming different orientations and identities. But we have a broader base of support from different activists and organisations who try to help us in different ways.

Our work has required a constant negotiation between the greater awareness and recognition that can be achieved through the public sphere, and the need for safety and privacy, both for the women we work for and for ourselves. The social conditions of living and working for sexuality rights in Kerala in fact create a series of paradoxes with regard to visibility and identity. Thus we have a publicly recognised organisation with no visible spokesperson; and a dependency on and engagement with the same media which creates more dangers for us. And in our attempts to create a greater understanding we must negotiate with a popular culture which simultaneously obsesses with lesbian identity and at the same time tries to deny its existence.

Our efforts to create supportive spaces for women to communicate demonstrate some of the advantages and disadvantages of visibility. Positive media coverage has so far been the most effective way to let women know about Sahayatrika; the majority of women approach us after reading about us, or being referred by someone else who has. To date, over 80 women have contacted our organisation through the telephone, letters, e-mail and word of mouth; and we have done follow-up or support work with at least 25 women, through the telephone or personal meetings. But for every one genuine letter or phone call we receive from a woman, we receive three or four contacts from men. While a small portion of these contacts are from gay/bisexual men (whom we support in solidarity) or from genuine well-wishers, a majority are sexual harassment calls, writers or callers sharing obscenities or sexual fantasies, or trying to use our service to arrange for sex or to meet a genuine 'lesbian'.

The invisibility of women-loving-women in daily life is countered by constructions of the 'lesbian' in the popular imagination; and a proportion of our callers seem to understand a lesbian to be, not a woman with same-sex attractions but instead a woman who will have sex with anyone. And our efforts to create safe, women-centred spaces are at risk of being overwhelmed by male sexual harassment/desire. So we do not give out our office space address or real names to initial contacts, and we take measures to protect the confidentiality of the women who approach us.

There are lesbian and bisexual women in Kerala who do not need a Sahayatrika, who prefer to be silent supporters, or approach this organisation with wariness. Some women feel that to associate with us openly might jeopardise a relationship, job or position in family/society. There is also an argument that increased lesbian visibility takes away safe spaces from women, placing public suspicion on both hidden lesbian relationships and close friendships between women. And yet the women who contact us speak of their relief in knowing that they are not alone, and tell stories of isolation, family violence, gender confusions and suicide attempts.

The women who contact Sahayatrika are located in cities and villages throughout Kerala, and more often than not they are living with families or husbands, and they contact us secretly. Because of the limitations to mobility that they face, as women who must answer to families, and sometimes because of a reluctance to become visible, most are unable to contact our office or attend a meeting. So Sahayatrika workers go to their locations and meet them when possible, and maintain contact through letters and phone. Recently we have also been making connections with women-loving-women who are less willing or able to hide, and who strive to live independently or with their partners. But this has posed a different set of problems, which I shall speak about later.

If political mobilisation is linked to people coming together in a group, especially around a shared identity, then we cannot say that there is a self-identified lesbian/bisexual women's movement in Kerala yet. For the time being, both the logistics of meeting as a collectivity and the dangers of visibility work against this. Even a group like Vaathil, which works for all sexuality minority rights, is not an identity-based group but open to every-one; as such, it gives space for queer people to choose when, where and if to 'come out'.

But sometimes seeing is believing. In the absence of visible lesbian bodies there has been the tendency to negate lesbian existence. Thus when we first tried to raise lesbian suicides as a political issue, a common response was denial: many people insisted these reports were another form of media sensationalism, and that these deaths must be due to poverty, sex rackets, anything but same-sex love. Now as both positive and negative representa-tions of lesbians are beginning to proliferate in the public sphere, there is a constant demand for us to produce these lesbian bodies, either as political spokeswomen who are willing to place their sexual identities before the tribunal of Kerala public opinion, or as the objects of research, journalism and activism. The time may be coming when more women-loving-women in Kerala choose to be visible. But in the present situation it is as likely, as the recent media furore indicates, that the women involved won't have a choice about it.

BEARING WITNESS: VOICES FROM THE MARGINS

Working for Sahayatrika, we have been privileged to receive a great many written testimonies of women-loving-women in Kerala, who survive in the margins, defying a hetero-normative and patriarchal social order. The stories I share here come from the women who write to us, though all names have been changed and quotations are paraphrased from the original letters. These narratives bear witness to some of the challenges and ordeals faced by a resisting but invisible population.

The letters don't speak only of sexual victimisation and marginalisation; sometimes they are also an assertion and celebration of lesbian existence. I still remember the first letter we got from a woman in our post box, with a green kathakali face drawn on its front page and the words 'Express yourself' (in English) written across the top. Or the young lesbian couple from a working-class background who wrote to us asking to help them to live together; across the bottom of their letter they wrote 'Love is great!' (in English) in big letters, an affirmation of their same-sex love. Or the woman-loving-woman in her forties, married with children, who wrote to assure us that 'love has no age limits'. Some women letter-writers wanted to help the organisation, offering money or assistance, and sometimes they sent us news clippings about lesbian issues. A student writing for the first time told us she had talked about Sahayatrika in her classes, as well as lesbianism. There are other women-loving-women in her classes, she wrote, who don't dare to contact us.

All of the women who have written to us must contend with the institution of marriage and compulsory heterosexuality. A small proportion of our letters come from older women, up to their mid-forties, who are often married and still trying to create a space for their same-sex desires. Some women manage to maintain same-sex relationships after marriage or even to negotiate an understanding with their husbands; but others are less satisfied. For example, one woman who was married at a young age writes that she 'hates family life', 'she wants to live with a woman companion'. Her family did not take into consideration her resistance to marriage; and now she feels trapped in a partnership in which she is unable to have sex with her husband.

The majority of our letters from women have come from a younger generation, in their early twenties or late teens, who often express an awareness that they would be pressured to marry in upcoming years. These women struggle with issues of depression and isolation. One 24-year-old who writes 'one of greatest tragedies in life is to be married', says that her parents are forcing her. She is afraid of the male species, and furthermore in love with a girl. Another computer science student writes that she thinks she is homosexual and dislikes sex with men; but all her friends are straight so she can't disclose her desires to them. She finds it 'difficult to endure a single day', and can't concentrate on her studies.

Many women who are having same-sex relationships yearn for the social legitimacy and acceptance that is given to heterosexual marriage. For example, a young woman whose family and community know about her five-year relationship with a woman her age, asks if it is possible for two women to be legally married. She writes that the couple 'doesn't want to elope or run away' but instead 'want to live in our own place with respect without people gazing gluttonously at us'. However, for the time being she and her partner are ostracised in the community, as 'Society doesn't understand us, nor the depth of our love'.

Often women who attempt to live together will have to choose between their partners and their families/communities. For example, 'Sunitha' tells the story of her partner and herself, and how they left Kerala for another state in order to be together. Their relationship started while they were students and although in the following years Sunitha tried to change her 'homosex nature' she couldn't; she discovered that she needed her friend to love her fully. When her partner's family came to know about their relationship and tried to police the young women's phone calls and letters, the pair found work in a neighbouring state and ran away.

However, Sunitha remains torn between having to choose between her lover and her family. She describes her family as worried about where she had gone, and sad that she had such a relationship. At one point the couple decided that they had caused enough trouble to their families, so they would consciously separate; but they were unable to stay apart. So the women continue to live together, but Sunitha agonises about the ways in which her decision affects her family. Who will help her in her old age, she questions, and how will society view her? And how will her sister's children view her, or her other siblings?

Women who are unable to find partners face different kinds of problems. We have several women calling us regularly, for example, who are grieving for the loss of a partner who was forced to marry. Others face the difficulties of finding reciprocal love with a woman in a hetero-patriarchal society. One student writes about how after sending a love letter to her friend, the girl mocked her, and showed the letter to others. Another expresses the frustrations of being woman-loving in an apparently straight world: 'I sometimes feel discomfort when my friends come close. I want to say words of love to them, but know that they won't reciprocate.'

At the extreme, women wrote of suicide attempts, self-harm, desire for sex-change operation or the desire to change their orientation. A 23-year-old wrote to us that, in the past two years, she has understood that she has the 'disease' known as homosexuality. She has always felt close to women and while studying, was painfully attached to female friends. After a sexual relationship with a female schoolmate who later rejected her, 'Reshme' tried to commit suicide twice but still can't forget her friend. Now she struggles with the knowledge that her father is trying to arrange her marriage, and asks to meet other women like her.

LESBIAN SUICIDES AND OTHER PROBLEMS: IN SEARCH OF A 'REMEDY'

Just a sampling of the letters Sahayatrika has received suggests many different aspects of emotional and institutional marginalisation that lesbian and bisexual women in Kerala face. Emotionally, these women are grappling with great internal difficulties which may manifest themselves in depression, self-hatred and self-harming behaviours, or physical symptoms. Socially and economically, they are constrained by the institutions of family and marriage. Some women opt to leave the family system in response, while others try to find space within family, community or even marriage for a same-sex relationship. Some women crave for societal change, such as the writer who seeks legal rights and community respect for her companion and herself. Others desire to change themselves, to change their sexual orientations through means such as self-restraint or psychiatry, or to cope with the non-conformation to gender norms by seeking sex-reassignment surgery.

Suicide may be the ultimate response to these dilemmas of difference. Many writers and callers have talked about histories of suicide attempts, or consider taking their lives as a way to end their difficulties. Moreover, although we are maintaining supportive relationships with an increasing number of women, many of those who contact us call or write once or twice, never to be heard from again. Frustratingly, we have no idea how these women are coping with the struggles they have shared.

This privatised and invisible suffering is paralleled by news stories of same-sex companions that appear with increasing frequency in the public sphere. Newspaper reports of double suicides among women companions who were unwilling to be separated are probably the most visible indicator of the difficulties endured by women-loving-women in Kerala. Other news stories have also appeared in the mainstream press, of women asking the courts for permission to live together, or students being evicted from schools or hostels for having lesbian relationships.

Lesbian suicides were an important starting point, in the workings of Sahayatrika, for bringing up lesbian/sexuality minority rights as a political issue in Kerala. We had compiled a list of newspaper reports of suicides, mostly occurring within the past eight years, which cited a same-sex relationship or had strong indications of it as the cause for death. At present the suicides of 24 women (and four men) are on this list, but it is far from being complete. Many more double suicides have been brought to our attention, through newspaper reports or word of mouth, but we haven't had the capacity to investigate all of them. Furthermore, we have only been able to gather information about suicides of people in relationships that have received media attention and become public knowledge. Excluded from such a list are single suicides committed by individuals due to their sexual marginalisation, as well as any suicides which have been concealed from the public eye.

When we first started talking about lesbian suicides, social activists and others raised a number of objections and doubts. First of all, as mentioned earlier, was the tendency to deny lesbian existence and question whether these suicides were actually committed by 'lesbians'. A related tendency was to invalidate lesbian suffering, to suggest that the numbers we were presenting were insignificant compared to the overall suicide rates in Kerala. The majoritarian notion that the importance of a social justice issue can be measured in terms of the number of people who are affected is in itself problematic. And in this case, newspaper reports of lesbian suicides must be viewed against the backdrop of a probably larger number of unreported suicides, as well as the broader spectrum of experiences and struggles that women with same-sex attractions have described.

It should also be noted that there **are** ambiguities involved in identifying and defining a 'lesbian' suicide, as it is often not so clear where a close friendship ends and 'lesbian relationship' begins. In many of the fact findings we have done, community members or confidants have described the women involved as having a love (*premum*) relationship. However, in other investigations, such as a case where two women jumped in a quarry after tying their bodies together with a dupatta, although the women were described as 'so close that... they couldn't bear to be separated', no one would articulate the romantic possibilities of their friendship. Social stigma and ignorance may contribute to this lack of articulation, and the women involved are no longer available to speak for themselves. But there is also the question of how one defines a 'lesbian' relationship: is it defined in terms of sexual intimacy, or in terms of same-sex love?

Another objection that was raised to our fact-finding investigations relates to the overrepresentation of women from marginalised backgrounds in lesbian suicides as reported in the media. A majority of the cases we have found involve women from marginalised communites (dalit, adivasi, other backward castes, and Muslim women) and/or women working in low-income occupations—such as factory work, tailoring or daily wage agricultural labour.

Arguments were raised that sexuality and sexuality minority issues are not relevant for communities dealing with issues of extreme poverty and daily survival. Implicit in such objections is the assumption of a dichotomy: that sexuality is a middle-class and/or theoretical domain, and that you can't work on sexuality issues with grassroots rural women.

These objections were raised most clearly around our first proposed fact-finding, of the suicide of two young adivasi women. It was a serious issue for ourselves as well, since it occured at the same time that adivasis were occupying the Secretariat for their land rights, and we wanted to support their struggle. We decided, after consulting with some supportive feminists, to write a larger report investigating many lesbian suicides; we didn't want to focus on barriers for sexuality minorities within a single community, especially within the most marginalised of communities in Kerala. As it happened, the media had already been interviewing community members and local people were themselves talking about the apparently romantic relationship between the two girls. And it was widely believed that the main reason for the suicide was the threat of their being separated.

Sometimes fact-findings have given us the opportunity to open up discussions about sexuality issues in different communities. In the case described above, we were able to talk about our efforts with the community people who seemed open to it, and we were invited to speak more about it to their kudumbamshree and other groups. However, it is a difficult and sensitive issue, and while in some fact-findings interviewees have found it therapeutic to talk about the loss of a loved one, in other cases we have had to stop our investigations because it was clearly traumatic or dangerous to those involved. In any case, the substantiating evidence for lesbian suicides in marginalised communities found in many of our inquiries demonstrate the absurdity of the argument that sexuality rights are only relevant for people in privileged positions. Such assumptions view sexuality as a luxury rather than as an integral part of life. But a question which remains unanswered is how to take discussions of sexuality beyond the realm of theoretical discourse and integrate them with community-based activism.

Another question that should be addressed is why there is this over representation of women from marginalised groups in the suicide reports? We know that, in contrast, the women who contact us through letters, e-mail or telephone are coming from all backgrounds, urban and rural, well-off and poor. One possibility is that women-loving-women from middle-class backgrounds have more resources and choices available, and may be committing suicide less. We can see the role that class and other differences play in our crisis interventions as well: women with financial assets, education or employable skills have a a better chancé of leaving the family system and living independently, and women who can speak languages other than Malayalam have more of an option to leave Kerala. But we also need to recognise that middle- and upper-class communities have more power to invisibilise the suicides of their daughters, and to protect themselves from media scandals, as well. As one doctor we spoke to noted, girls from well-to-do families who attempt suicide are often taken to private hospitals, so outside people don't know.

In another well-known case involving the suicide of a dalit woman student at a Kerala university, issues of caste, marginalised sexuality and also gender difference come into play. Here there was a history of harassment of the student by her hostel warden, which culminated in the warden accusing the student of being a lesbian, which the student denied. The student then ran away with a female companion, but later both returned to their hostel. A day later, the student killed herself. Student activists argued that this was a case of harassment of a dalit student by a high-caste school official, who had falsely accused the young woman of being a lesbian. But the interesting point for us here is that the public accusation of being a lesbian could carry so much stigma as to drive a woman to suicide. Caste marginalisation and sexual marginalisation also intersect in different ways. For example, after the student and her companion returned to the school after running away, they were immediately taken to the police. The student's family argued that, had they belonged to a different community, school authorities would have returned the girls to their families and thus spared them the public humiliation.

In this case, gender non-conformity was also a source of antagonism. The student's 'masculine' appearance and behaviour caused some isolation among students, providing a further reason for harassment by authorities, and this fed into the assumption she was lesbian. One student says the student's behaviour 'was like that of a boy towards other girls' and for this reason the hostel inmates disliked her. This sort of visible difference is an issue for many of the women we have done crisis intervention with as well. Women who look and dress like men or do not conform to other gender stereotypes face harassment on this basis and have difficulty in obtaining housing or employment; this is especially difficult for lesbians who are already economically disadvantaged. A lesbian couple also becomes more publicly identifiable if one partner is perceived as 'male'—although some women we know have managed to live with their same-sex partners because the community believes them to be a heterosexual couple.

Many of the women who contact us also grapple with gender non-conformity and transgender identity issues. The concerns of biological women who identify as men and sometimes seek to physically change their bodies to conform with this self-concept are too complex to be discussed in detail here. Such a discussion would have to take into account both the fact that gender norms are socially constructed (and disrupted) as well as the experiences of transgendered and transsexual individuals, who argue for the right to choose gender identity and/or to transform the body. At the same time, the pressures a lesbian couple might experience to become socially and legally recognised as heterosexual might also be a motivation for sex-reassignment surgery.

Another issue which has appeared with some frequency in the media is that of two women appearing before the local courts and fighting for the right to live together. Typically the women have been brought before the court on a missing persons charge, and if the pair are both over 18 years of age, the court sets them at liberty to live as they please. Decisions were made to this effect by a Paravur Magistrate in October 2000, and a Trissur Magistrate in November 2002. However, the apparently legal right of two adult women to cohabitate may be subverted by popular prejudices and misunderstandings at various levels of society, from the judiciary to the police to the family and community. Thus in a similar case that was reported in newspapers in February 2001, two women from Kilamanoor who had run away together were brought before the local court, but forced to separate against their wishes and sent home to their respective families. Or in a case that we were involved with in July 2003, two women were granted the liberty to live together, but only after the public prosecutor unsuccessfully tried to argue that they were having an unnatural relationship under Section 377 of the Indian Penal Code. Women trying to live autonomously as a couple may also face institutional and civil violence before ever reaching the courts; thus in a recently publicised case, the police tried to force a 24-year-old woman to return to her family in spite of her stated wish to stay with her companion. And in another recent incident we have been involved with, local people and family members of two women who had been cohabitating for several years burned down their place of residence, forcing the women to leave the locality.

Some other cases also show the way that lack of understanding in social institutions can work to deny lesbian and bisexual women other basic rights such as the right to education or the right to privacy. One common experience seems to be the expulsion of women-loving-women from educational institutions like schools or student hostels, to protect other students from the infection of lesbianism. In a famous case in 1992, several schoolgirls were evicted from a Trivandrum secondary school for forming the 'Martina Navratilova' club, a lesbian group; and in 2002 two female students were kicked out of their school for play-acting a Hindu marriage and exchanging *talis*. We have also received word-of-mouth information about student hostels where plans were being made to expel students for their lesbian tendencies. There seems to be no concept that students with different sexual orientations might have rights as individuals and deserve the opportunity to be able to continue their education. Also, in a fact-finding we did about a student suicide, we discovered that the student's surviving companion was forced to drop out of university due to the resulting trauma. It seems that Kerala universities and other institutions of learning are a long way away from providing support to students in such traumatic situations, which might allow them to continue their studies.

Privacy is another basic right that seems to be easily violated when it comes to women-loving-women. For example, in the recent incident where the allegedly lesbian relationship of two women was covered in the tabloid press, this information was leaked from a supposedly supportive transition house where one of the women was staying. And in general, media and popular attitudes seem to regard lesbians as some subhuman category with no claim to personal space; all personal concerns of women-loving-women are considered to be potentially public knowledge.

STRATEGIES FOR RESISTANCE

The newspaper stories and personal cases discussed here, from lesbian suicides to experiences with psychiatry and sex reassignment surgery, from women seeking to live with their partners to women getting expelled from their schools, demonstrate different areas of marginalisation. One strategy to raise awareness about such issues, widely used in LGBT activism across India, is to frame these marginalisations in terms of human rights that sexuality minorities, in this case women-loving-women in Kerala, are being denied. The right to life, right to autonomy and self-determination, right to fair medical treatment, rights to education and privacy all come into question in the situations narrated above.

It should be noted that this language of rights has itself been criticised, both within and outside of sexuality minority movements, on a number of levels: as a discourse with its roots in the European Enlightenment which presumes universal rather than culturally/contextually specific values and is bound to legal or institutional interventions (Menon 1999), or as an individualistic approach which masks structural/systemic inequalities. But as one possible political language among many, it has been effective for raising awareness in the Kerala context as well, simply because it draws attention to notions of 'humanness' and personhood that are popularly, politically and legally denied to lesbians and other sexuality minorities.

Another strategy that we in Sahayatrika have employed to raise awareness is to locate societal violence against lesbians upon a broader continuum of violence against women. Again, this approach has been attempted in other parts of India—for example, a recent flyer protesting lesbian suicides, signed by an array of Mumbai- and New Delhi-based social justice groups, reads:

> Apart from rape, sexual harassment, and bride burning, violence against women happens every time a woman is married against her will. It happens every time

a woman feels guilty for wanting to be happy and every time that a woman must die because she is unacceptable to society. Lesbian suicides are a result of society's attempt to restrict women's choices and control their lives.[1]

For me, such a statement represents something of a conceptual victory, first of all because it situates lesbian suicides not just as a sexual minority issue but as a feminist issue, and second, because it is endorsed by organisations engaged in a broad range of feminist, human rights, media, health, and sexuality minority activisms.

In the past two or three years since Sahayatrika was formed, there has been increased discussion and awareness around lesbian and sexuality minority issues among women's groups and other social organisations in Kerala. We would like to think that Sahayatrika has played a part in deconstructing notions of the lesbian as radically 'other', and in arguing for the integration of lesbian/sexuality minority issues into feminist and human rights discourses. But it must be acknowledged that, just as lesbian and sexuality minority movements are themselves in a nascent stage in Kerala, political support for such movements and issues is itself only developing. The support which we have received so far from other social movements has tended to be private rather than public, and at the level of individuals rather than organisations.

In this section I want to talk about some of the barriers that Sahayatrika has faced in its activism, particularly as it relates to social and political dynamics relating to sexuality in Kerala. Specifically, I want to look at legal and social barriers which prevent other organisations and activists from supporting us, and I will attempt to draw out some of the implications that our activism has for sexuality politics in Kerala. I would like to note here that theorisation about the social, historical and political constructions of sexuality in Kerala is in many ways a newly emerging area. My own remarks here are thus somewhat tentative, and based in the working experience of Sahayatrika.

It is not just sexuality minorities themselves but also the organisations which seek to assist them which undergo legal, social and political marginalisation. Legally there is the threat of state persecution: like other organisations in India doing queer activism, Sahayatrika has worked with the fear of being charged under Section 377 of the Indian Penal Code for promoting 'unnatural sexual acts', and the knowledge that in recent years all over India, organisations doing HIV prevention work with sexuality minorities and sex workers' movements have been arrested. Moreover, in Kerala, there has been a public preoccupation with 'sex rackets', a term which is used indiscriminately to signify both the brutal violence of forced sexual trafficking and almost any configuration of sexual activities, be it real or imagined. Because we offer letter-writing and telephone support for women, and try to develop a peer support network, we run the risk of being accused of running a 'sex racket', and need to document our work and correspondence as much as possible for our own protection.

There is in fact a constant conflation of sex work, sex rackets and lesbianism in the popular consciousness in Kerala that needs to be disentangled. I would like to suggest that the notion of a 'sex racket' in itself needs to be problematised, that the tensions between forced sexual trafficking vs. sex work, or between sexual exploitation vs. consensual sexuality that are *at play* within this signification need to be articulated. Moreover, perhaps because both the 'lesbian' and the 'sex worker' occupy the far end of the continuum of who is a 'bad woman' in Kerala, we have found in our work in Sahayatrika a repeated confusion between these identities. Thus in our fact-finding investigations of lesbian suicides, in several cases local people believed the deceased women to be either willingly engaged in sex work or forced into sex rackets, although we found no corroborating evidence for any of these charges. Such beliefs seemed to be informed both by constructions of women from marginalised groups as being sexually available, and a popular confusion that women's sexuality, when not conforming to hegemonic structures, must be read as either prostitution or sexual exploitation. The constant mistaking of our own organisation as a 'sex club', is yet another example of this conflation.

The stigmatisation and threat of violence implied in being labelled as a 'lesbian' or 'sex worker' in Kerala society in fact functions as a means of controlling the social, emotional and sexual autonomy of any woman, in a way which erases the struggles and rights of those who actually belong to these categories. The societal impact of being identified as a lesbian and all the connotations that go with it, as already noted, are a major deterrent to the visibility of women-loving-women in society. Yellow newspapers such as *Fire* which regularly carry stories about lesbians, illicit love affairs and sex rackets, also use the discrediting power of the media as a form of retaliation. Thus, when the two women I spoke about at the beginning of this essay fought back against their negative media coverage by holding a press conference and threatening a lawsuit, the tabloid newspaper responded by increasing their defamatory and falsified coverage, issue after issue, of both the young women as well as the activists who advocated on their behalf.

The perils of 'moral infection' not only limit the actions of individuals but also of social organisations. Perhaps the situation is changing—but sometimes even supportive organisations and activists have feared being tainted by the same social stigmas which are used to invisibilise and silence sexuality minorities, leading to a sort of isolation and ghettoisation among social movements. Thus, when we first started raising lesbian suicides as an issue among social organisations, there was a tendency to push us to work with those activists already engaged in controversial sexuality issues, especially the sex workers' movement. And while the alliance between sexuality minority groups and sex workers' movements is important and powerful, based on a common experience of sexual 'othering', it can sometimes lead to a compounding of marginalisations. For example, Sahayatrika has needed to share office spaces with other organisations for reasons of safety; but the only spaces that were initially available to us were with our allies in the sex worker's movement. Sex worker's projects are frequently evicted from their building spaces and therefore change locations frequently, as neighbours come to (mis)understand and oppose such projects' functionings. Sahayatrika's own efforts were thus affected by this structural instability, as we also lost our office space with each subsequent eviction. However, it is possible that efforts to rent space by a self-standing sexuality minority or lesbian rights organisation would also be subject to this same cycle of evictions in Kerala.

The fear of visibility and social stigma by association has also resulted in a reluctance for even sympathetic organisations and movements to publicly support lesbian/sexuality minority rights. Again, this situation may be changing; and it is affected by the invisible status of sexuality minorities themselves. For example, last year when two teenage girls who pretended to marry were kicked out of their secondary school, we wrote a complaint to the Kerala Human Rights Commission; encouragingly, many local activists endorsed our petition. But in this case we took care not to label the incident a 'lesbian' issue for fear of stigmatising the girls involved; and it remains unclear whether a petition about an openly 'lesbian' issue would have had the same support. Similarly, in the recent case of the two women who want to live together but denied having a lesbian relationship, this denial itself became the focal point for some of the media and public. In such cases, it is sometimes easier even for supporters to focus upon the damage of a supposedly false accusation of lesbianism, rather than articulate the implications of the marginalisation of lesbians themselves. Among women's groups, although there has been an increasing receptiveness towards lesbian and sexuality minority issues, at least conceptually, some argue that feminists, already designated as 'bad women' in society and burdened with charges of 'breaking up the family', are not ready to publicly support more controversial issues like lesbian rights. However, it is important to recognise that the ambivalence that some feminists (and other progressive activists) have towards sexuality rights are not only rooted in 'morality' or the fear of moral contagion but also in a very real situation of social and sexual violence towards women. The tendency, as evidenced by public campaigns against sexual harassment, rape and forced sexual trafficking, is to locate the politics of sexuality primarily in a paradigm of sexual violence or exploitation.

Sahayatrika itself, as already mentioned, has also tried to raise awareness by locating issues such as lesbian suicides within a violence-against-women framework. Both the human rights approach and the prevailing feminist practice in fact tend to emphasise violations of rights or experiences of violence. But the legitimacy gained through articulating lesbian issues through paradigms of violence or victimisation leaves unaddressed perhaps more challenging and disruptive notions of sexual and personal as well as socio-economic autonomy for women. Can we work for a lesbian politics that articulates the implications of giving choice to women about the types of relationships, families and economies they might form? And can we move beyond presenting lesbian existence as a site of violence and conceive of a lesbian (or a feminist) politics that is based on the right to desire?

Sex workers disrupt the sexual exploitation framework when they start to argue for their sexual services as a form of labour/work; and lesbians and sexuality minorities disrupt this framework when we start to argue for sexual rights in terms of the right to desire, or the right to have fulfilling relation-ships, regardless of gender identity. Regrettably, there is probably more of an openness among women's groups, at this point in time, to engage with the challenges presented by lesbian/sexuality minority movements than those presented by sex workers' movements. But I think that desire as a political issue for women still presents great practical and theoretical challenges, especially if we want to locate sexual autonomy not simply in a liberal feminist framework but also in an understanding that simultaneously recognises the intersectionalities of different relationships of power, violence or exploitation in the society.

In some ways the experience of Sahayatrika testifies to these multiplicities. For even the small spaces that we have tried to create for positive sexual activism—through our helpline, in building connections and networks, or in trying to find places for women-loving-women to meet, work and live—are constantly being intruded upon by the threats of violence and objecti-fication. And yet the sorts of spaces we aim to create seem to be vitally important—and not just for lesbians and other sexuality minorities. Even the overwhelming response of men to our helpline, be it in the form of sexually harassing or obscene phone calls, doubts about negotiating sexuality, or experiences of abuse (as victims or perpetrators), as well as calls from men with different sexual or gender identities, indicates a tremendous amount of anxiety and often dysfunctionality surrounding male sexuality. Although this is beyond the scope of Sahayatrika, there is a need for discussion and engagement with the problems of sexuality, heterosexuality and constructions of masculinity as experienced by men of all orientations.

The very fact that women contact our helpline, intended only for women, with less frequency than men gives some indication of different senses of entitlement and difficulties in coming forward that women experience with regards to such a service. Moreover, although some women in Kerala may be able to resist the patriarchal ordering of their bodies and find spaces to explore their sexualities and desires, be it same-sex or opposite, others speak about an absence of such locations. For example, when we were originally approaching women to be involved with Sahayatrika, we discovered a section of women who said that they themselves did not know what their own sexual orientations were, based on the experiences they had. And one of the biggest challenges that we have faced, working as a sexual rights project for lesbians, was that we were working in a sort of political vacuum, since there was no equivalent programme focusing on sexuality rights for all women. For this reason, we would give counselling and support to any woman who called us. Many of the women supporting Sahayatrika also did not identify primarily as lesbians or women-loving-women, but were drawn to the potential of a political and social space where one could articulate issues and experiences of women's sexuality more freely. In this way I think that Sahayatrika captured the imagination of many women—and men—not because they viewed it as an organisation working exclusively for lesbian rights but rather because they perceived it as a site for resistance and creating new possibilities against the confines of a constraining, patriarchal and heteronormative sexual morality in Kerala.

TOWARDS A POLITICS OF DESIRE? AN UNFOLDING OF QUEER POLITICS IN KERALA

I started this essay as an attempt to reflect upon the experiences of Sahayatrika. But as I try to construct some concluding remarks for these examinations, I wonder if the 'lessons' of Sahayatrika are not answers but instead more questions. This seems especially so because the activism upon which I am reflecting, an activism located in Kerala for women-loving-women in particular, and sexuality minorities in general, is very much in a period of change and transformation, with new events unfolding every day. My 'conclusions' here cannot be finite in any sense, but are very much the product of an engagement with an ongoing endeavour.

In the two or three months since I started writing this essay, a great deal of cultural and intellectual productions concerning lesbian and sexuality minority issues have emerged or are emerging into the public sphere. In this time period alone, a film festival on queer sexualities, a collection of theoretical and political writings on sexuality minority issues in Malayalam, and a book and a documentary film on lesbian suicides in Kerala have appeared. A feature film on a lesbian relationship in Malayalam is in production, and numerous articles continue to be published in the print media. It seems that we are on the brink of a still increasing public debate on sexuality, and sexual and gender identity, in Kerala.

More important developments are happening still, from the standpoint of women-loving-women in this state. When I began writing this essay I said that women with same-sex attractions in Kerala were not able to meet in collectivity or to develop political formations. For a long time as well, the public intrigue and media fascination with lesbian issues/Sahayatrika was developing much faster than our efforts to develop a network or women's community. But even this situation is changing. Small groups in Kerala have been meeting, and although some of the women's understandings of their sexualities and their relationships may defy and push the boundaries of 'lesbian' identity, these women are finding a sense of solidarity and community with each other. Some of these women have different visions for supporting and working for others who are like them. Whether they continue to work through organisations like Sahayatrika, or to invent new configurations, new possibilities for resistance, it is, all the same, a promising development.

Throughout the last year, other sexuality minorities, especially gay and bisexual men, have also been increasingly meeting and networking in different spaces, from Vaathil to the Internet, to more informal and local places. It is significant to note that at this point in time our core support as Sahayatrika activists has often come from other sexuality minorities or queer activists, more than women's movements or other social movements.

Visibility continues to be both empowering and disempowering for sexuality minority movements, and we all must grapple with its contradictions. On the one hand, when we make interventions and engage with discourses in the public sphere, we have the opportunity to create awareness and make our own positions and criticisms available. Such discourses and such activisms also help to create new spaces for people. For example, the increasing meetings and connections between women-loving-women in Kerala in recent months is directly related to increased media visibility. The two women who were widely slandered in the media fought back, holding their own press conference and giving other interviews. Although there was a backlash against the women, they also inspired many sympathisers; and new women approached Sahayatrika as a result of this incident and other media coverage.

And yet, for individuals who come under media scrutiny, there is also a tremendous cost. The women who held the press conference face considerable disadvantages in obtaining work or housing beyond the marginalisations that other same-sex couples are experiencing, if they stay in Kerala; and the very fact of their visibility prevents some people from helping them. That is to say, even sympathisers are sometimes reluctant to help very visibly stigmatised people because of the repercussions they themselves might face from landlords, family, employers, community members, and others.

Sexuality minorities engaged with an emerging queer movement are not the first social movement activists to face the dilemma of political actions in the public sphere vs. repercussions in private life. But because our marginalisations are based in our sexualities and, therefore, vulnerable to a type of extreme objectification, because many sexuality minorities in Kerala have found safe spaces to live and survive in the private realm, and because not everyone feels the imperative to attach their sexual practices to a political identity, the issue of 'coming out' into the public sphere may be different. So some of us still question if there are alternatives to the politics of visibility.

It seems we need to adopt a multiplicity of strategies; we need to create both spaces of safety and privacy, and continue to make interventions in the public sphere. Media and cultural productions, public debate, and other forms of awareness-building can also help to create greater conditions of safety for everyone. As an organisation that made statements in the public sphere without visible spokespeople, Sahayatrika tried to negotiate these tensions between visibility and safety by a sort of compromise—others who become activists may choose to be more visible, or less. But perhaps those who feel that the requisite for a sexuality minority political movement is visible faces and visible bodies, should consider the question: will you also help these spokespeople to find work or housing, or provide emotional support, when the backlash against them, which is inevitable, comes?

There are two fundamentally important, but opposing impulses involved in strategising for a sexuality minority politics. One is the impulse towards sameness, towards commonality. When we argue for integration into feminist or human rights discourses, for the inclusion of 'lesbians' into the categories of 'woman' or 'human', when we fight for legal rights and protections, we are appealing on some level to a sense of commonality that we share with other people regardless of our sexual or gender identities. When we choose to be visible, in the best-case scenario, we also appeal to the public's sense of commonality, of empathy or self-recognition—of being fellow humans living with courage and struggling, with experiences sometimes similar and sometimes different from those who see and hear us.

In the worst case, visibility makes us 'other', makes us the object of ridicule, exoticism, sensationalism, violence. But the impulse towards differ-ence, towards radical rupture, is a powerful political impulse too. For a sexuality minority politics (like a gender politics or a sexual politics) has the potential, as our critics charge, to deeply challenge prevailing notions of interpersonal relationships, gender hierarchy, community formation, prop-erty rights and family. Yet this destabilising impulse carries within it pro-foundly transformative possibilities, to rethink and relive these relations in ways that are perhaps less repressive, perhaps more egalitarian.

It is here that the notion of a 'queer' politics becomes useful, especially if we think of queerness in its broadest sense, as transcending a narrow identity politics to 'signify [any] practices which question the heterosexual norm, *i.e.* that the only valid way of sexually relating to one another is within the framework of marriage and procreation' (Narrain: 1). Such a politics can be embraced by anyone, regardless of sexual orientation or gender identity, who questions or subverts the emotional, sexual, and socio-economic marginalisations which occur when only the dominant modes of expressing sexuality, performing gender, forming relationships or creating families are given legitimacy.

One commentator has suggested that:

> In India though the word queer is not commonly used, the realities of the queer experience, *i.e.* lives and ways of living which contest the embedded nature of heterosexism in law, culture and society, have traditionally existed and continue to exist in the contemporary context (ibid.: 2)

Kerala society also encompasses a diversity of different sexualities and gendered existences, although very often there have been no names and identities for these queer lives. Indeed, the cultural specificities of queer life in Kerala, what sorts of sexual/gender identities (or lack of identities) may have been here or continue here is probably a rich area of inquiry. For our purposes we can begin by recognising the historical relativity of the construction of the 'modern' family in Kerala as patrilineal, nuclear and monogamous and the variety of practices which have existed outside of this. In the experience of Sahayatrika, when we have encountered, for example, a 'lesbian' couple living together for 10 years with some degree of acceptance from their rural village community, we see how different social worlds, values and practices survive alongside this 'modernity'.

It is not necessary that lesbian, sexuality minority or queer politics that emerge in Kerala be identical to those found in Western countries or even in other parts of India. Perhaps any new movements or communities which develop here will be influenced by global identities, Indian queer movements, and the specificities and conflicts of life in this region. But to me it is clear that, whether they are making press conferences, surviving marriages or creating hidden spaces to resist hetero-normativity, women-loving-women and other sexuality minorities are living and surviving in Kerala with great courage. Now, we can only hope that the larger society will be courageous enough to support them.

NOTES

1. From flyer against lesbian suicides, 'Right to Life: Denied', signed by Aashray Adhikar Abhiyan, Action India, Breakthrough, CREA, Human Rights Law Network, Jagori, Kriti team, Nirantar, Prism, Saheli, SANGAT, Vikasini, Lawyers Collective—HIV/AIDS Unit and WRI.

REFERENCES

Menon, Nivedita. 1999, 'Rights, Bodies and the Law: Rethinking Feminist Politics of Justice', in N. Memon (ed.), *Themes in Politics: Gender and Politics in India*. New Delhi: Oxford University Press.

Narrain, Arvind. 2004, *Queer: Despised Sexuality, Law, and Social Change*. Bangalore: Books for Change.

13

Fire, Sparks and Smouldering Ashes*

Gomathy N.B. and Bina Fernandez

 The film *Fire*[1] is about a relationship between two women, Sita and Radha, married to brothers. Set within the patriarchal framework of a middle-class Hindu family in Delhi, the film portrays both women as oppressed in their respective marriages. They turn to each other for tenderness and respect, moving into a sensuous and sexual relationship. They finally break out of the very patriarchal structures that threw them together, to form independent lives.

The film has four clear strands interwoven through it. One is that of the oppression that these two women face within the hetero-patriarchal institution of marriage—the violence and the absence of love or tenderness. The second strand is that of the nature of sexuality within Indian families and in particular, the repression of women's sexuality and desire within it. Interwoven is the sexuality of 'other' characters: the affair of the second brother with a Chinese sex worker; the hiring of pornographic films by young school boys; and the live-in servant who watches a pornographic film and masturbates in front of the mother-in-law (old and paralysed, unable to communicate her distress except by the ringing of a bell). The third strand is the evolving love between the two women, the dilemmas that this poses, and the strength that it gives them to break the patriarchal structures that bind and violate them.

The fourth strand in the film locates this story within the Hindu cultural context. The film reiterates religious icons that reaffirm patriarchal control over women and their sexuality. Only, the icons are placed in new configurations so that the old and new symbolisms are placed in juxtaposition. Thus

* This essay originally appeared in *Women in Action*, Vol. 1, 1999, an online magazine available at http://www.isiswomen.org/wia/wia 199/index.html.

fire that usually symbolises purity and sanctity, and is a witness to the marriage of women and men, is used to symbolise the passion between women. The names 'Radha' and 'Sita' represent popular mythological heroines/goddesses.[2] In Hindu mythology, Sita has to undergo a trial by fire to prove her chastity—here the trial by fire is also for Sita. In using these names, the film directly challenges the construction of female purity and symbols.

Fire was released in India in November 1998, over a year after it was internationally released. In this time it had also won 14 awards. Within the country, reviews and articles had been appearing in the media well before the actual release of the film. Much to everyone's surprise, the Censor Board of India passed the film without a single cut. It was screened for three weeks in the city and the country and ran to full houses. Special women's shows were organised every week in Mumbai.

It is without doubt that the film brought the issue of lesbianism into the public domain for discussion. For the first time, lesbianism moved from the grey areas of silence and half-murmurs, to the arena of the 'big' screen. It forced all kinds of people to make public their positions: people who may have never known about the issue; who may have heard about lesbians and held a healthy or morbid curiosity; those who may have taken a moral position about the sinful nature of such intercourse; those who have denied their own sexuality and sexual experiences; as well as those women who have known that they loved women.

The film screening was disrupted three weeks after its release by the Mahila Aghadi—the women's wing of the Shiv Sena (a Hindu fundamentalist party, currently part of the ruling coalition in Maharashtra). A handful of people broke the glass of vandalised New Empire, a local theatre in Mumbai, tore the posters and disrupted the screening. They also threatened to prevent the film from being screened all over Mumbai, as well as across the country, claiming that the film was perverted and was specially aimed at injuring Hindu sentiments. At the same time, similar vandalism occurred at the Delhi theatres screening the film.

After the initial period of shock, many groups in Mumbai, Delhi, Pune and other parts of the country organised to counter this attack. In many ways, the film acted as a trigger for processes all over the country. The nature of the reactions and organising in Mumbai and Delhi were very different. We understand from reports that in Delhi, the reactions were centred around the portrayal of lesbianism in the film. There was a strong wave of demand for visibility of lesbian rights, by lesbians, feminists and supporters of lesbian and gay rights. A candlelit protest was held. Meetings were called, and regular protests were organised. This effort coalesced into a group now known as the Campaign for Lesbian Rights, comprising lesbians, supporters and feminists.

In Mumbai, the home-turf of the Shiv Sena, the protests took on a different colour. The focus of these actions was the freedom of expression, and the need to protest against communalism. Even while the film was still being screened, there was a feeling of disbelief that the Shiv Sena had not moved to prevent the screening. We were looking over our shoulders even as we distributed pamphlets about Stree Sangam, our group for women who love women, at the women-only screenings. Then there were the attacks on the theatres that were showing the film. While we first experienced a feeling of shock, anger and helplessness at this attack, there was also a feeling of inevitability. Under the Shiv Sena's influence, more and more of us have had the feeling of sitting on the sidelines, ineffectively watching in a world where fundamentalist forces are gathering momentum to the point where no differences would be tolerated, where women would be pushed into corners.

The mass reaction to the Shiv Sena vandalism came as a relief. Concerted action from different parts of the city, not merely by activists and academicians, was initiated. In the past two years we had seen a series of 'clampdowns' on all art and events that offended the Shiv Sena dictates, and somewhere, the vandalism in this instance was the proverbial last straw. *Fire* literally sparked a concerted move to organise against the Shiv Sena dictate. A large number of women expressed publicly their displeasure about the film, and in doing so, re-emphasised their right to select the kind of films that they wanted to see. Spontaneous protests erupted in the city. Four days after the film was removed from the screen, 32 organisations protested in front of the theatre. People were arrested and harassed by the police for disturbing the peace during this protest (the same police force that was conspicuously absent when the theatre was being vandalised). Then there was an effort to launch a massive poster campaign. The poster focused on the freedom of expression and challenged the city's passive acceptance of each violation perpetrated by the Shiv Sena that finally culminated in the banning of the film. About 25,000 posters were printed. Efforts to put up the posters in the city were stopped by the police repeatedly. Men who were paid to put up the posters backed out at the last minute, expressing fear of the police Finally, members of the Republican Party of India volunteered to put the posters up, but were arrested. Those posters that were put up were torn and a handful of the thousands put up survived. Then there was an easing on the part of the state. Small-size posters were put up in trains, in the ladies compartment. Some of these survive to date.

This was followed by a public demonstration against the banning of the film. A long banner with protest slogans in five languages—Hindi, Gujarati, Marathi, English and Urdu—was held up. The English slogan on the banner was 'Bombay a city of freedom, not anyone's kingdom.' About 300 women gathered on a public beach in Mumbai, along one of the major crossroads in the city. The event was widely covered in the media.

The protests coalesced into a loose group of organisations, Committee for Action against Fascism, to continue protest action against the atrocities in Mumbai by the Shiv Sena, which still remains active. The protests also initiated an active debate within the press and around the Right to Freedom of Speech and Expression.

Dilip Kumar, Deepa Mehta and Mahesh Bhatt, well-known actors and directors, filed a court case against the act of vandalism by the Shiv Sena and demanded the continuation of the film screening. The film was referred back to the Censor Board and was passed once again with no cuts. However, the producer Jhamu Sugandh—to ensure that the Shiv Sena does not disrupt the film screenings again—made some cuts, and removed the names 'Sita' and 'Radha'. Despite the confusion caused by this lack of names, even in its mutilated form the film continued to draw crowds and broke even at the box office.

For those of us who identify as women who love women, that such a film should have been made at all and shown in India in mainstream theatres seems almost unbelievable. The experience of sitting in a theatre full of women and watching the film with its scenes of love and caring between two women, and not a man and a woman, was moving in a way that prevented immediate analysis or critique. Foremost was a sense of exultation that within the constant barrage of heterosexist imagery, there was one possible representation visibilising and validating the ways in which women can love women.

There have been several critiques of the film by film critics, feminists and women who love women. The most obvious criticism points to the directorial cop-out in portraying both women as situated in unhappy marriages. Their choice to seek each other seems more a result of an attempt to escape their marriages rather than a positive choice. In the arena of possibilities, one would wish that at least one of the two women were not married or in an unhappy marriage: then the point of positive choice could have been more deliberate. But on the other hand, there are very few women who come from situations that are not oppressive, and it is made very evident in the film that both women clearly assert their lesbian choice over their marriage.

Other critiques centre on the class-biased portrayal of the servant as a masturbating, comic figure (See John and Niranjana 1999). In addition, there is the clichéd portrayal of the 'foreign bitch' (the Chinese woman) who seduces Indian men for the gratification of her sexual appetite. In both cases, the director has resorted to common Hindi film stereotypes.

Another bone of contention is the lack of clarity surrounding the connection between the act of masturbation by the servant while watching porn videos where the mother-in-law is forced to watch, and the act of sex between the women. Both seem to come under the grey area of 'wrong' sex for a confused Radha, who is shown as unable to make the distinction between consensual and forced/violative acts of sex.

There have been many more critiques, but we will not go into those, given that this is one film attempting to portray a single story. To make it mean everything for everyone is a load the film (any film, for that matter) cannot carry. Instead, for us the critiques imply the absence of other cinematic images of women who are strong, who explore their sexuality and make choices about their sexuality outside the 'normal' paradigm.

What we would like to do, though, is examine the film in the context of lesbian existence and realities in India[3]—a complex issue, because women-only spaces and female friendships are woven into social practices and consciousness. Some feminists have contended that there are exclusively women's spaces existing within traditional Indian society, where women have had and continue to have the freedom to explore intimate and sexual relationships with other women. Such spaces would, the argument runs, be endangered if lesbianism was brought out as an open, politicised agenda. These silent spaces—along with the existence of ancient erotic sculptures of women with women, and the existence of many women-centred traditions and rituals—create a belief that as a society we are tolerant of same-sex relationships. It is necessary to explore the many strands underlying this belief.

Almost all women in our society have experienced women-only spaces— for confidence-sharing, healing, mutual comfort and support—at some point in their lives. Often deep bonds, intimacies and sensuousness—sometimes extending to the sexual—have characterised these spaces. At the interstices of a patriarchal society with the potential to maintain the structures that control women, or transform them, these spaces act as essential 'breathing spaces' and sources of energy for women to share and recuperate from the misogynist society that we live in. However, 'women-only' spaces are 'allowed' only if women in it are seen as sexually inactive within them. The possibility of women actively choosing women as sexual partners is thus denied.

These spaces can become autonomous, but only when women begin to challenge and transform the structures within which we operate. Sometimes both processes of maintaining and transforming happen simultaneously. Women have used these spaces to express choices, other than what is sanctioned by patriarchal structures of society. Often, these choices are a silent testimony of resistance. Lesbian women, by expressing sexual desire for each other, engage in acts of resistance that challenge the norm of female sexual passivity.

It is this shift from same-sex behaviour to the articulation of a lesbian identity that has tested the limits of the supposed 'tolerance' of same-sex relationships, and sometimes provoked negative, even hostile reactions. In *Fire*, although neither Radha nor Sita identifies as lesbian. It is not so much the several challenges to the hetero-patriarchal, Great Indian Joint Family set-up or even the fact that they make love that is perceived as threatening, but the final act of resistance in their walking out, together.

The point comes home when one takes a comparative look at the other well-known lesbian story in the Indian context, *Lihaaf*. *Lihaaf* (The Quilt) is a short story by the Urdu writer Ismat Chugtai which was first published in 1941. The narrator is a young girl who observes (though does not understand) a sexual relationship between two women (under the quilt). Obscenity charges were levied against the author by the moral brigade of those times. These charges were overturned in court by the judge who ruled that the story did not use any obscene language, and could only be understood by someone who already had some knowledge (and therefore could not be said to 'corrupt' innocent minds). Here, therefore, there is no hostile reaction, because there is no articulation of a lesbian identity.

The articulation of a lesbian identity in India has been taken a step further when women have attempted to register their marriages (with other women), in any way possible. In 1988, the marriage of Leela and Urmila, two women police constables, marked the start of a decade that has seen media attention given to a series of several women-to-women marriages, or suicides by women who refused to be parted from each other. In 1998 there were three instances: in April, two young women in Patna were reported to have filed an affidavit (witnessed by three persons) that they were married and living together. In two separate incidents, later in the year, a young couple in Bombay, and another couple in Orissa committed suicide. These are all women who have mostly had limited access to the resources necessary to enable them to live independently or even access the city-based lesbian and gay support group networks. They have been trapped in circumstances that have forced them to conform to compulsory heterosexuality, even if it means undergoing a sex change, or suicide. Despite this, some of them have had the courage to publicly assert their determination to love and live together.

It is our contention that speech, and images—especially those created by us—are vital in the definition of lesbian existence in India. In the absence of this, the accounts of lesbian existence are arid newspaper reports recording the punishments, denials, death, suicides, isolation and labelling of women who have acted on their sexual desire for other women. In so many cases, their silent acts of protest are registered as statistical details of suicide. This invalidates the lived realities of these women. It sends a message to other lesbian women to be silent or simply cease to be.

In the absence of self-created images and speech, it is possible for the director Deepa Mehta to back out 'under fire' with statements like 'Lesbian-ism is just another aspect of the film. It is probably the last thing they resort to when they derive a certain confidence out of the relationship' (*Indian Express* interview, 13 December 1998); and 'I can't have my film hijacked by any one organisation [with reference to the protests by the Campaign for Lesbian Rights in Delhi]. It is not about lesbianism, it's about loneliness, about choices' (*India Today*, 21 December 1998: 80).

Neither the Shiv Sena protest against *Fire* nor (by and large) the counter-protests are about conscious lesbian identity. Overtly, the Shiv Sena vandal-ism was justified by their claim that 'lesbianism is against Indian culture'. The subtext, though, was the definition of 'Indian tradition' as Hindu. The film, and, therefore, lesbianism, is okay as long as it is identified with the 'other'—if the heroines' names are changed to Shabana and Saira.

In retrospect, looking at our strategies of protest in Mumbai, in reacting to the communal threat and in protecting the right to freedom of expression, somewhere the lesbian lens on the picture got out of focus. There are two ways in which we feel this happened.

First, when some feminist critiques—in the media, and in the protest marches—questioned the hypocrisy of the Shiv Sena in protesting against lesbianism and not against violence against women and obscenity in Hindi films as being 'not part of Indian culture'. This is dangerous territory since an implicit equation is being set up between negative sex acts (rape, incest, and so on) and lesbian sex. The Shiv Sena could very well (at least hypotheti-cally) turn around and protest against the former, along with the latter.

Second, when we defined the counter-protest terrain as 'freedom of speech', somewhere the unquestioned equation was made with the 'freedom to love'. On closer examination, though, this equation doesn't hold, as long as the 'freedom to love' is criminalised through Section 377 of the Indian Penal Code. And here's the irony: Section 377 criminalises the act of sodomy. One cannot be convicted 'for being' homosexual, or 'saying' one is homosexual. One has to be 'caught in the act'. Supposedly, too, since the Section refers to sodomy, lesbians have the 'freedom to love'.

However, as long as there is a moral and social stigma attached to same-sex love, it can be criminalised under obscenity laws, whether or not there is a sodomy statute. Section 292 of the Indian Penal Code punishes obscenity and makes it a criminal offence. The definition of obscenity in the Section can lead to its misuse against gay men and lesbians.

Given this context, what is the liberatory potential of 'freedom of expression' for lesbians and gay men? Can the limits of the concept be stretched to include the right to pleasure and desire (and the expression of both)? Or is the maximum stretch only to the point of tolerance of sexual diversity? And so, in some sense, have we not come back full circle?

NOTES

1. The film is directed by Deepa Mehta, and has Shabana Azmi and Nandita Das in the lead roles.
2. Sita in particular also represents purity, first virginal and then monogamous, who is saved by her husband from the 'evil clutches' of another man. Then she passes through the test of 'fire' to prove her chastity to be accepted back by her husband. Her word is not enough. Her chastity is proved by her stepping into fire. The god of fire does not harm her (incidentally a man) and returns her to her husband. Upon her return, however, her chastity falls into doubt since she was in the presence of another man and away from her husband for a long period of time. Her word is not enough, and she passes through a test of 'fire' to be accepted as pure by her husband. The God of Fire (incidentally also male) does not harm her, and she passes the test.
3. The conceptualisation of these ideas about lesbian existence was done with Maya Sharma and Shanti.

REFERENCE

John, Mary and Tejaswini Niranjana. 1999, 'Mirror Politics: "Fire", Hindutva and Indian Culture', *Economic and Political Weekly*, Vol. 34, Nos 10 and 11, 6-13 March, p. 581.

14

Queering the Campus
Lessons from Indian Universities

Mario D'Penha and *Tarun*

INTRODUCTION

 In July 2004, a panel discussion was organised at the 2nd International Conference on Masculinities, Sexualities and Culture in South Asia, held in Bangalore. At this conference, a group of students, from universities as diverse as Jawaharlal Nehru University (JNU) and Lady Sri Ram College in Delhi to the National Law School of India University (NLSIU) and Indian Institute of Science, Bangalore, gathered. The writing below borrows from the presentations made at that panel, and traces the emergence, opportunities and challenges facing the queer student movement in India today.

The emergence of queer campus movements in recent times may be located within the larger scheme of the creation of new queer spaces, an effort that has come to bear prime importance at a time when queer people are in the process of constructing identities for themselves. The last few years have seen a radical shift in which queer groups by questioning traditional hetero-patriarchal constructs have begun asserting distinctive political identities for themselves. Recent authoritarian backlashes are largely a result of this radical assertion, and the creation of new queer spaces is all the more necessary and yet all the more difficult.

All mainstream societal institutions reinforce the primacy of heterosexuality by using silence, condemnation or criminalisation as tools for the purpose. The most potent of these, and also the most pervasive in the Indian context, is the silencing and invisibilisation of sexuality, which refuses to acknowledge the existence of an alternative way of life even if only for criticism, whether it be for single women, inter-religious couples, or queer people. The educational system in India is no exception. Our generally conservative educational system reinforces all societal norms, including gender and sexual stereotyping.

Campuses, although often the spaces within which student identities are created and asserted, are hardly the places where queer students can be themselves for fear of social ridicule and peer harassment. This reflects the reality of the world outside where many queer people are also forced to keep their identities closeted. The emergence of campus queer spaces thus comes to reflect a shared need to overcome both patriarchy and heterosexism by creating a safe space for interaction, discussion, being and belonging. They attempt to allow people to come out of their closets and be more confident and articulate young men and women.

What makes a campus queer-friendly? How does one take the first step to begin discussions on sexuality on campuses where the subjects are, at best, not talked about, or at worst, subject to violence and ridicule when raised? This essay includes narratives from two universities—the National Law School of India University, Bangalore, and Jawaharlal Nehru University, New Delhi— but is, at all times, about a larger story of a new generation of students for many of whom college life is the first exposure to politics, and especially to issues of sex and sexuality in any meaningful way. The narratives trace the struggles of activists to raise questions of gender and sexuality on campus, to negotiate both official apathy (or hostility) and social spaces, to find the language and space for sexuality activism on campus, all the while remembering that they must inhabit and live in the very institution that they seek to challenge and change. Many of the realities of being queer on Indian campuses involve tales of horrific violence and indignity, both physical and emotional. The battles facing queer activists are as much tied to creating safe spaces for queer students, as to changing the social and political thinking that allows such violence to be deemed legitimate.

The narratives diverge and converge on their approaches, and identify different factors that help them in their own contexts: the pre-existing atmosphere of political discussion both helps and hinders activists at JNU, while the conception of rights language and law is used by activists at NLSIU. Both spaces rely on political discussions using the language of human rights and larger understandings of patriarchy and gender in India, subjects that are linked to their academics as well. They identify the need for supportive faculty, and/or outside visitors that help make inroads into the student community, as well as allied students who, though not queer-identified, support the cause of queer rights.

Colleges and universities represent some of the most important spaces for political activism, and queer politics is no exception. For the success stories that are outlined here, there remain hundreds of institutions where queer people have no safe space, and no one to turn to. The lack of any activist narratives from engineering or medical colleges is one of the most glaring gaps in the movement today. Students from these colleges stress that they do not have access either to the political student spaces of social science colleges, or the academic space. What language and what spaces do they turn to then?

It is hoped that these narratives will provide some sort of inspiration to readers to critically look at the academic spaces that they themselves inhabit, either as queer or non-queer students, and wonder if the space of learning that they belong to is an inclusive space where all forms of knowledge and all expressions of desire are truly respected.

NATIONAL LAW SCHOOL OF INDIA UNIVERSITY

Most of us remember what it was like to be in school, where any mention of sex and sexuality was met simply with giggles and a stern admonishment from the teacher. The story is not very different in most colleges. However, what is different is the availability of space outside the curriculum for student activism. It is essential to claim this space if queer activism has to reach the college campus. Sometimes students need to educate the educational system instead of the other way round.

Laws deal with the entire spectrum of human behaviour, relationships and conduct, which then form the source of rights, obligations and punishments. A law school quite successfully mirrors this omnipresent majesty of law through its official legal narrative discoursed in the classroom. It deals with almost everything under the sun—from buying a car, to the ingredients of murder to formation of treaties between states. Yet, this comprehensive official narrative completely refuses to acknowledge even the existence of queer people. Even the provision of law criminalising homosexual conduct does so without uttering the word 'homosexual' but couching it in the vague terms of 'carnal intercourse against the order of nature'. To quote from a queer student at the Harvard Law School sharing his despair on the absence of queer ideas in the classroom, 'Don't gay and lesbian people make contracts? Don't we own property? Don't we commit tortuous acts? Wouldn't we make an interesting "class" for a class-action hypothetical?' (Reuther) Yet the law deals with us only while criminalising, and that too by using euphemisms.

208 • Queering the Campus

Of course, this discomfort of the official classroom narrative to a radical point of view is not exclusive to queer theory, but is shared by feminism, caste issues, etc., to varying degrees. So, a feminist view of international law or a queer critique of insurance laws are at best marginal to the subject, and at worst, irrelevant or even preposterous.

The resistance and reaction to such incongruous radicalism in the classroom are obviously dependent to a large extent on the individual whims of the professor, who is usually a straight male a generation or two older than the students he is teaching. However, the official narrative and its reaction to radicalism are also defined by the alternative out-of-the-classroom student sub-culture of the school. This sub-culture continues to mould the official narrative, usually marginally, but sometimes substantially.

The NLSIU, as a premier institution in legal education in India is itself quite young. It was established by a legislation of the Government of Karnataka in 1986 to cater to needs of legal education in India. Striving towards social justice was one of the avowed goals of the institution. Right from the beginning there was an exposure to issues like civil liberties, labour relations, and so on, within the human rights framework.

Unlike the resilient official narrative which is created by a largely unchanging group of professors, the sub-culture is supported by a fluid group of generations of students, and is, therefore, much more difficult to sustain. It is important that this sub-culture derives nourishment from more factors than the mere presence of a few politically active students in every batch. In the Law School, this nourishment has come from the largely unsuspecting official narrative itself. This is especially because this official narrative, particularly in social science courses like political science, history and sociology, is very much grounded in constitutionalism, the rights language and democracy. Once you recognise that abstract individuals have rights (the discourse of universal rights) it becomes very difficult to deny the rights to any particular group. The only way one can do so is to deny the humanity of gays and lesbians and that becomes a position which contradicts the core belief of universality. Once the intellectual challenge is overcome by the rights language, the stage is set for radical ideas to be articulated. Now, even a threshold-level tolerance of activism by the institution sustains the sub-culture. One should not underestimate the value of rights language as we can see that the coming out of sexuality itself has not been so easy in other academic disciplines and this is precisely because there is no language of entitlement with which one speaks of sexual orientation issues.

Though queer students were coming out in smaller circles to close friends, sexuality as an issue for public debate was not really on board in the initial years of the NLSIU. By the mid 1990s, feminism as an academic discipline was gaining more and more acceptance and generating heated debates within the student body, which ultimately provided the legitimate academic basis for articulation of queer rights. The real breakthrough in the sexuality front, however, came with a seminar on Gay Rights in 1997 by a few students held in the NLSIU. The idea came after a student came out to his friends who then decided to hold a seminar on the issue. This was also the first time the administration was confronted directly with the issue of sexuality, and to their credit, they let the seminar happen though not entirely happily. However, the seminar seemed to have tapped into some larger process of change as it generated enormous enthusiasm in the queer community in Bangalore with the community attending the seminar in large numbers. The media too picked up on it and it generated more publicity for the Law School than any other event in the Law School's history had done so far. I joined Law School two years after the seminar, and found that the incident had continued to live on in Law School memory through colourful t-shirts with slogans such as 'Don't think straight...Think people'.

Students started increasingly opting for research projects on sexuality-related issues covering decriminalisation, same-sex marriages, hijras,[1] adoption issues, the Hart-Devlin debate[3] and other jurisprudential aspects, queer sociology and politics, hate crimes, male sex workers, and so on. This became possible because the Law School usually allows students to work on any area of their choice for research projects as long as it falls within the scope of the subject. In one of the projects on 'Sexuality in Law School', a group of students conducted a survey by distributing questionnaires to both teachers and students. While the response of the student body was predictably positive, faculty responses varied from outright support to condemnation to ambivalence to even refusal to fill up the questionnaire. Since the seminar, therefore, the sub-culture had begun to confront the officialdom every now and then.

However, confronting the mainstream discourse could not be sustained without consolidating the sub-culture itself. The Gender Study Circle, a big student group which takes up issues relating to gender on a regular basis and organises sensitisation programmes, film screenings, article discussions, and so on, was one of the most important efforts to institutionalise the radical sub-culture. It did not take long for the students to recognise that feminists and queer activists, with the common enemy of hetero-patriarchy, were natural allies. The Gender Study Circle completely embraced queer issues within its folds. Issues relating to masculinity, lesbianism, politics of pleasure, hijras, identity politics, gender neutrality in rape laws, child sexual abuse, and so on, are recurring themes in its discussions. The Gender Study Circle also engages in passionate discussions on its online e-mail list, where issues like 'The straight person's guide to gay etiquette' and 'Is marriage a necessarily oppressive hetero-patriarchal institution' have been discussed in the past. This is clear evidence of the role feminism has played in facilitating the articulation of queer jurisprudence on campus.

In 2000, I witnessed a visit by Peter Lane, an 'ex-gay' from Australia who came to deliver a lecture on 'Opposing Homosexuality'. I thought the lecture was more successful than any other meeting organised in support for sexual rights, since about a 100 students landed up and vehemently opposed his views.

A couple of months after this lecture there was a visit by Justice Michael Kirby, an openly gay judge from Australia, and a respected and frequent visitor to the Law School; the first time while I was studying there. He was a regular visitor and a big source of encouragement for the queer students in the University. Justice Kirby in his visits always made it a point to come out before students and faculty members, ruffling a few feathers of course, but inspiring many others. His contagious courage made him our 'Queer Patron Saint'. A few of us requested him to talk to us about 'Sexuality, Morality and Human Rights'. At this talk, we revisited the Hart-Devlin debate 50 years after it had happened, going back to the role of law in society, and whether it included the enforcement of morals.

By mid-2001, there was a sudden spurt of coming outs within the student body whose reaction was quite accepting and supportive. By this time I was also practically out to most people on campus. Coming out really helped concretise the support of the student body since now the oppressed were people among them and not an abstract victim. Of course there must be a homophobic section among the students also, but the political correctness that the sub-culture has managed to establish ensures that outright homophobic views are rarely articulated in the public.

In the year 2001, the National Human Rights Commission (NHRC) of India had rejected a petition urging human rights violations of a young man who was administered electric shock therapy to 'cure' him of his homosexuality. The Chairperson of the NHRC, Justice J.S. Verma was visiting the University around that time. A petition protesting the decision of the NHRC not to recognise sexuality rights and act upon that complaint was signed by about 60 members of the student body and the faculty and submitted to Justice Verma despite the fact that authorities didn't take very kindly to the protest.

Around this time, Ashwini Sukthankar, an out lesbian rights activist also visited Law School to offer a credit course on law and literature. The course was scrapped by the then Director due to undisclosed reasons, but a group of students went ahead to do the course without the credits. Sexuality and queer jurisprudence figured prominently in this course.

A number of students also participated in a public protest which was organised in Bangalore in 2001 to condemn the arrest of outreach workers working with Men who have Sex with Men in Lucknow holding banners like 'Give us the Right to Love', 'Lesbian and Indian', 'Out and Proud', 'Love is a Basic Human Right', and so on. Justice Kirby was visiting Law School again in January 2002, and this time we organised a week-long queer film festival on campus in his honour. The films covered a range of issues including coming out, discrimination, celebration, relationships, and so on. The levels of tolerance and acceptance of alternative sexuality among the student body can be ascertained by the fact that an openly gay student was elected as the Vice-President of the student union. A number of factors are responsible for the radical sub-culture going from strength to strength.

- One of the most important factors is the largely democratic structure of the institution, which involves a great degree of student participation in most of its activities. The value of liberalism precisely lies in this respect of different ideas. So, even at times when the authorities did not like certain activities by students, there was no direct intervention to stall them.
- Possibly, the fact that the Law School student union is an autonomous body with absolutely no party affiliations helped us overcome the natural conservatism associated with political parties.
- The interconnections between issues also makes possible this kind of articulation. The NLSIU is not an overwhelmingly male space. This is due to the almost equal number of women on campus and the presence of a number of vocal articulate women who make it impossible to de-masculinise the Law School public space. That apart there is a tradition of thinking about other social issues which allows the emergence of alternative perspectives on sexuality as well. For example, the pro-Narmada Bachao Andolan sentiment was already strong before sexuality emerged as an issue and provided an activist supportive space. Women have always fought for and have largely achieved equal rules and discipline codes within Law School. Discrimination in curfew timings of hostels, and so on, which are often defended as protective, was done away with after a sustained demand by the student body. There are regular demands for regularisation and better work conditions for the labour force employed in the college. Students from the

University have also been a part of the anti-communal struggle and a number of them visited Gujarat to help with relief work in the camps affected by communal violence. Perhaps it is no coincidence that those supportive of the struggles of the people of the Narmada valley, gender equality, anti-communalism and labour rights were also supportive of queer rights. Maybe oppression of one sort does make us sensitive to other kinds of suffering as well.

Last, but of no less significance, was the value of coming out by some queer students to building a broader student culture sensitive to queer issues. Once a person is a friend then support is built. Also, coming out challenges the root of the problem with queer politics, i.e., invisibility.

Of course, the constant interaction of the sub-culture with the official narrative cannot leave the latter untouched, and we have had a few achievements. Queer issues are raised increasingly in the classroom, and a few teachers, mainly those teaching social sciences, have incorporated them in their courses. At this day, various aspects of queer theory are raised and discussed in a number of courses including sociology, history, political science, jurisprudence, family law, constitutional law, criminal law, and law and literature. In many courses where senior students work as teaching assistants, sexuality politics is usually dealt with by them, revealing greater acceptance of the issue within the student body than the faculty.

Another milestone was the declaration in the Official Prospectus of the University in 2002 that the University does not discriminate on the basis of, among other things, sexual orientation. The policy has entered its second year and is reiterated in the 2003 prospectus. Both these achievements were possible only because of student involvement in both the processes, owed largely to the democratic structure of the institution.

Again, in its official recommendations to the National Commission for the Review of the Constitution, the Law School suggested the inclusion of a non-discrimination clause in the Indian Constitution on the ground of sexual orientation, on the lines of the South African Constitution (http://www.nls.ac.in/ncrwc/ncrcw_index.htm). This was a result of the efforts of the students who worked on the recommendations and got them approved by the faculty.

At the same time, these achievements do not in any way indicate that we have been entirely successful, or have achieved a substantial part of what we set out to achieve in the context of the University. The NLSIU is certainly not the most queer-friendly space in the world, but at least in the Indian context it does stand out like an island where you can be yourself with dignity and talk about discrimination legitimately. However, we are currently faced with a number of issues and concerns, a few of which are the following:

- Global shift towards authoritarianism has its impact in the Law School, like all other educational institutions. One foresees that there possibly is a shift towards greater authoritarianism which is worrying. But hopefully the ingrained democracy is too resilient to be shaken.

- The gender balance has not been able to be fully resolved as there are fewer women coming out than men. This keeps reminding us that probably within Law School, and despite all the efforts over the years, women still have fewer spaces and security than men.

- Law School cannot entirely dismiss the claim that its social constitution is largely élite and metropolitan, though increasingly small-town students are enrolling. This social composition tends to validate claims that sexuality is the problem of the élite alone. However, there is no perceivable difference in response to the issue by students from urban and élite backgrounds and the ones from relatively modest small-town backgrounds. The argument also does not seem to hold in a context like India where even in élite settings, sexuality largely remains a taboo. And yet doubts remain if all this would have been possible in an entirely non-élite setting.

These and other issues will, hopefully be resolved in time, and the radical student sub-culture will continue to redefine and sensitise the official discourses of the educational system, continuing to take a stand against all forms of oppression, including sexuality. It is this radical sub-culture on college campuses which makes universities the harbingers of wider socio-political changes in a polity. The tragedy is that stories like that of the Law School sound extremely singular in the increasingly conservative student culture. The situation is particularly disturbing given the history of student association with the national movement for independence, the left movement in Bengal or the opposition to the Emergency. We, the students of this age, are the children of the post-socialism 1980s; a generation which has witnessed increasing political conservatism and the only popular movement we have inherited from our predecessors is the Temple movement. This notwithstanding, I retain my belief that radical sub-culture on campuses will continue to inform while being informed, and shape the course of the Indian polity for times to come.

JAWAHARLAL NEHRU UNIVERSITY, NEW DELHI

Jawaharlal Nehru University in New Delhi is an extremely politically active campus and from the 1970s onwards has served as the hub of the leftist intelligentsia in India. Student parties affiliated to the major Indian political parties are also quite active on campus and carry on intense debate among themselves through the judicious use of posters. Campus life usually revolves around long and often heated discussions over tea at one of the many *dhabas*, and the atmosphere is one that is usually well-informed and often opinionated.

Starting out as a group of friends studying at JNU, some of us had already begun discussions among ourselves about the homophobia and misogyny we had experienced first-hand on a campus that usually prided itself on its liberal values, and felt the need for the student community on campus to come together to begin the process of dialogue around issues of sexuality. The tangential need to combat regressive attitudes around sex, sexuality, desire, sexual orientation and sexual choice as well as to raise awareness within the student community around these issues was also felt. Therefore, in November 2003, as a result of this long process of consultation, Anjuman, the JNU students' queer collective was formed.

One of our first tasks at Anjuman was to redefine 'queer' from being just an easier, or perhaps more academic way of saying LGBT, to using it to describe any person who consciously questioned gender and sexual norms. Anjuman, in Urdu, refers to either a milieu or a space, and as a space that supported questioning, we found it important not to affiliate ourselves politically with any of the student parties on campus.

During our first meeting, some of the older LGBT students in JNU spoke about their experiences of harassment and often violent homophobia on campus, which was quite shocking to the rest of us. Although many at the meeting affirmed the importance of having a collective that spoke openly about LGBT issues and sexuality in general, some others at the meeting assumed that anyone who spoke about LGBT issues was bound to be LGBT, and conversely on being assumed to being LGBT, many others chose to avoid all further association with Anjuman.

Our first poster dealt with very basic LGBT issues, giving out the basic definitions of various sexual identities, information about Section 377 of the Indian Penal Code, which criminalises same-sex sexual activity, myths and facts about sexuality, and the history of the queer movement in India. The poster was in both Hindi and English, as JNU has two groups of students, usually divided on the basis of class, which also usually corresponds to the language spoken. The poster evoked quite a bit of curiosity on campus, as well as a host of reactions ranging from the elative and congratulatory to the offensive. Subsequent posters included one on the issue of lesbian suicides on International Women's Day.

As one of its first activities on its inception, Anjuman had also scheduled a film festival and discussion, and in the wake of the reactions to the poster, many of us were quite apprehensive about participation in the film festival, expecting not more than 20 people to arrive. We were quite shocked then, to see that over 200 turned up eventually, and we reasoned that people were probably just curious or perhaps it was just that we were screening a film like *Fire*, with all the controversy around its content and this drew people in. The other film screened was *Summer In My Veins*.

The discussion brought quite a bit of overt homophobia to the fore, and statements questioning the morality of homosexuality, and the possibility of the extinction of the family structure and the human race if it were allowed to continue, as well as comparisons of homosexuality to bestiality, child sexual abuse and criminality were made. This association is of course the result of society's vilification of any tendency that is against patriarchal values and the norms of heterosexuality. Gautam Bhan, our discussant for the day, ingeniously tackled most of these sentiments, and the discussion also veered well into the class angle of the issue as well as the importance of speaking about sexuality.

Discussions about the film festival and Anjuman were heard at *dhabas* and in canteens, among small groups of men and women. These discussions might have been derogatory, neutral or supportive, but the very fact that sexuality and queer politics had been brought out in the open was perhaps a welcome change.

Later in the academic year, Anjuman also organised a talk by Roselle Pineda, a Filipina Communist lesbian on the lesbian movement in the Philippines. Interestingly, the hostel in which the talk was to be held was one in which the Hindu right-wing students' party, the Akhil Bharatiya Vidyarthi Parishad (ABVP), affiliated to the BJP, had earlier in the year, lost the elections after a period of six years. One can imagine why a Filipina Communist lesbian speaking in a hostel that had until very recently been dominated by the Hindu right-wing was so irksome to the ABVP, whose leadership consequently initiated private efforts to have the talk stalled. When these failed, the volume of the hostel television was raised to such an extent that the talk seemed as though it was about to be jeopardised. However, Roselle, always the performer, shouted above the television to recount her very interesting and enlightening experience.

The continued harassment of many of the members of Anjuman, especially its male members, where they are called names, taunted and teased, as well as Anjuman, the collective, and Anjuman, the word itself, being the object of much ridicule on campus perhaps fits in with the idea that visibility often brings its own backlash. In this context, it is important, however, to classify such behaviour as harassment, as often, fixed notions of harassment and homophobia assume that these are only constituted through violence and not merely through attitudes. Violent homophobia is itself quite prevalent on campus where in an incident later in the academic year, a student's room was ransacked and dirtied and homophobic notices were stuck on his door. A few people have also written in to Anjuman and often the impression one gets is that many of them just seek a space to understand and talk about their sexuality and these opportunities are usually not available with their peers.

More recently, Anjuman has signed on to 'Voices Against Section 377', a Delhi-based coalition of various groups rallying to create public awareness about Section 377, as well as the recently-initiated 'South Asian Queer Students' Alliance' (SAQSA). These efforts will hopefully consolidate and represent student voices in the queer movement. The Anjuman experience has so far been enlightening and exciting though at the same time painful and worrying. Nonetheless, it certainly seems like the beginning of a healthy process of self-criticism, questioning, awareness-creation and discussion.

NOTES

1. The Hart-Devlin debate is a famous debate in jurisprudence wherein the question of the law's role in enforcing morality was examined. In 1957, the Wolfenden Committee in UK recommended the decriminalisation of homosexual behaviour which was opposed by Lord Devlin on grounds of public morality. H.L.A. Hart responded by saying that law had no business in enforcing public morality.

REFERENCES

Kevin S. Reuther, 'Dorothy's friend goes to law school', http://www.ibiblio.org/gaylaw/issue2/reuther.html. Accessed 12 February 2004.

15

Amitié
Organising LGBTs in Small-town India

Anis Rai Chowdhury

 Amitié is a friendship group for the sexual minorities. We are stationed at Chandannagar, a small subdivisional town in West Bengal, a suburb of Kolkata. We are a few faces who are tired of hiding behind the mask for so long. The pain of not being able to get in touch with others who were suffering was immense as well. We envied our friends in the big metropolitan cities who had support groups in times of need. Some of us were in touch with some of the groups in Kolkata, but never dared to think of forming our own group.

The present author is from a very conservative middle-class family brought up within the context of 20th-century Bengali culture where a same-sex relationship is considered a disease and a development disorder. It was always the same with all of us. Still, some could gather up enough courage to go out cruising. Naturally they came to know each other and formed a small network of their own.

But all were not that fortunate. Being children of overprotective parents, they were never allowed to go out alone after dark and explore life and its possibilities. Moreover, their family background and grooming led them to think of themselves as sinners and abnormal freaks. They tried to hide their true feelings and pose differently. But nothing can be more painful than living a false life!

Those who were already confident about themselves had their own share of problems. They were regularly harassed by neighbours and friends. Even the people who had enjoyed heartless, merciless, coercive sex with them the previous evening used to tease them the very next morning in public. Incidents of physical abuse were not rare either. Fear, shame and frustration were an integral part of their everyday lives. The risk of getting infected by deadly diseases was still something of an unknown threat. Many attempted suicide, and a few even succeeded. One very young kothi, who used to work at a roadside *dhaba*, died of some unknown disease. Many said that he suffered from cancer of the anus caused by regular anal penetration.

One of the persons from Chandannagar, leading a secret life, once got in touch with Counsel Club—a support group working in Kolkata. After meeting the groups, for the first time he felt confident and comfortable about himself and got rid of all his misconceptions. He started thinking about starting a telephonic-helpline to get in touch with other like-minded people and help them out. Within a few months he met others from his hometown at one of the Counsel Club meetings. Previously he thought he was the only one in his surroundings. Now this new discovery emboldened him to think afresh. The fact that he had to go to Kolkata to find out about friends from his own town was really an interesting thing. He realised that there might be others like him, suffering silently—alone, in the darkness of fear and ignorance. He felt that only a local support group could solve this problem.

When he became more intimate with his new found friends, who were already out, he came to know their side of the story. That made him even more determined to form a support group. But the most difficult hurdle was the unwillingness of many of the members of the community itself. They were scared of getting undesirable exposure. Some even thought that only economically independent people could think of such things. A few called it an urban circus.

Still, there were people who wanted this group to see the light of the day. They assembled on the Maghi Purnima day of the Bengali year 1408 (14 February 2003) and after some discussions decided to form a group to support the causes of the local LGBT people.

The process of finding a name for the group, getting it registered, getting a registered address and other formalities began. A very senior activist, Pawan Dhall, was supporting this effort from the very beginning. Since he was the CEO of SAATHII Calcutta, that agency also helped the new group in every possible way. New Alipore Praajak Development Society, a partner agency of Naz Foundation International(NFI), also extended their helping hand. Some members were invited to join a capacity-building workshop at Kolkata and then two office-bearers joined the NFI Regional Meet at New Delhi. Such exposures helped this group (already christened as AMITIÉ, a word that means 'Friendship' in French) to strengthen its foundation.

The members of Amitié tried their best to serve the people of the local community. The 'manly' men who used to abuse gay men and kothis verbally and/or sexually were taken care of. Most of them became friends after proper sensitisation. A few had to be brought under control by applying combined force. Amitié with its limited resources tried to supply members as well as non-members with condoms and information. Such activities brought friends, who first doubted or opposed the attempt, back into the fold.

In the meantime, some changes were taking place in the LGBT scenario of West Bengal. Most of the support groups and community-based organisations (CBOs) were coming together to form a network. Amitié joined this process and became the proud host of the first structural meeting of this network (now known as MANAS Bangla). As part of the said network Amitié participated in a needs-assessment exercise for an MSM (Men who have Sex with Men) Targeted Intervention for the West Bengal State AIDS Prevention and Control Society. At present, as a partner of MANAS Bangla, Amitié is playing an important role in running West Bengal's first ever MSM Sexual Health Targeted Intervention Project.

The Amitié team has always been the largest one to attend any relevant events (like the Rainbow Walk, India's first Pride Parade organised by the Integration Society; the Siddharth Gautam Film Festival organised by SAATHII Calcutta; the 4th West Bengal Sexual Health Conference organised by WBSAPCS; World AIDS Day and World Human Rights Day celebrations, and so on). In November 2003, on the occasion of Jagaddhatri Puja, an important local festival, Amitié ran an HIV/AIDS Awareness Campaign with the help of the West Bengal State AIDS Prevention and Control Society (WBSAPCS) and the event was a great success. The campaign was inaugurated by the Mayor of Chandannagar Municipal Corporation, which proves that Amitié has created a space of its own. Today it is also busy in helping newer groups to come up in neighbouring towns like Bardhaman, Rishra and Nabadweep.

But it has not all been only success. In this short existence of one year we have had our share of frustrations, failures and harassment. One of our members is dying today due to an anal infection caused by the fracture of the anal lining. Non-availability of lubes and condoms can take more lives. With the Targeted Intervention project taking off, the situation is supposed to improve. But a lot still has to be done.

On 20 November 2003, in the evening, our secretary Bikram Das, along with some other members of our group (Prabir Ray, Abhijit Ray and Abhishek Koley—all kothis) were sitting at Chandannagar Strand and were discussing the preparations for the World AIDS Day. At that time two women and two young boys were passing by. They passed by our bench and then suddenly the women turned back and without any provocation started uttering abusive words at our friends by calling them eunuchs and accusing them of sodomy in very filthy language. The boys were about to retort but Bikram told them to remain silent. The women, however, continued shouting.

Subsequently, two armed policemen appeared on the scene, asked the women what was the matter and whisked off our three young friends. When Bikram tried to intervene, they tried to take him along as well but later changed their minds. Bikram accompanied them to the police station in any case.

Within a few minutes other office-bearers of Amitié got the information and reached the police station. There they met the Inspector and informed him that we work with HIV/AIDS and were during the incident discussing related matters with the young people present there. They also informed him of the events that followed. The officer very rudely told us that we were not supposed to discuss such things in a public place as such talk could upset a lady and that NGOs need not talk about such things with young people as that is beyond their field of action—there are other people for that kind of work and he is quite aware of what an NGO should do and what it should not. He said that our friends would be produced in a court of law the next morning.

The boys were booked under Section 39 of the West Bengal Police Act—apparently for eve-teasing (Chandannagar Police Station G.D. Entry no. 824 dated 20 November 2003). We procured bail for them with the help of a local lawyer. The duty officer and the lawyer who helped us to procure the bail were willing to hush up the matter in return for a bribe and when we declined to do so, the lawyer suggested that the boys plead guilty, pay a nominal fine and close the chapter. He repeatedly told us that this case can't be contested and that was the only way out. But we felt that we should fight it to avoid further problems, save our boys from similar harassment later and establish our right of discussing HIV/AIDS, sex and sexuality and allied issues and also to highlight the officer's misbehaviour. But we definitely did not want to do so at the cost of the honour and freedom of our young friends. Moreover, it seemed most absurd that in spite of the constitutional provisions, the accused was not going to have an opportunity to defend himself!

So we sought suggestions and help from our friends. Aditya Bandyo-padhyaya referred us to a friend of his, Satyajit Mukherjee, a lawyer who practises at Chinsurah, our district headquarters. He helped us a lot. The case was heard by the Chandannagar Subdivisional Court on 10 December 2003 and 19 January 2004 is presently being contested.

We also informed the WBSAPCS and the State Management Agency and they in their own capacity too dealt with the matter. As a result, within a fortnight, on World AIDS Day (1 December 2003) we set our information dissemination and condom promotion pavilion on the Strand, exactly opposite the Police Station. The Police did not trouble us at all. Instead that very officer, who only a few days back told us that talking about HIV/AIDS in public was none of our business, paid a visit to our pavilion and praised our efforts. But the battle was not yet fully won. We are looking forward to the way the case actually ends.

Our wish list includes a tele-helpline that will enable people from the surrounding areas to approach us more easily. We have mainly worked for the gay, bisexual and transgendered males till now. But we are really eager to help the local lesbians and transsexuals as well. We have our plans ready for the documentation of the process of becoming a 'launda'. But we have no funding and very few friends and little introduction. We are struggling hard and success seems to be very distant. But we are not going to lose heart and we intend to go on and on and on...

III

Personal Narratives

16

A Hijra's Own Story*

Revathi

My Childhood

Who am I? I was born in Tamil Nadu and grew up with the name Annadurai. Ever since I can remember, I would help my mother with housework. I would sweep the entrance clean and cover it with *kolam* (an auspicious art of decorating courtyards and prayer rooms in south India, almost always done by women or young girls of the house). Sometimes, I tried on my sister's clothes and looked at myself in the mirror. I usually kept company with girls of my age and played with them. People—my brothers, friends, the neighbours—would call me names such as *ali, onbathu, pombalasatti* (all derogatory references to hijras). My teacher would pinch me in the thigh and ask 'why do you act like a girl?' 'Behave like a proper male child.' That was when I understood that I was behaving like a girl. I was happy being that way.

When I turned 15, I began experiencing various feminine desires. I began to feel shy and self-conscious when men were around and felt a growing need to dress up and look good like women did. I was male but also womanly. Was I the only one who felt this way? Questions and doubts such as these came up all the time. I simply could not understand what was happening. Since I was male in body, I concealed my femininity, my desires, and found myself deeply shaken by my inability to hide these things for long. I could not concentrate on my studies. I failed my tenth standard examination and spent a year studying at home because of this.

* This piece was originally written in Tamil and translated by Arul Mani. Arul Mani teaches English at St Joseph's College of Arts and Science, Bangalore.

Could I find somebody who felt the way I did? I began to seek people like myself. I once visited a hill-fort close to where I lived. I met people like myself there. I spoke to them of how I felt. I learnt from them of men who had become women.

I would visit this hill-fort often to meet my new friends and to express myself freely. I would sing and dance and spend time with them happily. My family began to restrict 'me. They began asking questions about where I was going and what I was doing. I was ordered to work as a cleaner on the lorry we owned. They would scold me while the people who worked for us were around and leave me feeling humiliated. I was asked to do all the difficult jobs that men normally did. They also beat me now and then. I was unable to bear the physical and emotional torment inflicted by my family and so I ran away from home in search of the places where hijras lived.

MY DISCOVERY OF THE HIJRA WORLD

I found refuge with a hijra community in Erode, some 50 kilometres from my native place. For the first time, I met people who had had the operation and dressed like women. They would dance in the *Karagattam* (a form of religious offering through dance). They also made periodic visits to Bombay and Delhi. I wanted to become a woman, to become like them. I asked if I too could wear a sari. They said I needed to grow my hair and get my nose and ears pierced before I could wear a sari. How long would it take for my hair to grow sufficiently long? I would weep silently because I needed to dress like a man till this happened. At Erode, I did whatever work they gave me. I also learnt to cook and to dance. Three months later, I travelled to Delhi.

I got my ears and nose pierced, wore women's clothes and lived the life of a woman in Delhi. A hijra elder adopted me as her daughter and I would accompany her when she visited the shops for money. I didn't like doing this. I accompanied her because there was simply no other option.

My family found out that I was living in Delhi as a hijra and visiting shops for money. I returned home when I received word that my mother was seriously ill. I took off my hijra clothes in Salem railway station and went home dressed in male attire. I was apprehensive about my mother's health taking a turn for the worse if she saw me dressed in any other way.

At home, I found my mother was in good health. My older brother began beating me with a cricket bat without a care whether he hurt my head or my limbs. I screamed in unbearable pain. My mother urged him on: break his legs, she said. Prevent him from going with hijras again. I began to bleed from the head. I wept uncontrollably; my body was covered entirely with swelling bruises. I did not have the courage to stand up to my family and express my womanliness. I could not get over the fear that they would beat me some more and perhaps kill me. They took me to the temple the next day and shaved my head. They had struck me several times, but their blows did not hurt as much as losing my hair did.

I was at home for about three months and then I ran away to Bombay. I joined a hijra community in Vikhroli, near Ghatkopar. It was here that I learnt of hijra life, of our culture and our traditions. I learnt of relationships within the community such as those between the *guru* (teacher), *chela* (disciple) and *nani* (maternal grandmother). The hijra community has seven houses. Each house has its own *nayak*. To become somebody's *chela*, it is necessary to bring the seven *nayak*s together in a *jamaat* and place a *reethu* in their presence.

I also learnt that I could become *chela* to another guru if I was dissatisfied with my present guru. I learnt further of the rules of hijra life, that we never cut our hair, that we touch the feet of our elders when we begin and end each day, that we must be careful about even our clothes coming in contact with elders. I learnt of how I was supposed to conduct myself in the presence of my *guru* and my *nani*.

I would visit shops. I also helped with housework. Six months passed in this fashion. They sent me to Dindigul in Tamil Nadu for my *nirvanam* (salvation: in this case the actual castration). Another hijra from the group whose *nirvanam* was due travelled with me. We completed our *nirvanam* and returned to Bombay suffering much hardship. Forty days after the ceremony, they performed the milk ritual. I went back to visiting shops.

I was very happy after my *nirvanam* because I felt that I had finally become a woman. I wanted to marry somebody and become a family woman. But who marries hijras? It was also not possible to live alone—that was against the rules of our community. Such a life, even if I attempted it, would be one without any security.

I·began to desire sex with men. The rule in our house was that we shouldn't see men or speak to them. This was a difficult situation. I couldn't hold myself back for very long. I broke with my house and joined another group which was involved in sex-work as *chela* to another hijra in that house. Joining another house while you are still a *chela* can lead to fights and violence. The only way to avoid such a situation is to become a *chela* to another hijra in that house.

I began to seek sex-work. I was able to have sexual relations with men but it was not very satisfying. With customers, you have to do what they want if you want to get paid. I was forced to have sex even when I didn't feel like it because I needed the money. Even though I made good money and handed it all promptly to my *guru*, I never was given good clothes. And sometimes, local *goondas* would force me into sex without paying for it.

Once a *goonda* forced himself on me in a way that I found inappropriate. It hurt in more ways than one. My guru did not lift a finger to help me. Sex-work was possible in our locality only if you did what the *goondas* asked you to do. I barely survived that experience. I didn't want to stay there any more. I wondered where I could go. Society looks down on us. We don't get jobs. We are treated badly. To add to all this there is the nuisance caused by policemen and *goondas*. After thinking about all these things I decided to return home to my native place.

I went home as a woman for the first time. You could say that an earthquake shook my home. My brother tried to beat me again. I yelled that I was a woman. That I would go to the police if he laid a hand on me. I displayed the result of my *nirvanam* to them. They told me that I must wear men's clothes. I declared that I couldn't do all that any longer. My father who understood my feelings said let him be as he wishes. I was however not allowed to step out of the house. I could not take part in functions on public occasions. My relatives and acquaintances visited me as they would visit somebody who was ill. They began to look at me in a strange way. Everyone began gossiping about me.

I did not wish to continue living there. I left home and joined a hijra group in Bangalore. I became a sex-worker in my new guru's *hammam* (spaces for bath as well as sex work). I understood that I would get respect only if I had money. I worked in Bangalore for five years and saved the money I earned.

I gave my guru and my family money occasionally. I got treated with respect only when I did this, both by my family and within my hijra group. I would go home now and then and give my father the money I had saved. I told him that I had begun dancing, and that my earnings came from this activity. I did not tell them anything about my sex-work. These visits home would sometimes last as long as 10 days. Now, they let me move about freely and did not try to restrict me in any way.

When I travelled by bus, women would not sit next to me if they guessed that I was a hijra. People in the bus would tease me mercilessly. Some men would try to grope me or try funny business with their feet. My life went on in this way every day, fearing society, *goondas* and the police.

POLICE ATROCITIES

I would venture out of the *hammam* into the streets of Bangalore for sex-work. I pretended to be a woman while seeking customers. Nobody would have come to me if I had let the fact that I was hijra be known. People in cars would pick me up. On several occasions other hijras and I were chased by policemen who were following me in *mufti*. They would slap me around and chase me away before getting money from my customers. They would also take money from me—sometimes fifty, sometimes hundred. Even before I had made my *boni* (first earning of the day), they would turn up and say let's go to the station. I would give them money because I was so frightened.

I've been dragged into their vans while walking the streets. At the station they would beat me and kick me and humiliate me with questions like 'how do you have a woman's body? Show us'. They would keep me there for two days and torture me—no case was ever registered. They would then drag me to court. At the entrance, they would make me give them money, say two hundred rupees, and tell me to get lost. I had to live in fear of the police while seeking sex-work. Whether I went out for sex-work or not, I had to give my guru a hundred rupees every day. Only then could I stay at their house.

Once while I was looking for customers, some policemen stopped me and forced me to trap people for them. They lay in wait and collared the customers who approached me to discuss my rate. A few people who stopped to ask for directions also got arrested. They caught some 10 people this way and then beat me up and said get lost, if we see you here again, we'll put you in jail for six months.

Once, at Cubbon Park police station I was beaten up, tortured, and forced to eat off the floor on a cold winter day. I was made to sweep the entire station clean. Whenever something like this happened I would ask myself why am I am suffering like this and whether all this trouble is because I do sex-work. If other jobs were possible, I could live like other women. I would weep bitterly because I knew that these options didn't exist.

Goonda Trouble

At the *hammam*, local *goonda*s would turn up for some free sex. If I refused, they would make threats. We won't let you live here.... We'll take a blade to you.... Once, two men stopped me on a street and tried to make me go with them. When I refused, one of them pulled out a knife and tried to stick it in my face. I warded off the jab with my hand-bag and the knife landed on my hand. I yelled the words 'police, police' loudly and they ran away. I have to live with my heart in my mouth from the moment I step out till the moment I return home.

I decided not to do sex-work. How long could anybody deal with all these things? Police, *goonda*s, everybody. I returned to my native place. At home, I helped my parents around the house. My strongest desire was to live the life of a woman, to marry the man I liked, to find a job I could do. In trying to become a woman I had ended up living the life of a hijra among other hijras. I needed money to live with respect in society, to wear nice clothes, and to meet my daily needs. Having no real option, I was forced to take up sex-work to make enough money for my needs. I had to buy the love of those around me with money. I had to deal with policemen and their torture. This society does not look on me favourably. The legal system refuses to provide either facilities or assistance. My family treats me well only if I give them money. I grew sick of life thinking of all this and wanted to do something to end my life.

Seeing me in this state, my mother asked why are you like this, why are you in this state of collapse. 'This is why we beat you, because we didn't want you to become a hijra. What is the use of being depressed now? Are you now unhappy in this woman's guise?' I said it's not what you think. I want to live the life of a woman. I am what I want to be. I am unhappy because I can't find a decent job or get married. My mother said, marriage for you? With a man? Can you bear a child for him? Your being a hijra is enough humiliation for us. If you get married the little dignity we have will also go.

Even if my dreams had to be bundled up into a gunny bag and forgotten I felt that others like me should not end up the way I did. What could I do to ensure that? And how? I didn't know. At this point I found a job through Sangama, an organisation in Bangalore.

SANGAMA

Sangama is an organisation that fights for the rights of sexual minorities. I am now able to work for my people because of Sangama. I am not at fault for the way I am today. I think it is society and its laws that look on me in a prejudiced manner.

I shared my experiences—of hijra life and police atrocities—with various organisations and spoke of them at public functions. I am thus bringing about some awareness about what it is to be hijra. I got married, but it broke up in about a year. I wanted to live like a woman but was not allowed the rights of a woman by my husband. He wanted his freedom. We parted ways because of these things. It may be more correct to say that I was divorced by my husband than to say that I divorced him.

I am now writing a hijra's life story. I will soon publish it in English, Kannada and Tamil. I now have a passport through Sangama. After a long struggle, I have got a passport as a woman. I take pleasure in describing myself as a woman. I desire to see our society and its legal system accept us as women, to accept all of us.

17

Leaving Home to Go Home

Sandip Roy

 My mother's eyes are shimmering with tears. In the harsh fluorescent light of the Kolkata airport, she looks tired. Hunched on the hard plastic orange seat she clutches my carry-on as if she was holding me. It is late at night and smog engulfs the city outside, the sulphurous street lights glowing amber. My little nephew is bored and roaming around the airport staring at the flickering orange and gold fish in the aquarium. His father tries to entertain him with sodden paper cups of Coke. My niece stares at the magazines in the bookstore. 'When will you reach San Francisco?' my mother asks distractedly. In the middle of the bustle of a departing international flight, hidden in the heart of our banal chitchat, there is a well of deep sadness. I am leaving again—going home to San Francisco and leaving home behind.

The first time I left India at the end of the 1980s, I couldn't wait to get to America. I already knew I was gay but my gay life was a string of hurried encounters in dark cruisy parks, behind trees and benches, ducking from strolling couples and roaming cops. At that time there were no gay groups, no bars in India, only shadowy circles of 'friends of friends' or men who changed their names in the parks. It was lonely being gay in India. In America I was going to be 'properly' gay. I would just walk into a gay bar and it would be nobody's business. The first time I brought someone home, it was utterly thrilling. The sex was almost secondary. Just walking into my apartment with this stranger I had met in the bar two hours ago felt like a small act of revolution. No more 'When will you be back?' No more 'Who is that friend of yours? I have never seen him before'. My independence was intoxicating. I was finally myself, not someone's brother, someone's son, someone's grand-nephew. Just me.

I could buy porn. I could answer personal ads (and get them sent to me at home without worrying who would read them). I could talk openly on the phone. I could have my boyfriend stop by in the middle of the night because he wanted to make pancakes.

America was all that and more. I found San Francisco. I found gay friends. I discovered gyms and chat rooms. I went dancing all night long at clubs filled with fog machines and glistening muscled boys, bottled water shoved into their back pockets. I found other gay Indians like me. We draped scarves around our heads and pretended to be tragedy queens from old Hindi films lip-synching our sorrows in lilting song. We marched in Pride parades in our shiny sequined peacock-iridescent Indian vests while the Toyota pickup truck draped with sarees blared Bhangra music.

And yet deep in me, that loneliness of being gay still remained like a hidden mirror I tried never to look into. When I came out to my parents, my mother said, 'Well, this is all very well when you are young. What's going to happen when you are older? Who will look after you?'

I told her brave things about how that was why we needed to come out, to build community, to have support structures. But the words remained—etched in me like an invisible script. I realise I don't know how to build family. When I visit my family in Kolkata, I just dive right in and the love closes over me like a warm tropical sea. But I know I am just a visitor. I see my nephew clambering onto his mother's lap to show her a drawing and I know I am just passing through. I see my mother scolding my niece for not doing her homework and wonder what will happen to me when I am my mother's age. Will I have someone to scold like that?

Every time I go back there is a little less left for me. My old books are falling to pieces and have been thrown away. Another aunt had died. Another friend had married and moved away. Next time I return even the house I grew up in will be gone, replaced by a much more practical block of apartments.

'Your nephew misses you. He mopes around,' my mother says the day after I leave. But the hustle and bustle of everyday life catches up and all traces of me are gone—like ripples from a stone falling into a pond. The kids are growing older. They are shyer now—they say 'Hello' on the phone and run away.

When I call home, my mother tells me about what they had for lunch. 'It must be your dinner time' she says. 'What did you cook?' I somehow can't tell her I just had cheap Chinese takeout. I imagine leftovers for her—cauliflower and dal and chicken curry. An imaginary meal for our imaginary family.

I wish it wasn't this way. I wish they could accept my gayness as unquestioningly and easily as they accept my sister's marriage and children. But it's not going to be so. We don't fight about it anymore. Living thousands of miles apart we have no time to waste on fights that no one can win. But it remains—its prickly edges butting into our conversations.

It remains in the questions my mother faces when she goes to weddings. 'When is that son of yours getting married?' In a culture where everything is about family, where family values are just ingested with rice, its hard for her to admit that my family doesn't fit the model she has imagined. I know it hurts her every time she knits little woollen coats for the latest new baby born in our extended family. But I also know I cannot do much about it as long as she cannot bring herself to call my partner more than my 'friend'. I listen to the long and involved tragic story of a cousin's divorce while the pain of the dissolution of my decade-long relationship lies unacknowledged.

I want to say it's her fault for not being broad-minded enough. But I cannot. I stand at the airport and look at the gray in her hair. She smiles at me and timidly holds my hand. It's a small private family moment and like an old photograph it fades a little more every time I get onto that plane.

When my friend meets me at San Francisco airport I hold him a little tighter than usual and don't want to let go. He is my family. As is my cat and dog. It's a fragile uncertain web we are spinning. Out of men I have met at bars, through ads, out of potlucks and outings to Hindi films, out of trips with friends to Mexico or Russian River, out of cocktails, drag parties, and India Day parades, I am trying to make myself a family. But I never know if I have got the recipe right.

18

She Came from the World of the Spirits

Maya Sharma

 At the turbulent confluence of three northern rivers, Ganga, Yamuna and the mythological Saraswati that pushed its course underground a millennium ago, stands the ancient town of Allahabad, considered holy by Hindus. On the newly developed periphery of this old town, between the bungalows and flats of the rich, past the crossroads of village Beli to the right, is a forgotten space sloping over a wide *nallah*. On the slope a creaking door opens onto a courtyard. Right in the centre, towards the back, stands a rectangular building constructed in the colonial style, with a verandah running alongside supported by pillars. From it stare five unblinking rooms.

In two of the rooms live Hasina Bano, her friend Fatima and Fatima's friend Choti. Untangled from amongst these lives, this is the story of Hasina Bano and her relationship with Fatima.

The norms and pressures of marriage, traditional family structures and daily struggles of material survival intersect with moments of inexplicable transcendence, built around the love between these two women. Their difficult times, their giving and taking, their mutual support, their interdependence, cannot all be classified as one identity, or contained in one. Therefore, our effort in presenting the facts as they are is problematic. We see the intimate connection between these two women as an example of how fluid the lines are between a sexual relation and an emotional bond. We read a lesbian identity, impose an orientation, rely on a conditioned perception. We admit that our purpose of rendering this particular 'lesbian' identity visible comes up against peculiar complications. Such a deep-rooted, flexible and sustained interweaving of consciousnesses and destinies, evidenced in this story, defies the simple narration of supposedly simple facts.

Our own ideological need to establish a single identity for our subjects in this context is countered by our interaction with such women, whose lives are proof that no one identity fully expresses even limited truths. Facing these inevitable contradictions, we have tried to narrate the story of Hasina Bano, a story that refutes easy interpretation and convenient categorisation.

When we first walked down the narrow lane into the courtyard and from there stepped into Hasina's room, neither she nor Fatima nor Choti was there. But there was a spirit of happiness hovering around the place that day, and it persisted through our visit.

Tahira, Hasina's youngest daughter, warmly welcomed us. Serving us tea and a snack of *murmure*, she introduced the people who shared that space. 'The government has banned the use of plastic bags, that is why we are all sitting here now, making these packets of paper. We'll earn something sitting at home. At least something is better than nothing.... That little thatched hut you see there, right in the corner of the compound, that is where Fatima keeps the load of bananas for ripening in a certain powder before selling them. She made the hut in the corner because the powder in which the bananas ripen has an overpowering stench. From here she carries them to the *kachehri* compound for sale.'

'Who helps her? Does she carry them by herself?' we asked.

'No, her relative from her village and her friend Choti also live here, together they take them,' Tahira said. She put her arm around the young girl sitting next to her, about twelve years old. 'Adjoining Fatima's room lives Hiralal mistri. This is his daughter. When she was very young her mother passed away, and now there are just the two of them, father and daughter... In the room near theirs lives the tempo *wala chacha* with his wife Vimla and three children.... That room there, the only one with a door, that locked iron blue door, the first one from the other side, it belongs to our landlady. She is the third wife of her husband. This space, land, house, everything, her husband has given her. Inside where she lives there is a bathroom, kitchen, everything. She is more fortunate than we are, we all have to sleep in one room, only Ammi and Fatima sleep outside. The landlady worked in a school as a teacher. She lives alone now. Though for some time now she has not been living here, she has gone to her daughter....

'Last year when there were floods and our house was inundated we climbed up and sat on the roof, you see these walls of bricks,' Tahira added, pointing to the unfinished door frames, windows and walls above us. 'After the floods the old landlady came and started to get these built, but without completing the work she left. At that time we pleaded with her to get our part repaired first. This house is old and falling apart, it is not in such a condition that anyone can just add another floor to it. Anytime it can collapse. What will happen to us then? We alone will have to bear the brunt. If there is a flood again we won't be able to sit on the roof even. This year it didn't rain much, otherwise what would have happened! Fatima and Hiralal mistriji worked on this construction themselves.' Tahira's voice had a ring of complaint, as if these two had somehow let the occupants down.

Along with the many humans in the congested compound live Fatima's faithful dog Moti and Hasina's pets: hens, rabbits, chicks, a parrot, and a charming little frisky baby goat. Before we left, we asked Tahira to tell her mother we had come and would return to see her.

The next time we went Hasina was home. She wore a saree. Her head was uncovered. Her long earrings chimed to her movements as she greeted us with a 'Salaam!' She rose and pushed aside the heap of clothes piled on the string cot, inviting us to sit. She was just a little over four feet tall, and seemed much younger than her 40 years. Perhaps she gave that impression because of her smile—it spread in the happiest way I have ever seen, mocking the lines of tension around her mouth, while crinkles at the corners of her eyes deepened mischievously, almost dangerously. In contrast to her daughters who spoke standard Hindustani, she spoke mainly in the local dialect mixed with Urdu, sweet to the ear, lyrical and intimate.

Lifting her smiling brown eyes, Hasina shared the moment of her first meeting with Fatima, in a whisper. 'I was standing by the well in the kachehri compound one day, all dressed up in red. At that time he emerged from the well and told me, "I love you". He came for me disguised as a woman and cast on me a magical spell I cannot explain. I cannot live without her. She has not come from your and my world, she has come from the world of the spirits.'

When she spoke of Fatima, Hasina sometimes referred to her as a man and sometimes as a woman. A bit stunned as well as moved by her description, we were silent for the few seconds and she remained lost in her reverie. Then she continued in a normal tone:'I was born in a village called Chitaymau and grew up with two sisters and one brother. Our father was poor. He had ten bighas of land. In my childhood I got a chance to go to school. I can read Urdu. My sister lived in purdah but I would go around without wearing any burqa, nor did I cover my face. I used to take the goats out for grazing. My sister would grumble that I did nothing in the kitchen except want food all the time. At that time I could not hold back my hunger. And today...' she paused thoughtfully, '... today it has all changed. The man my sister is married to, his family wanted me as the bride. I was fairer than my sister and they wanted a fair-complexioned girl. But my family decided I would not be good for that house because there was no woman there, and since I did not show interest in household chores, they thought I would not be able to manage the domestic work. But look at me today, I not only do the domestic work, I also go out to work. I am running my own life. I am proud of myself.

'Days passed, years went by, now only our mother is alive. She lives with my sister in the village. My brother is in Bangalore in a casting factory for brass. And I'm here, with each passing year growing older. I am no longer as fair and agile, you know how with age everything changes. My whole body aches. Each day I have to take a pill that costs two rupees, so that the pain eases. I have this nervous feeling inside me, there are times when I just feel like running away. Previously I was always cheerful. Even now I don't like to go around with a long face. But at times I can't help it....

'I came to the city for my livelihood. I took up massaging as my job. But I cannot count on it, there may be work, there may not be work, nothing about it is certain. Now I have taken work in two houses where I work for Rs 300 a month in each house, sweeping and swabbing floors and cleaning utensils. Both mistresses stood by me in my recent hour of need. Just now I went back to work after a month but they did not hire anyone else in my place. They said, "We'll have only you to work for us." They like me because it is not my habit to gossip or carry tales from one house to the other. The master of one of the houses works in the Middle East. When he is here he says, "Don't use so many utensils, Khala will have trouble washing so many." They respect me in that house. It's there that I have my first cup of tea in the morning, and *nashta*. They don't let me leave without eating something. They even come to my house to inquire about our welfare....

'You can't imagine this house when Fatima and I moved into it, it was very filthy then. This compound was used as if it was no more than a toilet. All the neighbours from around came here to ease themselves, morning and evening. We cleaned it with our own hands. Then only did this place become fit for human occupation. Our second daughter Sahira—you know Sahira, the one who works with me in your friend's house, the friend who told you about us—Sahira does not understand, she does not want to understand. She keeps saying, "Look for another room somewhere else." Tell me, how can we take another room, just like that, simply take another room, how can we? It is not that simple, take another room, indeed. Admitted that a door is missing and the rain drips from the ceiling. I've put a curtain in the verandah, it blocks the cold in the winter and in summer the breeze blows in freely so it is cool. For the rainy season I've tied a plastic sheet under the ceiling, that takes care of the dripping water. A room anywhere else costs nothing less than Rs 500– 600 per month. We're paying practically nothing here. Whatever we save I put away for Sahira's wedding. The woman who is to be her mother-in-law wants her married on Id, after the *rozas*. I want it postponed a bit, When our little goat Chandni gets all her teeth she will fetch Rs 1,000–1,500. We will sell her on Bakr-Id, for the sacrifice. God willing, we can earn a little bit.'

We said, 'We have heard that the boy Sahira is engaged to does not work. Is it necessary to marry her off to him?' Hasina explained, 'The work one does comes and goes, but it is the duty of all parents to get their children married off. The command of the Lord is that women marry and beget children. On the Day of Judgement I will have to give an account of all the things that I had to do and did not do. Our Sahira, she can read and write. She regularly recites the *namaaz* and observes the *rozas*.' She said it in a flat tone, as if she was not impressed with all that reading. I looked at her to ascertain from her face what her tone indicated but Hasina had moved on. 'Ayesha, my daughter older to Sahira, was married off to my sister's *devar*. A daughter was born, and a few days after that Ayesha passed away. The daughter is gone but one feels like giving things to the granddaughter, she is the only memory of my daughter. I've bought things for her. These things alone cost Rs 300–400. I've only one son, Firoz. He always manages to find some job or the other but he doesn't regularly work. Someone has cast a spell on him. So I sent him to the *maulvi*. He has given him a talisman. Thank God he is working now. He is employed in a biscuit-cake factory at Rajapur. His pay is not in proportion to the labour he is asked to put in. But I think the regularity of work will make him disciplined. Attending to a job daily will slowly put an end to his vagabond habits and also keep him away from the bad company he's fallen into.

'You see, now I'm the only one around to look after all my children. Alone, I have to take on all the work that has to be done. That is why I say I cannot leave Fatima. She is really brave, what man can match her courage? When we were on the roof during the floods, a snake crawled up to exactly where we were sitting. All of us were so shocked, we couldn't move. It was Fatima and Fatima alone who could have done what she did. With the presence of mind she has, she caught hold of the snake with her bare hands and killed it. No man, old or young, can stand up to her. One night some youths were being chased by the police and they jumped over the wall into the compound. They were wandering about the streets and the patrol got after them. But Fatima settled it well and proper, while we all slept.'

We expressed our wish to meet a strong woman like Fatima, and asked Hasina if she would mind our writing about her. Hasina raised a restraining hand, quickly explaining, 'Fatima is not the kind of person who will talk to anyone. She stands no nonsense. She is a stern woman. If a fellow even slightly suggests anything improper to a woman, or tries to swear or whistle or sing a line or make a pass, she puts him in his place there and then. One cannot take liberties with Fatima. At times when I work longer than usual or am held up somewhere and do not return home on time, she comes looking for me from house to house. She would not approve of the way I am sitting and talking to you now.'

We wanted to see Fatima, so the next day we went to the *kachehri* compound, the site of the well where Hasina had first met her. The *kachehri* was entirely a man's world. The well was hidden from view by the crowds surrounding it, concealed in the same manner that the well-water was hidden by the structure's walls and canopy. Only on pushing our way close to it were we able to see the circular empty space between the bodies of dozens of men. 'The water dried up many years ago,' someone told us, 'but no one has boarded up the well.' The advocates in their white ties and black coats, holding pens and paper and thick dusty files, though busy with their clients, could not keep their eyes off us. We were a distracting and unaccustomed presence in this place of men where Hasina and Fatima, two women, had instantaneously accepted their love for each other.

How had it come about, the chance of their finding one another among this busy, alien throng, how had they recognised the nature of their profound connection? Given the context, almost impossible! Yet we accept this as the true account of their meeting. Our observation of the actual well and Hasina's description of it, her transformative encounter with Fatima, the radical moment of the other's emergence from unseen and unknown depths underground, 'the world of the spirits', did not coincide. Interweaving her facts with the logic of fantasy, sublimity, dream and magic, Hasina had gone beyond the limits of the socially permissible. Paradoxically, in a male-dominated location where male-inspired and male-authored laws were interpreted and applied by men in favour of men, her vision was rooted in the realm of the illegal. Somehow, either miraculously or through sheer strength of will, she had generated possibility from the matrix of the impossible. Her private world materialized its substance from the very same public ground that completely excluded both her and her desired other.

Barely a few yards from the wrangling disorder of the *kachehri*, vendors and peddlers stood along the road. Among them, as far as the eye could see, Fatima and her friend Choti were the only two women among men hawking their goods. Short and stout, wearing a cotton saree, Choti stood talking to Fatima. Somewhat dark and lean, in a *salwar-kameez*, *dupatta* tied around her head, with one raised foot set on a sack and the other on the ground, Fatima stood sorting bunches of bananas. The large man's watch strapped on her wrist caught the August sun in the middle of its round dial and shone back little signals of light.

We went up to Fatima and asked her the price of the bananas. Pointing to different heaps she stated the various prices for the various kinds. We asked her to reduce the price. But she refused. Ignoring us, she went back to the task of pulling out, arranging and rearranging the different piles. We bought the bananas at the price she demanded, and left. The next day we told Hasina we had met Fatima. She smiled and asked, 'Did she ask you anything or say anything at all?'

'No,' we replied.

Hasina said, 'I told you, she will not talk. Where does she have the time? Her work is so hard. Carrying that load morning and evening, there is a pain in her ribs. She does not keep well. In the morning the man with a *thela* drops off the bananas, shouting "a thousand bananas". And he pockets the money for a thousand bananas. But the number always turns out to be less. No one can do anything about this thievery. How much can you fight? They will give the bananas to someone else if you argue. Her income depends entirely on what she can sell. When she can't sell them all in the *kachehri* she stands at the Beli crossroads. It is best when the entire lot of bananas get sold by the evening. If they are not sold and have to be kept overnight, we run into a loss because they become dark and pulpy. The next day they have to be sold at a much lower price. Fatima's son and her friend Choti both help her. But they don't wait till the evening at the Beli crossroads. They return home and Fatima comes later when she has sold them all....'

'But', we interrupted, 'Tahira was saying that the person who stays with Fatima is her relative from the village, not her son. If Fatima did not marry, who is that...?' We left the sentence unfinished. Horrified, Hasina tugged at her earlobes with thumb and forefinger, exclaiming, '*Tauba, tauba*! What are you saying? Fatima was married. Her husband died. That is the truth. My Tahira, she does not know. Fatima was married and this boy you think is her relative is her son.'

Observing Hasina's shock and her instinctive response to our query, we realised how sensitive this ground was. Such marginalised women struggling for daily survival had broken the traditional paradigm of the one-man/one-woman family, yet in no circumstances could they freely articulate their choices. Hasina was well aware of the extent a woman of her class, whether Muslim, Hindu, Christian or Dalit, would be permitted to live in the way she wanted to. She was also aware that to violate the social norms was, in literal and psychological terms, a dangerous action that could have serious consequences. Hence there was also a strong need to claim the protection of the traditional paradigm. Maybe that is why she repeatedly referred to marriage as the right thing to do. She was simultaneously making Fatima out to be different from the norm by claiming that she came from the world of the spirits, and erasing that difference by asserting that she had once been married, and thus was assimilated into the norm. It was clear that Hasina felt pressured to seek legitimacy for her friend and for herself.

Whatever the facts, it was also very clear that the two women depended on each other. Hasina said, 'Her support is crucial in my life. I count on her. One day some years ago, as usual I went to work. Tahira was busy in the house. I left at seven in the morning as I always do after having my quota of *paan*. Fatima told me later how Firoz and Tahira had quarreled. Tahira told Firoz to carry the lid of the container when he went to get milk, so the milk would not spill over. Firoz ignored her. He does not like to get up early in the morning and do errands, and on top of that, take orders from a girl. Reluctantly he stepped down from the verandah to go for milk, and as he pushed his foot into his slippers Tahira rushed out calling after him, but he was not listening. She called out to him again, then she ran after him carrying the lid in her hand. When she was about a foot from him she reached out to grab his arm, and he lost his temper. He turned and jerked her hand so hard that the lid fell. Brother and sister took hold of each other like wrestlers, circling like the lid spinning on the ground. When one lifted a hand the other seized it and swore retaliation. Who was there to intervene? Fatima heard them shouting and came out from her room. Just then accidentally Firoz's foot fell on a sharp piece of broken glass. He began to bleed, and bleed profusely. Fatima took hold of him and sat him down, winding a cloth tightly around his foot. Then she took him to the hospital, got the dressing done, got medicine, got him a tetanus shot. On the way to the hospital she told one of our acquaintances to let me know there was a serious fight in the house, that I was not to worry but I must come home as soon as possible. When I reached home after receiving the message, I got nervous seeing so much blood splashed all over. After they returned home from the hospital I started scolding the children, but Fatima told me not to shout otherwise the situation would flare up again. I kept quiet.

'Do you see? After all, why should she be concerned in my affairs! Yet she intervened in the fight, bandaged my son, took him to the hospital, got him treated. What would have happened had she not stepped in? She cares for me. There seems to be some previous connection between us, I cannot explain it. Sometimes when I've gone to my village or when she goes away and I don't see her, it seems as though I've lost something that is integrally mine. One day early in the morning I left for work. On the way I met someone coming from my village. He informed me my father was not well. I immediately set out for my village. Fatima returned home from selling bananas in the evening. She did not find me in the house. She had some food prepared by the landlady and fed Firoz. Next morning at six o'clock she left for my village. She came to find out how I was. She cares for my feelings. I join her family in times of happiness and sorrow.

'We have lived together for nearly eight years and not once have we fought. With my husband there used to be a fight every day. She came to live next to us, in the place I lived in earlier. Then she was selling vegetables. She saw my husband, the trouble he created for me, the daily thrashings and bickerings. That set off our friendship. My husband has left me and gone. Now I have no support except for her. She does not leave me, nor do I leave her. She has a heart of gold. If she were rich she would help with money as well. Anyone may ask me to leave her, but I will not leave her ever. Why should I not live with someone who supports me in all ways?'

We asked, 'Why is this coming up again and again, the question of your leaving Fatima? Has anyone said anything to you?'

Hasina would not meet our eyes. She busied herself pushing her bangles up and down her arm. Finally she remarked with reluctance, 'I'm just saying it, that's all. My husband left me and went away. People have ideas of social status and family honour, they are critical of me, saying that I go out of the house and work for other people to earn my living. But if I don't work, should I eat the mud off the walls? My husband has gone, I need to eat, don't I? I have to work and I work honestly and with self-respect. What wrong am I doing? I tell you, my flesh and bones may turn to dust but I won't marry again.'

Observing her defensiveness and discomfort, we began to understand what she was struggling to conceal, the grudge her family held against her for her unwavering commitment to Fatima. We learnt of the actual tension in more detail when Hasina and Sahira began to keep different work times at the house of our friend, a local resident who had functioned as our intermediary. Our friend asked Hasina for more time and help. But Hasina worked elsewhere also. So our friend asked Sahira to help. Now that the daughter's work took more time, she began staying after the mother left. Alone with our friend, she was able to build a bond of greater trust and confidentiality.

One day she finally gave vent to her feelings. 'I am fed up with Ammi! I wonder what spell Fatima has cast on her, Ammi has turned insane. Thank God I read my *namaaz* and pray, if Fatima tries to work some black magic on me, I will be protected. What nonsense Ammi goes around talking! After she met this woman, this Fatima, she turned Abba out of the house. I don't even talk to her now. How many times I've told Ammi to take a house somewhere else! Live away from Fatima, get away from her! But she won't listen. She won't leave her. She will not listen to any of us, her own daughters, she listens to Fatima only. No matter what her children tell her, she will not listen. I don't like all this…!'

And then gradually, as Sahira began to work for our friend for longer periods, it became harder and harder to talk to Hasina about Fatima, or ask her anything about herself or their relationship. When the subject came up, she evaded it. Gradually she withdrew. Then one day after completing her work she pulled her veil over her face and left. She did not return.

'Ammi is running a fever,' was all Sahira would say.

19

Death of the Gay Man

Devdutt Pattanaik

 What you are about to read is fact. You have the freedom to call it fiction. There will be no references, no testimonies. Just stories. Real stories of men who have died told by men who survived them. Men who prefer to be identified through initials: FR, PG, DL, RP, JP, MK, AC and NT. Not all of them are gay.

He slipped and fell under the local train. Was cut to pieces. His old arthritic mother and his paralysed father performed the last rites. There were many people at the funeral, family and friends, horrified by the incident. 'Mercifully, he had no wife or children.' 'But he had dependents. Who will look after his old parents, he was their only support. The younger son is away in USA with his foreign wife.' Tears rolled down as people struggled for answers, tears of pain, and fear: how would *they* cope in such a situation.

FR was a gentle man, in his early 50s, who chose to remain single. A man of varied interests from music to literature to cooking. He loved movies, was obsessively organised, hated Hindi movies, felt that India was going to the dogs, had very strong views on religion and politics. He was also gay.

At the funeral many of his gay friends were there. Four at least. Two of whom were married. All of whom were firmly in the closet. They did not look into each other's eyes. They pretended they did not know each other. They did not sit together as a group. 'What if someone finds out about us. About FR,' they said to themselves. 'Why upset his mother and father even more,' they rationalised. And so at the requiem there were speeches of how wonderful a man he was, a great friend, a dependable nephew, a devoted son. Nobody spoke of the many men FR loved and of the many men who loved FR. Love that was certainly not platonic.

Nobody mentioned FR's loneliness, his frustration, his yearning for a lover. Nobody perhaps knew that FR spent hours walking the street, cruising in parks and stations, hoping to find that perfect lover: dark, strong, masculine, raw, whom he would civilise. That part of his life was known to very few people. Only four such people were at the funeral. Four who chose to remain silent. And so an entire aspect of FR's life went unacknowledged. It never existed.

It was a fortnight before the news of FR's death spread amongst his wider friend circle. 'Oh god, I have his books.' 'I hope his parents or friends don't find that secret file on his computer.' 'He never kept those magazines in his parent's house but he did have that photo album in his own house. What will they do when they find it.' 'I had borrowed the file of newspaper clippings on gay issues he maintained meticulously. No one will find that, for sure.'

Friends poured in to offer their condolences. The old mother was surprised to find so many men, just a few women from the office, but mostly men, coming to her house, all strangers, with tearful eyes offering their condolences. She was too much in grief and too tired to bother to find out who they were. All men. All dark and handsome, not from the same community, not from his office or the neighbourhood. They all mourned for her Babu. But Babu had never even mentioned their names.

Out there was one PG waiting for FR to call. 'I am uncomfortable giving my number but I promise to call you every Monday,' FR had said. And every Monday, FR had dutifully called him. At 10 AM precisely after settling in his office and clearing his email inbox. FR and PG met every Tuesday at Sewri station and spent the evening together, sometimes even the night. Then the phone calls stopped. PG wondered why. Weeks passed. Frustrated, he landed up at the Sewri apartment. The doorman said, 'Saab died two months ago. Did you not know?' PG shook his head. 'His mother stays in South Mumbai. Do you want the address?' PG took the address. FR had a mother! FR had never mentioned her. They had shared so much. But he had never told him that he had a mother, a father, that they were old and sick, that his only brother, twice married, once divorced, was in the US and neglected his parents. So many secrets. When PG met FR's mother, she was polite. The condolence was accepted. PG wanted to scream, 'I loved your son. I held him in my arms as he complained about the cruelty of life. We would have been lovers, even partners, had he not withdrawn the moment I told him I was married with two children.'

During a condolence meeting organised by FR's friends, everyone shared their experiences of death of gay friends/lovers. DL spoke. 'You know the other day I received a phone call from this guy, RP. He asked me if I knew his brother JP. I said, "No." He replied, "Your name was in his diary. There was a star next to it. I thought it meant you were his special friend. Anyway, he died last week in a motorcycle accident." I was shocked to hear this. Who was this JP? I could not remember his name. I could not remember his face. Maybe he had given me a false name to protect his identity. I don't know if I should grieve for him, even if I were his 'special' friend with a star next to my name in his diary. Imagine we exchanged kisses, hugs and body fluids. For a few hours, or maybe minutes, we were intimate. Maybe I was his first or his only same-sex encounter. Now he is dead. And the man who once made love to him cannot even remember him, let alone mourn for him.

After DL spoke, others came out with their stories. MK said, 'It was only four weeks after AC died that we learnt of the accident. He kept his gay and straight worlds totally separate. And no one in the gay circle would have even known he had died. It just so happened that a colleague in AC's office was also gay. He had spotted AC at a party but had kept a discreet distance. This colleague was in UK at the time of the accident. When he returned and learnt of the tragedy he immediately told all those who knew AC about the event. Most people knew AC as Bobby. Bobby was a cheerful boy, very horny, constantly looking for sex, afraid of any emotional entanglements, even friendship. They felt sad he had died. But then since he had not shared his life with them, they felt no great urge to visit his house and convey their condolences.'

MK did not tell his friends or his family that he was HIV-positive. One day he would die of AIDS complications. His parents would perhaps learn the truth then. They would in all probability conclude that he had sex with a loose woman. They would then cope with the situation by blaming his 'bad' friends. And then they would cremate him. He wished he could tell them how he actually got HIV, how it was one of those many nameless men he loved to be intimate with. Men he met in trains. Men he cruised in parks. He wondered if he could ever tell them of his quick furtive encounters in dark alleys with men he would never associate with socially—truck drivers, labourers, peons, delivery boys, street vendors. MK had not even told his gay friends about his status. He feared they would pull away from him. He would lose that one space where he could share his feelings and frustrations, his desire for a relationship with one person but his inability to be sexually faithful to one man. So he chose silence. His secrets would die with him.

NT had accompanied one of FR's friends to the requiem. 'Funny. I did know FR, for 12 years at least. We were members of the same club and had many common friends. I never would have suspected he was gay. He was so straight looking. I should have guessed. Even he did not broach the subject.

Maybe he was not comfortable with someone as open as me.' All this talk of death worries NT. He and his lover have been together for 22 years. NT is now retired. His lover is 12 years younger than him. 'I have cancer. What will happen to him when I die. I cannot give him the flat we have lived in for 20 years. It belongs to my community and can only be passed on to my wife or my children. And I don't have enough money to buy him a flat. At least not in South Mumbai. And while my family is okay with him as a "friend" they will never let him take my property. That is the only reason why I even bother with issues like gay rights and gay marriage. Otherwise I am okay with the Indian indifference to all things non-heterosexual, which is any day better than organised homophobia in Western societies.'

20

On Being Gay and Catholic

Mario D'Penha

Life, they say, is full of seemingly contradictory or opposite things—
Mars and Venus, Yin and Yang—which need to meet, merge and
create confluences and harmonies so that the world can spin
around like it always has. However, these confluences are not
always harmonious, and many of our lives are testament to the negotiations
and questioning that govern the manner in which we handle contradictory
attitudes, behaviours and identities within ourselves. For me, choosing to be
both gay and Catholic has involved a great deal of understanding of what
constitutes these two experiences as well as constructing the rules I choose
to live by. In the process, I have taken ideals not only from my Catholic faith
and my understandings of sexuality, but also from the other influences my
life has had, such as socialism and feminism.

I come from a very devout Catholic family and so religiosity and spirituality have always been a very important part of family tradition. My parents
regularly prayed the Wednesday novena at St. Michael's while they were
dating. My mother, in particular, was part of several parish organisations,
juggling collecting funds for the Sodality of Our Lady and composing prayers
for the Parish Liturgical Team with doing the readings at Sunday Mass. As
a child, I was fascinated by all the stories from the Bible, and the lives of the
saints. I had learned to lead the family Rosary by the time I was seven, and
the nuns were especially proud at the prospect of me being a promising future
catechist, or even priest.

Following therefore in the family tradition of service to the Church, I
joined the Altar Boys' Service in the fourth class. The idea of wearing long
red robes which could be swished around like dresses and taking part in all
the important rituals of High Mass seemed very appealing at the time,

although in retrospect, I cannot imagine how anyone can get so excited about waking up at five in the morning to ring the bells at Mass or to swing a potful of burning incense.

This was also the time when I learned about homosexuality. I don't really remember where I heard the word for the first time, although I do remember looking it up in a very old version of the *Oxford Dictionary* that we had at home, and concluding that that was not what I was, either because the reference was too complex or because at that time when puberty had just hit and I was going through my first embarrassed bouts of sexual curiosity, I needed to reassure myself that I was no different than the other boys in class.

However, it didn't take me long to realise that I was different. While boys in class were getting all worked up about boobs and condoms, I was getting it up thinking about them. Thankfully, my older brother was gay as well, which I realised even more quickly, and the early copies of *Bombay Dost* which he left, very accessibly in his cupboard, and the copies of Marguerite Yourcenar and Shyam Selvadurai which he slipped onto my bookshelf, helped me to learn more about homosexuality. I come from the kind of family, however, which like many other middle-class, urban Indian families, gets terribly embarrassed by any overt mention or depiction of sex and sexuality. Kissing scenes on rented videos were always fast-forwarded by my parents when I was a child, and growing up in such an atmosphere where sex was both about embarrassment and shame, I reached adolescence feeling dirty and guilty about my homosexuality. However, having a gay brother in that same family and witnessing his constant struggles with my parents' ideas on propriety, also gave me a great deal of confidence as well as a yearning for independence.

As an altar boy, discovering my sexuality—and my city's cruising spots at the same time—I met the first person I was to fall in love with. This was a fellow altar boy who was to get very close to me as a friend, and although our relationship was always non-sexual, we were common accomplices in teenage lunacies as diverse as exchanging friendship bands (I keep mine to this day) to cheating on mass service points. He was also the first person I was to come out to—and quite dramatically at that—on the altar, during Mass, in a whisper drowned by the choir singing. He was initially shocked, but accepted it as information. We never ever discussed the subject again, but neither did he let it affect our friendship. I was to discover to my shock, however, that I wasn't the only one who fancied this guy. The priest in charge of the altar boys as well as another altar boy also wanted in, evidently *fida* (besotted), like me, over the thin, scrawny, long legs that emerged from his tight schoolboy shorts.

By the time I reached college, I had to quit the Altar Servers' Association (now appropriately renamed after girls were inducted—something that I had stood for uncompromisingly). St. Xavier's College was a huge change from school. And surrounded as I was, by liberal ideas, in an often illiberal, misogynistic and homophobic environment, I ventured into some of the first questioning I ever did in my life. In the second year of college, I came across a great deal of feminist writing while researching for a seminar paper on religion and sexuality. The Levitican taboos against homosexuality and menstruating women in the Old Testament, and the Pauline misogyny in the New, convinced me that the Bible could not be the 'Word of God'. I came to believe that God, like the Bible, was a construct of the human imagination and gave up over a period of time all the beliefs of the Catholic faith.

After my mother's death, it became easier for me to attest to my newfound atheism, although I chose not to flaunt it, because I was afraid of the consequences for my family. Individuals and families in Catholic circles who are seen to 'leave the Church'—often embracing Protestant sects—face a great deal of social ostracism, as sermon-induced paranoia about Protestants usually means that many Catholic families are afraid of the influence that these families may have on them. My father did enquire if my American Protestant pen-friend had anything to do with my decision. In a funny and deeply ironic way, many of our personal choices, be they about sexuality, marriage, or religion do have consequences in that they renegotiate the relationships not only between ourselves and our families, but between our families and society at large.

The Catholic Church has another great way of ensuring conformity and a lifelong loyalty and commitment to it and this is done by stressing the importance of prayer and spiritual observance at the level of the family. Sunday Mass is an opportunity for the family to receive the Eucharist together and this bond is strengthened through appeals to emulate the values of the Holy Family, and the recitation of prayers such as the Rosary and the Angelus, which is often done at home. This was perhaps one of the main reasons why my decision to choose atheism was so hurtful to other members of my family. My absence at daily prayer and at Sunday Mass meant a loss of familial unity which had been achieved through spiritual unity. My father kept telling me how he prayed for my 'return to the Church' and in his constant appeals to rethink my position, I perceived the challenge to the family's lifetime of shared ideals that my decision wrought and which he now felt.

A little more than a year ago, however, a string of incidents left me desperate for spiritual succour. The first was one in which I was arrested for having sex in public. At that time, after I was nabbed and while I was being paraded on the railway station, I could think of nothing else but asking God for help. Terrible stories I had heard or read about police encounters with gay men or kothis in cruising areas flashed before my eyes. Thankfully, for me, the police let me go after taking all my money and delivering their litany about how a 'nice boy from a nice family' should not be in a place like this as it is frequented by thieves and how I should get married instead. Another event that changed the way I saw things was getting into Jawaharlal Nehru University, something I had wanted for over three years, but was denied on an initial previous attempt. God had come through for me when I was in the direst of straits and these incidents led me to rekindle my faith in God.

When I assess what it means for me to be both gay and Catholic, I realise how hugely important the period of questioning-within-atheism that I went through was. If it hadn't been for that time, I might have accepted the doctrines of the pope as final, might have perhaps repressed my sexuality, and might have joined the priesthood. What I do realise today is that there is a great deal within established Catholicism that is worthy of being questioned—from the hierarchies that the Church promotes, the misogyny and homophobia that it legitimises, as well as other fears, biases and hatred that it furthers.

A central part of what I draw from Catholicism and Christianity, however, is the doctrine of unconditional love that it preaches. My affirmation of the Catholic faith is not so much an affirmation of Church dogma, which needs to be constantly questioned, as much as it is a channel through which I affirm my faith in God, who I now believe, exists, in spite of the constructs that humans have created around him. This affirmation is itself questionable, as are the incidents that prompted it. However, the very nature of faith and belief lays them both inaccessible to the niceties and proprieties of human reasoning. Therefore, I choose to believe in God as part of my faith, but I also question the structure of the Church that supports this faith.

My piecemeal inculcation of Catholicism also extends to my piecemeal inculcation of what it means to be queer and gay, in which case it is becoming increasingly important for us to question how class, gender, religion and other identities intersect with and interact with one's sexuality. This assessment and questioning of our positions must therefore extend to our other identities as well. My choice to be both gay and Catholic has been possible only through such a questioning.

21

Islam and Me

Ali Potia

 'Of all the creatures in the world, will ye approach males, and leave those whom God has created for you to be your mates? Nay, ye are a people transgressing!'... We destroyed them (the people of Sodom and Gomorrah) utterly. We rained down on them a shower (of brimstone): and evil was the shower on those who were admonished but heeded not.

Qur'an 7: 80–81

'When a man mounts another man, the throne of God shakes. Kill the one that is doing it and also kill the one that it is being done to.'
'*Sihaq* (lesbian sexual activity) of women is *zina* (illegitimate) among them.'

*Hadith*s of the Prophet Mohammed

As I started thinking what this piece would be about, I was reminded of the word 'journey'. He had said to me, 'you could just reflect on your own journey in negotiating your faith and sexuality.' Little does he know that it's hardly been one at all. I guess my journey with regard to my faith and sexuality has only been equivalent to me picking my mode of transport and strapping myself in. It's far too early for me to look back on the road I've travelled and comment on it, but I will try.

My ruminations on faith and sexuality started recently when I read a brilliant piece titled *The Invisible Queer Muslim* by Bushra Rehman which was published in *Curve*. I then proceeded to read this piece out loud at an open mike event organized by the Nigah Media Collective in New Delhi. It was extremely well received by the audience. Ms Rehman asserts that 9/11 and its fallout for American Muslims made her realise that even though she was queer, there was no way she could ever deny her Islamic identity in the post-9/11 United States of America. She unequivocally states that she is Queer and Muslim, so there!

This got me thinking about what my identity was. Do I really identify myself as a gay Muslim? I have struggled with this question of identity for a few months. Every single time I posed the question to my inner voice, the answer was a resounding, 'NO WAY'. I decided that I would use writing this piece as a cathartic attempt to explain why I don't think I'm a Queer Muslim.

As is evident from the quotes from the Qur'an and the *Hadiths* above, as well as the writings of every modern-day Islamic scholar, the Islamic religious tradition leaves very little room for the interpretation of homosexuality as legitimate within the orthodoxy of the faith. Even though there are liberals within Islam, the debate among Islamic scholarship is not about whether homosexuality is acceptable; rather, it is about how severe the punishment should be for sinners. I was told once that with regards to homosexuality, liberal Islam simply advocates the lesser of two evils—social ostracism instead of death. As far as I'm concerned, the religion is very categorical—buggery is a sin, and I will burn in hell for it.

When faced with such overt hostility, why should I even bother to find legitimacy within the faith? It's actually far easier and more convenient for me to reject it. The primary reason 'Muslim' is part of my identity is because I was born into the faith. I certainly haven't had any spiritual epiphanies attracting me to the prophet's message. There were many presumed identities I was born with along with my Islamiyat: Gujarati, middle-class, Indian, male, heterosexual. I've chosen to reject or at least redefine practically all of them, so why should my faith be any different? As queers, we do this all the time. In fact, we even encourage thinking outside the box when it comes to enforced identities. My favourite is a sign worn by a hijra protester at the World Social Forum that said, 'My gender; my choice'.

If an identity as innate as gender can be reworked, and the proud holder of a new gender identity be welcomed and celebrated, then it baffles me that there should be so much shame attached to people who discard their cultural identities. I choose not to be a Muslim, just as I make a choice to be gay. (For the record, I believe that homosexuality is an orientation and not a preference. My use of the word 'choice' here is deliberate, because there are thousands of people in India whose orientation may be gay, but whose preference is not).

Ethnic chic has made us all subscribe to the notion that 'culture' needs to be given pride of place in our personal identities. It is not considered liberal to criticise culture and religion anymore. In fact, it is more appropriate to constantly apologise for the hypocrisies and inconsistencies of our faiths—especially the minority ones. I have decided not to do this.

I may be a bad Muslim but I'm a perfectly upright human being—and I'd rather not be a Muslim at all than be a bad Muslim.

Overcoming the guilt of turning my back on Allah and Mohammed's message has not been easy. The first big step towards this was when I stopped referring to my inner voice as a conscience. Stephen Strauss of the *Toronto Globe and Mail* had asked me about my inner voice, and he had used these prescient words, 'it always amazes me how often people who are Christian and Jewish refer to their inner voices as their conscience, and others don't. What's it like for Muslims?'

It's the same for Muslims. It's not that I don't have a conscience; I just don't believe that it's Islamic. That way, I can overcome the Muslim version of Catholic guilt, which is anyway far more pernicious than the Christian one.

Ultimately the 'progressive' message of Islam boils down to a few basic truths—be good, don't hurt others, don't indulge in behaviour that would be harmful to you physically or emotionally, and the most universal truth of all, respect. Have respect for individual choices, respect for society, respect for life in all its forms. If it's spirituality I need, I should be allowed to make an informed adult choice instead of sticking to a faith I was born with. There's enough spirituality out there—I could dabble in Buddhism, tantric mysticism, earth-centric pagan ideas or even feminism!

I drop the word 'Muslim' from my list of identities precisely because if I subscribe to an identity, I would like to embrace it completely. I can't be a proper and correct Muslim the way the term is defined, and also be a homosexual without exposing double standards in my beliefs. The two terms, Queer and Muslim, are mutually exclusive right now.

In order to be a good, spiritual, and wholesome person, I don't need to subscribe to an otherwise ritualistic and rigid faith that leaves no room for who I am as a sexual being. I trust my body's physical message, and it tells me that I am attracted to men. Since Islam seems so intent on telling me that this is wrong, I have walked away. Aside from all the crap I have to deal with just being gay, I don't need the additional crushing guilt of thinking that I am unclean every time I fall in prayer towards Mecca. Abstinence is not an option for me, and neither is sinning. If my religion reinforces the fact that I'm sinning every time I kiss my boyfriend, then I don't want the religion to be around. I'd rather look for a worldview that's a little more supportive of my choices. The only path left to me then is to try to simultaneously be a moral and sexual person outside the umbrella of Islam.

If you turn around and tell me that I am basically being a wimp and running away because I don't want to confront ugly truths and stand up for myself as a Muslim, you are absolutely right. That does not make me less of a human being. I don't see any merit in trying to change Islam from the inside. I just feel that there is too much ideological baggage in the religion and this automatically disallows any rational discourse about sexuality and faith.

I have enough on my plate battling the powers that be and established fundamentalism just by being gay. It's hard enough for me as an urban queer to get a job, find an apartment, and even walk down the street unmolested. At least I don't have to also deal with *fatwas* because I'm blaspheming about the Qur'an. No *fatwas* against me because I'm not Muslim, get it! The *mullahs* hate me because I'm gay anyway, so why try and show them that I'm a gay Muslim?

There is entrenched homophobia in Indian society and in Islam. I feel my chances are better taking on urban, middle-class India than Islamic ideology. The orthodoxy and hate of organised religion is simply too much to bear. Besides, I know that the emotional satisfaction I would get from having homosexuality de-criminalised in India is far greater than if the Shahi Imam said that I wasn't a sinner anymore. I think it's pretty obvious that I should be petitioning the Delhi High Court and not the Shahi Imam.

One of the biggest struggles of any queer organisation is the facilitation of safe spaces for queer people to express themselves. Usually, the safest spaces are those we associate with religious tradition, but if my mosque is not a safe space for me as a queer person, how the hell can I be a Muslim? I'd rather sit at a Nigaah meeting in a dingy, cramped office in Defence Colony, which shakes every time a truck passes overhead, than pray with the masses at the Jama Masjid. Knowing that mosques all over North India are delightfully cruisy gives me no comfort at all.

I haven't completely rejected my Muslim identity. I know how and when to use it and when not to. I definitely play up the shtick when faced with men who have a fetish for all things male and Muslim (you know who you are!). Apparently there is a certain, how do you say, *je ne sais quoi* about being Muslim and gay in some quarters of Indian queer society. Most everyone, except hardened RSS types, find Pakistani, Kashmiri and Afghan men hot. That works in my favour to attract attention, but it's a precise masquerade— no different than someone being 'masculine' or describing himself as 'gym-fit' on his online profile. Thankfully, most of these admirers are satisfied just knowing that I was born a Muslim—they don't ask me whether I fast or how many times I've said *namaaz* that week, because they'd be in for a rude surprise.

I guess the only reason I'm stuck with the identifier of Muslim now is because of my name, and a certain missing piece of my anatomy (something I didn't have a say in).

Several erudite and rational (definitely more rational than mine) attempts have been made to argue that Islam does not expressly prohibit homosexuality. There is definitely a wealth of documentation out there arguing a historical tradition of queerness within the Islamic world. Most of this body of writing has a strong basis in fact. The Al-Fatiha Foundation, a non-profit grassroots organisation dealing with queer Muslims 'promotes the progressive Islamic notions of peace, equality and justice'. And they do a fantastic job. The claim is that there is sufficient leeway within the faith for spirituality and sexuality to co-exist quite peacefully; and therefore there is a much-needed place for Al-Fatiha on the Islamic stage.

Now, homosexuality definitely has a historical basis in Islamic society. Sure, it's great that the bushes behind the Sphinx in medieval Cairo made for the hottest cruising spot this side of the Vatican, but honestly, how many devout Muslims believe that? It's practically impossible to change a fundamentalist notion of 'culture' by citing history. Try telling the Bajrang Dal and Durga Vahini that women in India wore saris without blouses until about a hundred years ago, and they will burn your effigy in public and try to stop your film festival. The same principle applies to the *mullahs*. They're not going to buy your historical argument, no matter how legitimate it is, because their definition of Islamic culture and values stems from a very rigid understanding of what is right and what is wrong.

The same goes for using the position that homosexuality is widespread today in practically every Islamic society. This has been written about at length. My personal experiences in a *hammam* in Damascus bear witness to this. However, the orthodox Islamic leadership and their followers won't acknowledge this—even though men are picking up each other at (after?) Friday prayers at the Grand Mosque in Lahore, let's leave hypocrisy out of this for a moment.

So there's a dead end at every turn. You try to convince them by saying that queers have been around in Islamic society since the beginning and they don't believe you. You point out that massive numbers of Muslims, both men and women, are indulging in same-sex sexual activity under their very noses, and they simply shrug and say you are lying because they haven't seen it.

So what do you do? Obviously my approach to this quandary is the deliciously simple one I've outlined above, which is to simply turn our backs and walk away from the faith. That works great for me! And there are enough queers from Islamic backgrounds out there who have done precisely this; they just won't acknowledge that they have basically dropped the 'Muslim' from their identities. As I said before, the terms Queer and Muslim in their current avatars are mutually exclusive.

But what about people who really do want to keep their faith and reconcile it with their sexuality? What if they truly, in the purest and most proper sense, really WANT to be queer and Muslim?

When Queer Muslims turn to other Muslims for support, they should not be going out of their way trying to say, 'Look at me, look at me, I'm such a great Muslim, I pray five times a day, I fast, I give my *zakat*, I may even sign up for the next *jihad*. There's just one teeny-tiny sexual detail. But don't let that bother you, after all, Haroun Al-Rashid was a pouf too.'

The pitfall of this approach is that even if you do gain acceptance (highly doubtful that you would also get approval) within the Islamic mainstream, almost every single other inconsistency and anachronism within the religion will have survived intact without being questioned. You cannot critique Islam's approach to homosexuality without simultaneously demanding reform in every other aspect of the religion.

What queer Muslims should be doing is not striving for legitimacy within the current framework of Islam, but consciously trying to redefine the parameters of the faith from the outside. They should be celebrating and highlighting everything that makes them different from orthodox Muslims instead of constantly treating their sexuality as an insignificant detail on the road to spiritual awareness.

Culture changes, it evolves, and so do religions and social mores. As queer Muslims, we should form the vanguard (oops, just included myself in the Muslim category there!) of this evolution of Islam into a more inclusive and progressive faith. It isn't an easy task at all, but we must stand up and say that along with our belief in Allah and his Prophet, sexuality also forms an important path of who we are.... And that we are willing to stand outside in the courtyard with our rainbow flags and Cher CDs telling everybody our message. We will enter only when you also let in that big contingent of unveiled, single women and don't make us put the rainbow flags away or mute the Cher.

So what is identity after all? I'm not even going to attempt to go there. I don't identify myself as Muslim, and I definitely identify myself as gay. So have I chosen to substitute my Islamic identity with (in my opinion) a stronger queer one? What else am I besides queer? Am I narrowing my choices by only identifying myself by my sexuality?

I find 'Indian' too jingoistic and Sunny Deol-inspired. I show an overt loathing for labels like metrosexual, urban citizen of the world, liberal love monkey, slutterina, geographer (which I am, incidentally) and their ilk. All I seem to be left with, in the immortal words from Clueless, is, 'I'm a cake boy—a disco-dancing, Oscar Wilde-reading, Streisand ticket-holding, friend of Dorothy.'

Yes, I'm playing up the stereotypes....

What kind of a shallow person defines himself only by his sexuality? Many queers feel terrified by the prospect of being caught with a label that is so narrow, which is why they rush back into the comforting arms of the socio-cultural-religious identities that they are familiar with. Then you have the circle complete again, with queers blindly embracing identities without questioning them—some queers become liberal fundamentalists, some become actual religious fundamentalists, and still others wander around searching for meaning in a religious tradition that says they don't have a right to exist.

I see no problems in defining my identity exclusively in terms of my sexuality. After all, being gay is about so much more than just sex. My queer, urban family and I have much more in common with each other than just the fact that we sleep with members of the same sex. We face the same discriminations, we fight the same battles, and we share the same spaces. In fact, everybody else also seems to think we are identical—look at our portrayal in the mass media—so maybe we do have just that one identity after all. We are all just queers.

22

Is Being Gay about Multiple Sex Partners?

Pawan Dhall and *Mr A.K.*

 The following is a letter exchange between the father of a gay man who is confused about what it means for his son to be gay and a well known Kolkata-based queer activist. The exchange was posted on the *lbgt-india@yahoogroups.com* list.

Dear Mr PD,

Well I read your articles posted in the group. It is only last year that my son told me what he is. I have no problem with it rather i would like to say to all the papas to be proud that their child is something very special, as they know how to love a man. Love by itself is a wonderful experience in life and when it's between two persons of the same sex it is indeed great. But I have some questions regarding some facts for which I need some answers.

My son always complains to me that he is being changed by his partners time to time, and when he asks his partners why they can't remain fixed with one person, they laugh at him and say that in the gay world every one is for everybody and there is no fixed thing as it's not a world of straight people. If this is true then comes the question, whether all this coming out and rainbow walks is to get affection or right to have multiple sex partners only? Is the gay movement concerned only with safe physical pleasure? I have asked my son to settle down with the guy he likes, but in return he said that papa, I am ready but they are not. I think now is the time that we must come forward to see what is our real objective, is it a healthy society where every one can live as a human being with the human qualities, or just a world of animals ruled by the natural instincts resulting in to a great chaos!

If you are moved to respond, please reply.

faithfully yours
AK

Dear Mr AK,

Please excuse me for writing to you late. Many people have already responded to your message, and indeed, your message is a milestone one. Not just for this group, but for a lot of gay people off the net also. Yours is the kind of understanding that a lot of us yearn for, and very few are lucky to have. So thank you for being there for Rupam, for us and for writing in.

In response to your query as to whether the gay movement is only to gain the right to have multiple sex partners, the answer is no. The movement is for gaining access to rights which are already enshrined in our constitution. Right to freedom of expression, right to privacy (including right to sexual autonomy) and right to equality. I feel you would agree with all this, but what is perhaps problematic is the right to sexual autonomy. Please for a moment ignore what the rest of the gay world is telling your son (that your son can't have a committed relationship with another man because gay people can't/don't believe in being committed).

Please also try to ignore what social customs say—that a person can be happy and responsible only if he or she is in a one-to-one relationship. In my experience, both sides are wrong, because what they are saying does not reflect the lived realities of a whole lot of people. There are several gay and lesbian couples who even if not living together have been far more committed to each other than many heterosexual couples. There are also many individuals looking out for a committed relationship, some on this group itself. One of the members of this group has even gone to the extent of leaving his country to be with this partner. So commitment is very much a part of many gay people's lives, even if not all. It is a matter of time before Rupam meets the right person, and even if he does not meet a romantic partner, I'm sure he will be able to strike out several good friendships which need not be sexual in nature.

On the other hand, there are several individuals who have multiple sexual partners, but seem to be more honest, hard working, brave and considerate than many people in committed relationships. Do you think it would be fair to look down upon them just because they have several sexual partners? What is it that qualifies a person as good and responsible towards society? To my mind other qualities are more important in a person than monogamy.

Ultimately, it is upto Rupam to decide what kind of life he wants. You have accepted him for what he is. But he has to believe in what he says, and stand up to it with a lot of patience and courage. I feel that will make him happiest and you even more proud of him.

My best wishes to you. If you feel like talking over phone or in person, please let me know. If needed, I can also introduce you to other people who work in the fields of sexuality and sexual health.

PD

23

An Indian Christian Kothi Speaks Out![1]

Prathiba Sixer Rani

 Hi folks, I'm Pratap Patrick Paikaray, a.k.a. Prathiba Rani Sixer, after Prathiba Parmar, the British lesbian director; Sixer because we kothis or queens are called *chakkas* in the North and I wanted an English surname; Rani, like they say, is my middle name. Kothi is the word used in South Asia for queens and comes from the Persian language, which as you know was the last court language of independent India. Kothis are either transgendered women or queer men with strong personality traits traditionally ascribed to women. The former, i.e., transgendered women are nirvana kothi or hijra while the latter are zenana kothi or drag queens. Just as Kinsey saw sexuality as a continuum (1948), we kothi see gender as a continuum. Nirvana kothis, when asked if they are men or women, say they are women but that they are different. We zenana kothis are men, yet we are different. Our sexuality varies from asexual through homosexual to bisexual and our sexual behaviour in bed is much more varied than the PUCL-K report seems to suggest.

We, as kothis, have always seen our sexuality as inextricably linked with a common spirituality which finds uncommon expression, particularly for hijras, in the Chaitra Poornima feast of Lord Aravan, son of Arjun, who had his desire for marriage (before being offered as a *narabali* or human sacrifice for victory in war) fulfilled by Krishna who had sex with him in the form of Mohini. The other kothi goddesses you may have heard of are Yellamma of North Karnataka, Kalimamma and Annamma of Bangalore and Botraji Mata of Hyderabad, who symbolically enough, mounts a rooster: kothi release live cocks to mark the feast. The symbolic interpretation thereof I leave to you. As an Indian Christian kothi I am particularly influenced by Ardhanareshwara of the Shaivaite tradition, Gay Irish Sacred Heart

Missionary, Fr. O' Muruchu's exposition of androgyny as the basis of integral human spirituality and the Song of Solomon Chapter V, verses 7 and 8:

The watchmen found me as they went about in the city
They beat me, they wounded me, and they took away my mantle,
Those watchmen of the walls. I adjure you, O daughters of Jerusalem,
If you find my beloved, that you tell him that I am sick with love.

Exile is a recurrent theme in our lives. Jewish, Christian, Muslim and Bahai kothis will be familiar with the themes of exile in Egypt, Babylon, Syria and Azerbaijan. All of us know of Sita's exile from Ayodhya and feel the poignancy of her second exile in our own lives. My kothi sisters will forgive me if I touch on our culture very sketchily for want of time. Today being Stonewall day, or World Queer Pride day, I will start with Friday, 27 June 1969, at Stonewall pub in the queer Greenwich Village of New York. Besieged in the pub by cops, drag queens spilled out into the streets and rioted with the police for three days, marking the beginning of the modern queer movement. In Asia, Pride *Morchas* from Tel Aviv to Tokyo mark the day. Thomas Waugh, leftist gay film teacher at Concordia University, Montreal sees drag queen performance, as performative, a word he coined for the subversiveness inherent in drag. In kothi gossip, we subvert patriarchy by re-enacting it satirically in our own contexts. Thailand and Cambodia are the only Asian countries which have given queers the legal right to wear drag to college. India and New Zealand have transgendered teachers, activists, actresses, corporators and legislators. Dana International, the transsexual singer from Israel, successfully fought Jewish orthodoxy to represent her country at an international music competition in Europe, and win.

Zenana kothis tend to find more freedom in southern India. In Delhi, where Indira Gandhi gave the hijras a colony, Rafiq Nagar, and the ration card, the local culture has a special place for hijras at weddings when their *badhai* (gifts/money given to hijras on auspicious occasions) and *ashirvad* (blessings) are considered mandatory. The joyous association of the hijra with the *dholak* is a celebration of the song of life. Pre-*boni* offerings from shopkeepers present us with a cultural paradigm for social responsibility. Lucknow, for Hindustani speaking kothis, conjures up the image of the *tawaif*[2] as a feminist spiritual metaphor. The *badhai* song in Umrao Jaan, *Kahe ko byahe bides, arai lakhyan Babul more*, resonates with the theme of exile in our own land. *Bhaiya ko diyo babul, mehela o mehela, array tumko diyo Pardes, Arai lakhiyan babul more.*[3] In Bangalore, *hamam*s or bath houses for men have offered a degree of shelter to kothis, particularly nirvana kothis.

Our fascination with straight black women singers and their songs is enduring. Salma Agha's *Fazaa bhi hai jawan jawan*, Alisha Chinai's *Lover girl*, Aretha Franklin's *Respect*, Roberta Flack's *Killing me softly*, Tracy Chapman's *Baby, can I hold you tonight* and Gloria Gaynor's *I will survive* strike an immediate resonance in my heart. The last, which acquired the status of a queer anthem following the release of *Priscilla, Queen of the Desert* , I will quote from to conclude:

> *Once I was afraid, I was petrified*
> *Didn't think that I could live without you by my side*
> *But then I spent so many nights thinking how you did me wrong*
> *And I grew strong and I know I'll get along*
> *O! I know! Walk out of the door!*
> *Just turn around now coz you're not welcome any more*
> *Weren't you the one who tried to hurt me with your lies*
> *You thought I'd crumble, you thought I'd lay down and die*
> *O No! Not I! I will survive! As long*
> *As I know how to love, I know I'm*
> *Still alive and I got all my life to live*
> *And I got all my love to give,*
> *I will survive! Yeah!*

NOTES

1. This is the transcript of a talk given at the Sexuality Minorities Speak Out Conference organised by the Coalition for Sexuality Minority Rights in Bangalore on 1 July 2001.
2. Loosely, inadequately, and ahistorically translated, *tawaif* means sex worker.
3. Traditional farewell song sung when a bride leaves her home after a wedding to go to her husband's house. The essence of the song means: Why did you send me away from my home? My brother you kept by your side, why did you send me away?

REFERENCES

Kinsey, A. 1948, *Sexual Behaviour in the Human Male*, Philadelphia: Saunders.

24

In a *Loongi* in Chimbhave

Satya Rai Nagpaul

MY GENDER MY RIGHT

The wish was to tell Noor Sahib. It's no substitute, telling it to you.

For over a month now, innumerable *masjids* and *dargahs* have been looked at. we haven't got permission to shoot in even one of them. it is a sudden realisation that I haven't seen one Indian film centred around the location of a *masjid/dargah*; that I have no visual reference to even begin my imagination. Of course, this is my last attempt at the search. I am dreading the inevitability of having to shoot in a studio.

It is 3 in the afternoon. We are at the Mahad Busstand. SHE, her lover, her lover's cousin are boarding the bus back to Pune. I am staying; against her wish; in search of a *dargah*; I am doing it for myself; which is the same thing as doing it for the film SHE is directing and I am the cinematographer. I am definitely not doing it for HER. I must know it…this is our last project…some coming togethers must be impossible.

'Chimbhave' sounds like the name of a bird. Noor Mohammed, the *sarpanch*, appears just like that—flying in from nowhere and immediately taking me to see the *dargah* of his village. I can't believe the moment. I see the *dargah* and I can't believe the moment again. This is the *dargah* of HER imagination and I want to call her right away. I decide to stay the night at Chimbhave; I want to photograph and study the *dargah* for at least a day.

Noor Mohammed is sitting on his sofa as i dig into my bag, not coming up with any fresh trousers or even a *pyjama*.

'Aap loongi pehnegein?'
There are things you have never done in your life and there are moments that offer you exactly that. I seize the moment, with a reluctant
'ji, shukria.'

As I wait for Noor Sahib to come back with the *loongi*, the lights go out. As in the innumerable pasts, time, once again, stretches itself and fills the darkness. HE enters the door, with a candle in one hand and a *loongi* in another. it is a blue-checked *loongi*. I open the cloth and realise it is stitched into a circle. Noor Sahib is watching.

'*Aapne kabhi loongi nahi pehani?*'
Of course I heard him. I was willing. It was the answer that wouldn't come. How could a man of 32 concede to such a truth? How could he have not gone through such an ordinary rite of passage? Telling Noor Sahib could have been the first moment of a coming out that can't ever be a possibility. He caught hold of two ends of the *loongi*, pulled them towards himself and began to tie the knot.

This could be a moment between a father and a son, between two lovers, even between two men, strangers to each other.

As I stand at one end of the cloth circle, I am unable to look up. I am looking down. I see what he sees. My bulge, in the circle of that cloth. My bulge that HIS eyes glance across in a moment of confirmation. a moment whose duration is immeasurable. I can now look up. The first knot comes and hits my stomach. The view is gone and not a trace has crossed his face. I relax. HE is doing the second knot. His hands, like my father's. Thick hair. Two clumps on every finger. Full fingers. Full palms. Tying the knot, like my father's brother, hair sprouting from the first button of his *kurta* across a length. I watch like Noor Mohammed himself, the thick beard with hard straight outlines running down a long full face.

Noor Sahib has no idea of the moment that is passing. This is a moment between a man and a transman.

the lights come on....
the wish is to tell Noor Sahib.
It's no substitute, telling it to you.

25

I am Out and Here's Why

Vaibhav Saria

 I am Indian and gay. This oxymoronic identity is a bewildering, and often a sad experience at many levels. From having to nego-tiate thousands of years of culture produced as 'Indian' that say that same-sex love is wrong, to confronting many images and textual traces of same-sex love in that same 'Indian culture', or from falling for narratives that place it all at the door of the British (and those that portray gayness as a Western corruption) to accepting that we hated homosexuality much before them (and have our own homosexual histories). The bewildering questions for me as an 18-year-old gay man is: what is it to be gay and Indian? How do I situate myself?

For as long as I remember, I was always referred to as *chakka*[1] in school. After years of feeling bad, I grew indifferent. They so overdid the whole derogatory thing, thinking I might change or feel ashamed. It was in school that I heard the word 'Homo' and people at school called me that and I went home and opened the encyclopaedia and searched for the word and found out what it was. And that I was a homo. It was nothing exceptional, I thought. In my ignorance, I imagined that some people are homosexuals and there is nothing wrong with that. Little did I know that being gay in India and discovering that at my age was like a butterfly landing on a land mine. And then I went through the whole usual thing of having secret crushes on boys in school and my friends and having a secret life of my own.

I wasn't the unusual one in a country of 1 billion people that had less than 100 of them being completely and politically out of the closet. Secret lives are very common and sordid in India. But my sexuality kept building in me the anger that arose from this unjust world that gave medals for killing hundreds of men, but killed you if you kissed even one of them. At 17,

I decided to come out first to my best friend and then to my mother and my father.

The actual event of my 'coming out' is very humorous if you take away the messy emotions from it. Anyway, it was a summer afternoon in a posh flat in south Calcutta, the sun beginning to set and the much-sung-about summer breeze was making the curtains dance. The golden, steely rays of the sun entered the room with me as I went and sat down with my mother. Not trusting the knowledge levels of upper-middle-class Marwari women who are unwanted and created for marriage and reproduction alone, I asked: 'Mamma, do you know what a homosexual is?' She replied: 'Yes' and then, after a few seconds, we both started to speak together. I shut my mouth and she says: 'It's when two men are attracted to...' I said 'Yes and I am one.'

She immediately screams: 'Don't be an idiot, please don't do this to me.' I, as usual bereft of emotion, find myself thinking: 'Do this to *you*? I am the one who is gay and you think you have problems?' but I desist from talking and my mother goes into this whole Nirupa Roy mode with the flailing hands and the tears. And for the uninitiated Nirupa Roy was the legendary actress who played a mother in every movie and she wailed a lot.

Then, she composes herself, armed with the normal questions: 'How do you know? Whom have you slept with? How have you slept with them? Have you had oral sex? Oh my god, you are young, your brother is not gay how are you gay?' I remember thinking 'wow you stripped me of my individuality right there...are you a communist?' And then she says with dramatic aplomb: 'Indian society won't accept this. You must change because Indian society won't tolerate it.' I was thinking: 'I was not talking of Indian society, I was talking about you. Will you still love me?'

After ten minutes I did mouth that question: 'Mamma, will you still love me?' She evaded that question every time I asked her throughout the evening. She said: 'That is not important, you must change and you will.' I was thinking: 'Thank you, Mamma, for that answer.' It was my first lesson in the depth of family love, my first taste of the battle ahead of me.

I am different from all these other closeted gay men who marry women and are sad, in at least two respects: the first is I will not ruin a woman's life by making her marry me because of the age-old customs of this desperately lying culture and second, I do not want to live my life in accordance with other people's dictates, making choices I do not want to make.

I am different because I scream when many people opt for the so overdone silence. I have no qualms about screaming how I want to suck a man while I am wearing flashy pink leather jeans. I want to and will scream about my difference and live it. When people ask me why I have chosen this path down which I sashay like a beauty 'queen', I am most willing to point out that the old cyclic routine of the perpetuation of Marwari patriarchy and family values should be broken and I am going to break it.

Every middle-class family is like a can of worms with the picture of healthy growing beans pasted on it. From the dirty uncle who molests his nieces to the alcoholic father who will not refrain from using violence to prove his manhood; from the depressed child who contemplates escape through committing suicide to the mother who was made to believe that the family that she creates will be perfect and she will love them but who, in her heart, knows that she has no life except for her family and she hates them, the story of the family is a story of lies and deception.

The repressed sexuality of people, the repressed individuality of people. That is what it is all about. Living in the fear of the tolerated perversity of so-called 'respectable' relatives. Is that what a family should be? A man who brings AIDS into the house through his visits to the brothel, the son who gets into drugs to escape the world, the daughter who knows she has to marry so as not to be a 'burden'. Why did anyone expect me to stay in an institution that permits everything beneath the façade of perfection, why did anyone expect me to hide (which I can safely do as a man) behind the 'security' of the social image of being married while I can do what I do behind it? No thank you, I am very happy alone with a man I love, studying and working in the field of psychology. I know it's unheard of that any Marwari from a business family should do that. But do I care?

So while I am being laughed at for choosing to sway my hips like my mother would do and while I am being stoned for kissing a man and generally hated by every straight man because I make them question the illusion of strength that they are holding on to like desperate pathetic drowning men, I can only feel sorry for these people who have to bear so much bullshit in their house, their 'safe zone'. They are trying to grip a losing illusion that says that everything is fine when their sisters and mothers and daughters are being raped by people they know and respect or have to respect. They do work because everyone tells them money is important—'you must earn it, stop dreaming!' And so they live the nightmare of an unsatisfying job and live that nightmare with a woman as two people who don't want each other even in their shared bed.

Thus the contradictions are many. Homosexuality existed in ancient India and as usual it was hated by some and liked by few. Gay identity may be a western identity but many Indians want it: can they change, can they not? Should they change, should they not? Should the still pond of tradition be disturbed by this stone of change that will ask what is hidden under the seemingly calm surface? But it all boils down to the fact that there are people, who believe it or not, like people of the same sex and are going against the traditional norms and they are exposing the illusion of perfection and asking for a more livable reality. They are screaming and they want change, which is inevitable and I am one of them, because the past cannot be relived but it can be built upon.

What should India do to change all this? What do I see myself doing to change all this? Discover that you have a voice box and start screaming and don't stop till you die. What these hegemonic ideologies give people is the right to use and abuse you with their self-conceived moralistic 'authority'. And I say no, please, no one owns you and death, the worst solution, is better than this secret life of terror. No, I will not spend my entire life working in the family business; instead, I will study psychology and don't get me wrong I am grateful for the bread business puts on my table but it's really boring. No, I will not marry a woman because I am gay and in love with a man and, no, I will not shut up, because I have a voice. Sooner or later, a lot of people will start screaming and change is inevitable.

So, if you want to don a pink leather suit, go right ahead, honey, because that one second has more fun than wearing your father's ugly grey suit for the rest of your life. You live for 60 years and you need 20 to get somewhat of an idea of what you are. Don't waste the other 40 with what you 'should do' that is making life shitty. Live it with what you want to do. On your own terms.

Whip out the leather, the necklaces, the pink glossy lipstick, then, and take that man's hand and walk down Camac Street, and if you die in the process, its better being dead than actually living a compromised life. And compromised on someone else's terms at that. Live your own life. It is all you've got.

Notes

1. *Chakka* is a term that literally means 'sixer' and is used as a derogatory expression to refer to hijras, transgenders, or simply men who appear effeminate.

26

Convivial Misgivings

Sheba Tejani

 Sitting in Mr Thariani's living room, I watched as his granddaughter skated around in her pyjamas in the narrow space afforded to her between the coffee table and imposing sideboard. She glided across the room when the doorbell rang, deftly taking the plastic bag brought by the delivery boy. Mrs Thariani sat splitting pea pods at the dining table. I glanced at my watch impatiently in a barely concealed gesture and was relieved when I saw Mr Thariani emerge from the recesses of the house. A sharp old businessman, slightly bent with age, he quickly dismissed my pleas about returning the sum of money I had paid him just a few days back. A rather hefty sum it was too, that I had submitted as a token to confirm I would rent the apartment he owned in the adjoining building. Now I had changed my mind, but it seemed that even his granddaughter would give up on her skates sooner than he would relent. The last time I was there she had slept fitfully on the couch, with the wheels safely strapped onto her soles. Mr. Thariani decided I deserved to get only half the sum back and even a laminated prince Aga Khan seemed to be chuckling at me from inside the sideboard.

I had dusted and folded up my dreams about moving to Bandra, for the time being at least. But when I had not, there were many compelling reasons why it had seemed like the perfect place. The apartment we had seen was airy, on a higher floor and had one of those rare qualities in the teeming city of Bombay: an unobstructed view of a large, open maidan. It was well connected to the bus route, highway, close enough to the railway station and a stone's throw from the vegetable market. The conveniences were attractive, especially after our previous apartment, which was tucked away behind *kuchcha* roads on which it took you long minutes in a rickshaw to reach 'civilisation'. Bandra was also uniquely placed where urban Bombay becomes sub-urban;

it had the feel of a neighbourhood but was still ensconced in the city. Its cosmopolitan culture was alluring, peppered as it was by a sizeable Christian population from Mangalore, Goa and the rest of the Konkan coast called 'east Indians', for some inscrutable reason, although they are from the west.

But Bandra was so much more than a sum total of positive attributes: it was my mother's first love and our destination during every summer vacation. My cousins and I had eaten bright green 'baraf *golas*' here on hot summer afternoons, and cycled for hours on unwieldy cycles rented from St Theresa's cycle shop. Meticulously chalking out squares on the stone tiled foyer of the neighbouring building, we had played *langdee* almost everyday, breaking only for sweet frothy *lassi* from Welcome Milk Centre. The narrow winding roads tucked into the heart of the suburb, the roar of Linking Road, the jagged seascape at Bandstand were inseparable from the filigree of childhood memories that had captured my imagination. In what is now a dilapidated building, I remember being awakened by a *koel* and watching the first rays of sunlight casting a lattice of light on my grandmother, as she sat by the window, oblivious, immersed, swaying gently to the prayers that fell in whispers from her mouth.

Subsequently, my vacillation and finally panic about moving to Bandra, when the opportunity presented itself, baffled me nearly as much as my girlfriend, who had been subjected to extended epiphanies on the virtues of the suburb. In retrospect, I wondered if I had been naïve, oblivious or just immodest to not have grasped the implications of the impending move. A family hub— Bandra, 'queen of the suburbs', was generously strewn across its length and breadth with the assorted pedigrees of my various aunts and uncles. As for my parents, their relationship with my sexuality can best be described as a work-in-progress. But this was not simply about being in the closet or out, it was about walking a tightrope between asserting identity but preventing spectacle, between assimilation on one hand and exclusion on the other.

My mind hinged on the details. Now, if my cousins decided to 'drop in' what would I do about my multi-coloured postcard, which had just one word printed on it in large font: 'homo'? So how does one go about this: shall I simply put up the postcard on my door so everyone knows and I am spared the ordeal of repeating the same banal detail to each one? What happens if I bump into Ruksana aunty when I go vegetable shopping with my partner on a particular Sunday morning on which I am feeling especially amorous (she had mentioned that she does her shopping at the same place)? Would my uncle, driving back from work, catch a glimpse of us leaning towards each other through the glass façade of the corner coffee shop? How would various family members understand my absences at some, if not at all significant family get-togethers; so far distances had provided me impunity, but what would be my excuse now? I was too close for the imaginative, 'I was working late', 'I had a flat tyre', 'I have a stomach upset'. How many times could I refuse invitations without sounding disinterested or even insincere?

In the cracks and cleavages in the spaces of this city, my girlfriend and I had found the freedom to be bold, to be indifferent and absorbed. We had actually come to believe that we were not extraordinary, even as we existed on the margins of the heterosexual rule book. We held hands on Marine Drive, we kissed in the elevator and we laughed at prejudice. We had managed to create an impenetrable exterior in our previous home that was as curious for our neighbours as it was safe for us. Now, I thought, for my cousins I might even come to represent the world of new sexual exotica that could be enjoyed from the outside, vicariously. I had a little sample of this already: as we drove by billboards announcing a new masala movie, featuring a lusty lesbian pursuing her straight and virginal 'girlfriend'— a first in Bollywood after the *Fire* fiasco—one of my cousins declared eagerly, 'I love lesbians.' I thought to myself, 'Yes, I do too.'

Whilst in the throes of indecision, a cousin who I am out to gave me some well-meaning advice in the event I decided to make the hallowed by-lanes of Bandra my home: 'Be careful', she said. Did 'being careful' mean walking with a measured distance from my girlfriend on Bandstand, looking away when I accidentally catch her eye at one of those family dinners, entirely transforming my body language so people cannot discern we are having sex? Did it mean appearing as if we had separate and mutually exclusive lives, so that when I'm digging into the *dalgosht* at Naseem aunty's house, all I am actually thinking of is how I will ravish my girlfriend when I get home. Did it mean undoing the myriad ways in which we apprehended each other, or the ways in which our bodies declared familiarity? Mask the knowledge that you have of each other privately, when in public. Be discreet. No it was worse, be neutral. Yes that's it, I thought, I have to learn how to be 'neutral' about my girlfriend.

The answers were obvious. Until the time I gathered up the resources to deal with the entire morass of issues that the simple decision of moving to a suburb such as Bandra threw up, I would have to stay put. Status quo. Find another place, in another part of town that allowed me access to the family but also numerous routes of escape. The escape implied a certain sanctity, it precluded the fissures that were bound to surface when reprieve was limited and scrutiny relentless. Besides, my girlfriend and I were not ready to subvert the illusions we harboured about being invincible, just yet.

27

Sum Total
A Matrimonial

Sonali

 One Indian Woman
Plus
a lesbian
Minus
a dutiful obedient wife
Minus
a tall, thin, slender eligible girl
Minus
long beautiful hair
Minus
a doctor, an engineer, or even a businesswoman
Minus
timid and speechless
Plus
determined and opinionated
Divided by
abusive demons
Multiplied by
a will to survive
Sums me up

Notes on Editors and Contributors

EDITORS

Gautam Bhan is a queer rights activist and writer based in New Delhi who writes extensively on queer issues and social movements. He is a member of PRISM, Voices against Section 377, and the Nigah Media Collective.

Arvind Narrain graduated from the National Law School of India University, and did his LLM from Warwick University. He is currently working as a part of a collective of lawyers at the Alternative Law Forum based in Bangalore, a young group working on a critical practice of law. He is the author of *Queer: Despised Sexuality, Law and Social Change.*

CONTRIBUTORS

Vinay Chandran is the Executive Director of Swabhava Trust which provides various kinds of support to sexuality minorities including a drop in space, a help line and training workshops. He may be contacted at <u>swabhava_trust@hotmail.com</u>

Anis Ray Chaudhuri came in contact with the Counsel Club in 2001, and felt that he should do something for his community. After he came out to his parents, and received their support, he became an activist. Around this time, through the Counsel Club, he got to know others from his community in Chandannagar and together they started Amitié. Chaudhuri may be contacted at <u>samakami2001@yahoo.co.in</u>

Deepa V. N. is an activist of Malayalee origin who has been living in Kerala for the past five-and-a-half years. She is engaged with queer politics, teaching, and other creative mischief.

Pawan Dhall is a well-known queer activist from Calcutta. He has been involved with queer issues since the early 1990s and was instrumental in founding the Counsel Club, and the magazine *Pravartak*. Now he is associated with an NGO called SAATHII (Solidarity and Action against the HIV Infection in India). He may be contacted at pawan30@yahoo.com

Bina Fernandez is an activist and researcher. She has previously edited *Humjinsi*, a comprehensive resource book of LGBT issues in India.

N. B. Gomathy is an activist and a graduate of TISS, Mumbai, where she completed her research on violence against lesbian women in India.

Alok Gupta is a law student in Mumbai. He may be contacted at galok@vsnl.com

Akshay Khanna is presently pursuing a Ph.D. in Social Anthropology at the University of Edinburgh. He is a founder member of PRISM, New Delhi, and is presently thinking up strategies to queer-ify Scotland.

Elavarthi Manohar is presently Director of Sangama, an organisation which works for the rights of queer people. He may be contacted at manohar@sangama.org

Nivedita Menon teaches Political Science at Delhi University and writes mainly on gender and politics. She has recently published *Recovering Subversion: Feminist Politics beyond the Law* (Permanent Black, Delhi and University of Illinois Press, 2004). She is politically active in non-funded, non-party citizens' initiatives in the field broadly, of democratic rights.

Satya Rai Nagpaul is a transman. He is a cinematographer by profession. He moderates an e-group for transgender, transsexual and intersexual persons of Asian and Asian diasporic origin called Sampoorna. He may be contacted at ekdoorbeen@yahoo.co.in

Dr Devdutt Pattanaik is a medical doctor by education, a manager in the pharma industry by profession and a mythologist by passion. His passion has led him to write books and lecture extensively on the relevance of mythology in modern times. In the process, he has unearthed many narratives in India that accommodate non-conventional gender identities and behaviours. To know more about him and his work, visit www.devdutt.com

Mario D'Penha is originally from Bombay, and a disco queen on the dancefloor. A leftie when it comes to personal politics, he still wonders whether he prefers 'gay' or 'queer' as a terminology. He is currently pursuing modern history at Jawaharlal Nehru University, Delhi.

Ali Potia grew up in Bombay, where he attended St. Mary's ICSE and was clueless about life, love and sex. Since then, he has had as many jobs as he has had boyfriends. Ali's current job as a corporate trainer has given him the opportunity to travel widely. He is presently single and lives and works in Colombo. Despite having resolved his issues about identity, he is still clueless about life, love and sex.

Prathiba Sixer Rani has been a long time member of the Bangalore queer group, Good As You (GAY). She lives and works in Bangalore.

Revathi is presently working in Sangama. She is an activist not just for the rights of hijras and other queer people but is also actively involved in working on women's rights, dalit rights and in the anti-communal movement. She is presently working on documenting the life stories of hijras as well as her own autobiography. She may be contacted at revathibangalore@yahoo.com

Sandip Roy is a US-based gay activist and one of the founders of Trikone, the largest South Asian queer space in the US.

Vaibhav Saria is an Undergraduate in Psychology at the University of Arizona in Tucson. He hopes to become an AIDS activist and counsellor and is, for the moment, a gay activist and patron saint of oppressed Marwari children.

Chayanika Shah is an active member of Lesbians and Bisexuals in Action (LABIA, earlier known as Stree Sangam) and Forum Against Oppression of Women, both voluntary, non-funded, autonomous women's collectives in Bombay. She identifies as a queer, feminist activist and has worked and written extensively on issues of sexuality and sexual rights, the politics of population control and reproductive technologies and feminist studies of science. She has a doctorate in physics and teaches at a college in Bombay.

Maya Sharma, a feminist, is an activist in the Indian Women's Movement. Born in Rajasthan, where girls rarely get the opportunity to go to universities, Sharma completed her post-graduation. Her life changed radically when she came in contact with the women's movement. From being the staid house-wife in an urban middle-class home, she chose to be an activist—within that identity she found the space to grow and nurture her skill of listening, observing and writing. Most of what she has written stems from her work as an activist. She has co-written a book on single women's lives, *Women's Labour Rights,* and several articles and reports. The narrative in this anthology is part of the research she undertook in response to developments in the women's movement and the ongoing and growing gay movement.

Currently she is working with a grassroots women's organization, Vikalp in Baroda, Gujarat.

Sonali is an activist and filmmaker who has made several films including *Sum Total* and *Barefeet*. She may be contacted at sonalifilm@yahoo.com

Ashwini Sukthankar is a labour rights advocate and lesbian activist.

Tarun was a student of the National Law School Of India University, Bangalore.

Sheba Tejani is a queer feminist. She lives in Bombay and works for the *Economic and Political Weekly*. She may be contacted at sheba_tejani@hotmail.com

Muraleedharan Tharayil is the Head of the English Department at St Aloysius College, Trichur. He completed his doctorate on British Cinema at CIEFL, Hyderabad. He has published various research papers on Indian cinema and is currently working on a book about the queer dynamics in mainstream Indian cinema.